Learning to Weave

Learning to Weave

DEBORAH CHANDLER

INTERWEAVE PRESS

For my students, who have taught me everything in this book, and a lot more.

Photography: Joe Coca, except as follows: David Crossley, pages 57–73;
      Eric Redding, pages 28-52
Illustrations: Kim Jonas, Susan Strawn
Design and production: Marc McCoy Owens, Sharolyn Eitenbichler, Elizabeth R. Mrofka
Cover design: Signorella Graphic Arts

Interweave Press LLC
201 East Fourth Street
Loveland, Colorado 80537-5655 USA
www.interweave.com

Library of Congress Cataloging-in-Publication Data

Chandler, Deborah, 1949–
    Learning to weave / Deborah Chandler. —Rev. ed.
       p.   cm.
    Includes index.
    ISBN 1-883010-03-9 : $24.95
    1. Hand weaving.   I. Title.
TT848.C417 1994
746.1'4—dc20   94-22905
                                                    CIP

15 14 13 12

Acknowledgments

Oh, such thanks I have to give . . .

to those who started me weaving and got me to the point of understanding it: Bill and Louise Chandler Green, Eric Redding, Jeanne Schenk Steiner, and Sherri Smith;

to the teachers who helped me be a better teacher: Louise Bradley, Judy Steinkoenig, Lynn Dhority, Eric Jensen, Ismael Garcia, and many others;

to six weaving guilds*, four in Colorado and two in Houston, who have provided me with inspiration and entertainment for more than 20 years;

to the illustrators Kim Jonas Reed and Susan Strawn, the photographers Eric Redding, David Crossely, and Joe Coca, and the weavers listed throughout, who made the visuals visible;

to the entire staff of Interweave Press, who have been among the most enthusiastic supporters of Learning to Weave since Day 1, and who have worked as a team to get my words and ideas into your hands since 1977 (when I was Debbie Redding);

and at Interweave, extra enormous appreciation to Jane Patrick, editor of the first version, who took a lot of raw material and turned it into a beautiful and user-friendly book that exceeded every fantasy I ever had; and Ann Budd, equally hard-working and remarkable editor of the revision, who has managed to fit a lot more material into the same numbers of pages while keeping it friendly and beautiful; and Linda Ligon, publisher extraordinaire, mentor to all of us, and friend;

and finally, to the many weavers I've met and students I've had who have shared so much with me, including many of the good ideas in the pages that follow.

Thanks beyond measure to them all.

—Deborah Chandler
November, 1994

*Pikes Peak Weavers Guild, Northern Colorado Weavers Guild, Handweavers Guild of Boulder, Rocky Mountain Weavers Guild, Contemporary Handweavers of Houston, Tall Pines Weavers.

Many thanks to the following students and friends who generously loaned us their weavings to illustrate these lessons:

Sharon Alderman, Jean Anstine, Selena Billington, Louise Bradley, Lisa Budwig, Awyn Combs, Ardis Dobrovolny, Betsy Holdsworth, Wanda Holmes, Helen Irwin, Janice Jones, Audrey Kick, Barbara Layne, Linda Ligon, Helen Menzel, Jane Patrick, Mary Peterson, Katie Potter, Maggie Putnam, Eric Redding, Donna Reilly, Louie Ross, Lynda Short, Yvonne Stahl, Judy Steinkoenig, Beth Thomas, Annemarie Tucker, Margie Wortzman, and the unknown weavers who left pieces at the Weaving Shop for the continued inspiration of others.

Preface

When I first started teaching weaving, I knew a little about weaving and less about teaching. Since then, I've learned quite a lot about both, mostly through experience. While this may not be the most efficient means, it is practical. As I try new things, anything that doesn't work I reject immediately; that which does work I keep and let grow.

As a new teacher, my single greatest frustration was students' lack of self-confidence. It was a total block to their absorbing the information. These adults, mostly women, were so full of "I can't", "I'm not clever enough", and "I don't know how", that getting them to try anything was a major accomplishment.

At some point, a great truth became clear to me, and it has been the life force of my teaching ever since. I had thought I was in the classroom to teach weaving; I learned I was there to teach people. This understanding has affected my style of teaching, completely and forever.

I don't recall ever having students who wanted to weave ugly things, make pieces that would fall apart, or create anything that they couldn't be proud of. On the other hand, at least 25 percent of my students have set such high standards for themselves, based not on knowledge of the subject but on a general attitude of inadequacy, that they are perpetually frustrated and self-discouraging. It isn't better standards I need to teach, it's acceptance of and gentleness with one's self, one's creations.

I encourage my students to understand what's happening and then make their own decisions as to how to proceed. While I am more than willing to help with structural problems, functional understanding, I go to great lengths to resist answering questions like: Blue or green? What size? Is this correct? It's a standing joke among my students that the answer to most questions is, "What do you want?"

Many aspects of weaving are not covered in this book, some because they aren't appropriate to a beginning class, others because I don't know enough about them myself. You'll find all of them in other books, in weaving magazines, in the minds of other weavers. This book is only the beginning, the very beginning.

I want you to relax, to have fun. Being easy on yourself is not contrary to good craftsmanship. Learning from and being inspired by others is not counter to originality, creativity. Enjoying something does not mean you're not taking it seriously. Mistakes are as valuable as successes, one for learning and growth, the other for reward and encouragement. A poster hanging in my classroom says, "You have failed only when you failed to try." So go out and try something, and if it doesn't feel just right try something else. The journey is as important as the destination.

Table of Contents

Introduction

Welcome to your own home study four-shaft weaving course. More than anything else, I want you to have fun and enjoy learning to weave. There's not much point in it otherwise. Second, I want you to understand what you're doing and feel comfortable with the weaving process so that you are able to solve problems as they arise. If you understand the loom, the yarns, and the rest of the ingredients of weaving, you will be able to decipher most surprises easily. I hope that by the end of this course you will be able to plan, execute, and complete a project from start to finish with full understanding of each step of the weaving process—and do it with confidence. What you will find here is the information you need to make decisions, rather than the specifics for making a particular project.

I believe that taking a class and having a teacher there in person is a better way to learn than from a book. Feedback on questions is immediate, and many things you didn't know you needed to ask about are answered before they become problems. Also valuable in a classroom setting are the unique interpretations of each assignment by other people interested in the same subject you are. It's a good way to meet new people, sometimes start new friendships, and always learn more than you anticipated. If you can't or don't want to take a class, it is my sincere hope that this book will help you to learn the things you need to know to become the weaver you want to be.

This book, first published in 1984, is based on the classes I've been teaching since 1972. As I've learned more about teaching and about how students learn, I have continually revised my classes to encompass this newfound knowledge. With this revised edition, I've tried to include some of the many things I've learned in the past ten years; I expect to learn even more in the next ten. So here is the best I have to offer right now, with my hope that you will grow beyond it, just as I intend to do.

Each lesson begins with an overview of the basic concepts presented in that lesson followed by an in-depth discussion of the technique or process. At the end of each lesson, you'll find a few assignments to try, along with project ideas. Try them all, or only a few, or make up your own. The more you weave, the more you will know! Below are some guidelines for how you might proceed.

1. Make up your own class schedule, one that is realistic for your lifestyle. Set aside a time every week or every day for your class. Go to class at that time and don't allow yourself to be interrupted for anything less than you would if you were attending class elsewhere. Take this as seriously as a class you'd paid for and arranged your schedule around.

2. If you have friends who also want to learn to weave, get together and form your own class. Use this book as your teacher; meet and learn together. You'll have one of the greatest advantages of a classroom situation: seeing other interpretations of the same lesson. It will also help your motivation and enthusiasm stay high, both for learning and for getting your homework done.

3. Keep notes. We've left some wide margins so you can take notes as you go along. You will also come up with questions and discoveries that don't seem to be covered in the book; keep those in a separate notebook that you can take with you when you go to your weaving shop, guild meeting, or weaving friend's house. And read over your notes occasionally. You'll be pleased to see how much you've learned (early revelations will become core knowledge that you will take for granted and think you've always known), and discoveries forgotten will be rediscovered. Reading your notes from time to time will save you some relearning.

How long it takes you to learn to weave will depend on how much time you devote to it. In my classes, students complete one of these lessons each week. They spend two to three hours in class and perhaps four to twelve hours on their homework, more at first, less as the weeks go by. You may want to take a leisurely approach or a more intense one. It's up to you how many of the homework assignments at the end of each lesson you do.

You may want to go through the whole book first fairly quickly, then repeat it with more study of each lesson, or you may want to spend a month on each lesson the first time through. How fast you go doesn't matter a bit, as long as it works for you and is a pace that lets you enjoy it, balancing satisfaction of accomplishment with not feeling pressured.

If you already know something about weaving, you may want to skim the first lessons or skip them altogether, at least for now. These first lessons were written for people who know absolutely nothing about weaving.

I know only one person who has read her weaving books from start to finish, and it isn't me. I'm assuming that many of the people who pick this up will start somewhere in the middle and read only the lessons that interest them. Therefore, each lesson is as independent as possible and can stand on its own. I've repeated some ideas and facts in various places as seemed appropriate.

This book does not contain everything you need to know, not even close to it, so I hope you'll read lots of other weaving books for all of the interesting and useful things they include that aren't here. I tell my beginning students that it would be ideal if they could take at least two beginning classes from two different teachers, for they would then see that they can interpret most things in many ways. The same is true with weaving books. They will appear to contradict each other; you can also say that individual perspective is another word for contradiction. There is room for us all, and in fact, a need for us all. Let's get started so you can become the weaver you are meant to be.

PART I:
For the Very Beginner

LESSON 1

Getting Familiar

What is weaving?

The anatomy of a loom

Equipment you will find useful

Weaving vocabulary

Knitted fabric.

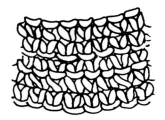

Crocheted fabric.

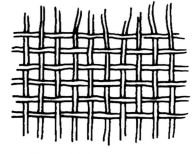

Woven fabric.

14

In writing this book, I've placed myself in the classroom, imagining you, the reader, as a student in my class. Students arrive in class with different levels of understanding about what weaving is. Some have woven a little already; others aren't so sure they know what weaving or a loom is. I'll proceed as though you know nothing at all about weaving and give you a bit of background information. If you already know these basics, you may want to skip this part.

What is weaving?

First, the *very* basics. There are many ways to make cloth. Most of you know that knitting involves two needles and a continuous strand of yarn. A knitted fabric is a series of interlocked loops, as is a crocheted fabric. To crochet, however, one uses only one hook instead of two needles. In addition to looped fabrics there are those made by twisting yarns together, knotting them, felting unspun fibers, and others.

Woven fabrics are easily the largest and oldest category, and what we are interested in here. In woven fabrics two sets of yarns cross perpendicular to one another. One set is called the *warp*, the other set *weft* (or *woof* in some locales). You may

remember as a child making potholders on a small frame or using a needle to weave through yarn stretched on cardboard. Using cotton loops or a needle threaded with yarn, you pulled the threads over and under, over and under the threads held taut on the "loom". You were weaving then, and the only difference now is that you'll be using a more sophisticated loom.

A *loom*, whatever kind it is, is a device to hold a set of yarns taut so that it is easy to weave other yarns over and under them. The yarn attached to the loom is the warp. The weft is the cross threads that are woven over and under the warp threads. Looms that are more elaborate than potholder or cardboard frames have some kind of mechanism that raises or lowers some of the warp threads at any given time, so that when the weft is passed across, it automatically goes over some warp threads and under others. The space created when some of the warp threads are raised or lowered is called the *shed*, and the tool that carries the weft through is called the *shuttle*. Different looms have different ways of making sheds, depending on what kind of fabric you want to create or how fast you want to create it. We aren't going to bother with any but the four-shaft loom here. While floor looms have some features that table looms do not have, what they will do is essentially the same, and this course is intended to be equally applicable to either. See the discussion of looms in Part IV if you are totally unfamiliar with your own loom.

The anatomy of a loom

Let's look at your loom now and get to know its parts and what they do. First, find the front of your loom, where the frame that moves back and forth is. That whole framework is called the *beater,* and within the beater is the *reed,* the metal piece with lots of slots (called *dents*). A beater may hang from above or it may be mounted from below, bolted to the sides of the loom. The reed determines how close together the warp threads are and keeps them straight as you weave. The beater and reed together are used to beat the weft into place as you weave.

The *shafts* are the rectangular structures hanging or resting inside the major frame of the loom behind the beater. This largest part of the loom is called the *castle,* easy to re-member because it is central and oversees all the rest. Hanging within each shaft you'll find *heddles,* strips of metal or string with eyes in the middle through which the warp threads will be threaded. (If your loom is old and the heddles are very rusted, throw them out and buy new ones; heddles with corroded surfaces can cut your yarn.) On most looms in the United States and Canada the heddles are on heddle bars made of spring steel, a steel that will flex for removal without bending perm-anently. Older looms and some new ones have other kinds of metal for their heddle bars, and to remove them requires lifting the shaft out of the castle and sliding the bar out rather than bending it. If you don't have a spring steel bar, don't bend it, for it will never be straight again.

A floor loom has *treadles* down near the floor that are used to raise or lower the shafts. (For this reason these are also called foot-powered looms.) The lifting mechanism on a table loom is a series of *levers* mount-ed on either the front or side of the loom, one lever for each shaft.

Across the front and back of the loom, about halfway up, run two large rotating beams which may be round, hexagonal, or made of four flat pieces of wood attached togeth-er. The one in the back will have the warp rolled around it before you start weaving, so it is called the *warp beam*. The one in front is called the *cloth beam* (or *fabric beam*) since this is where the cloth will be rolled up as it is woven. These two rotating beams allow you to weave great long lengths of cloth, something not pos-

Table Loom

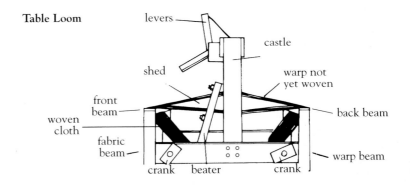

Floor Loom (also called Foot Loom)

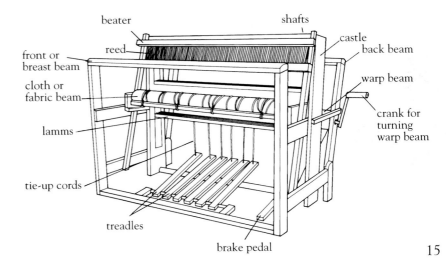

Warping pegs

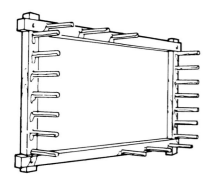

Warping board

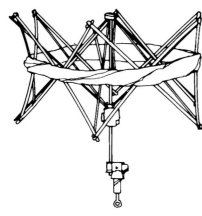

Umbrella swift

sible on frame and cardboard looms.

Also at the front and back of the loom, higher and probably outside of the warp and cloth beam, are two flat beams, used to elevate and level the warp for weaving. These are called the *front* or *breast beam* and *back beam*. On most floor looms, one or both of these beams can easily be removed so that you can get close to the castle when you thread the warp. On table looms, you can reach through or over the framework to the castle. In addition, many floor looms are designed so that the entire back section will fold up or drop to the floor, getting it farther out of the way. Play around with your loom to see what will and won't move.

One last part of a floor loom that makes life easier looks like another treadle but is off to the side, usually to the right. This *brake* or *tension release pedal* is used to release the mechanism that keeps the warp beam from turning. (Some looms have cords to pull instead of a foot-controlled release; the principle is the same.) A brake is needed on both the warp and cloth beams to keep the warp taut while weaving is under way. Most looms have a ratchet and dog, or pawl, in front that is a toothed gear and a straight or slightly curved piece that falls into the teeth of the gear to hold it still. The warp beam may have another ratchet, or a friction brake, a round piece held tight by a cable (both are pictured on page 88).

A relatively recent development is a brake that utilizes worm gears for infinite adjustment of both warp and cloth beams. It's a nice feature but more expensive and at present found on only two looms that I know of.

These are the basic parts of your loom. You'll understand more about them and what they do as you begin

using them, so don't be concerned if it isn't all clear now.

The loom is only one of the pieces of equipment needed to weave, and while other tools vary in their degree of necessity, I want you to at least be aware of a lot of them. Look through the illustrations on the next few pages, read the descriptions of each tool, and then decide which would be useful to you. You may already have some of them. Not everything available is shown here, so browse through shops and catalogs when you have the opportunity to see what else exists, especially if you find yourself having a problem that you suspect a tool might help solve. The glossary, too, is here for your initial exposure. Read through it but don't feel compelled to memorize it. Use of the words will come as you get into weaving and encounter them in context.

Equipment you will find useful

Warping pegs are the most basic of all warp measuring devices. Clamp them to a table the appropriate distance apart and wind the warp thread around them.

A **warping board** is a nice piece of equipment to own, easy to figure out, comfortable and efficient to use. This warping tool is very common and the one I refer to in this course.

An **umbrella swift** is both invaluable and fun to look at. It holds a skein of yarn and keeps it from getting tangled while you unwind yarn from it onto your warping board, bobbin, shuttle, or whatever.

A **ball winder** is the tool to acquire right after you get a swift. In a couple of minutes, a ball winder will wind a solid, stackable, center-pull ball. It's also useful for winding multiple strands of yarn together.

Loom benches come in a variety of styles, each with something that makes it more than just a bench. Most have some storage area for yarn, shuttles, etc. Some are adjustable in height or angle of seat.

Bobbin winders come in different shapes with different drive mechanisms and different prices. Their purpose is to rotate boat-shuttle bobbins so that yarn can wind on evenly, smoothly, and quickly. Many people use other tools such as drills or electric mixers as substitutes, all of which work, but none of which is as easy or efficient as the real thing.

Electric bobbin winders go faster than manual models. They are particularly useful if you're weaving with fine threads. Speed is controlled with a foot pedal.

The **McMorran Yarn Balance** is one of the cleverest inventions for weavers since the loom. Made of clear plastic, about 6 inches tall, the arm is calibrated to measure yards (or meters) per pound of any yarn, except possibly a very heavy thick-and-thin yarn. It's a tremendous help to those who collect a lot of miscellaneous unlabeled yarn and wonder how much of it they have or, more significantly, if they have enough.

The ***reed*** has two functions, the spacing of the warp and the packing in of the weft. Reeds come with different spacings, called dents per inch. A 12-dent reed has 12 slots per inch (all the way across). A 36-inch reed is 36 inches wide and can accommodate a 36-inch-wide warp. Reeds are made of steel and can rust if they get wet. If you live in a coastal area, buy stainless steel reeds, the added expense of which is your trade-off for the joys of living near the water. Reeds were originally

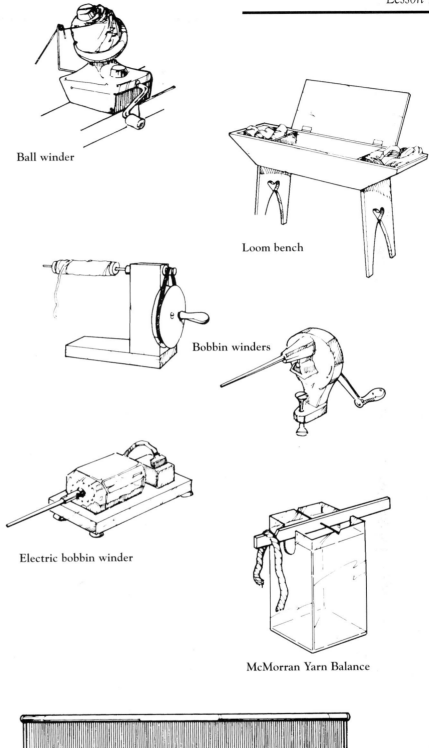

Ball winder

Loom bench

Bobbin winders

Electric bobbin winder

McMorran Yarn Balance

Reed

Getting Familiar

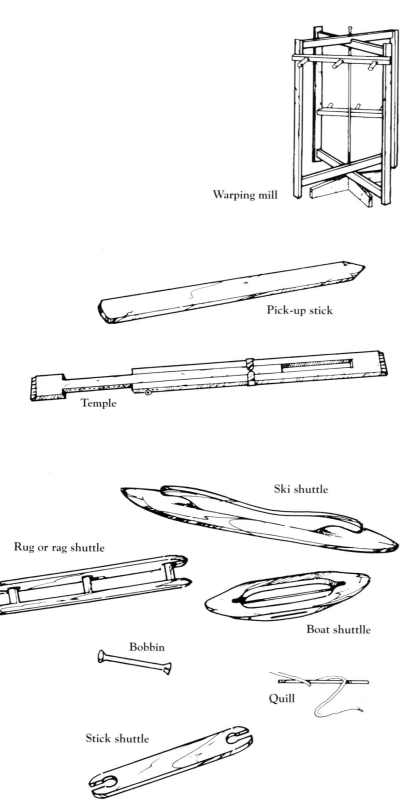

Warping mill

Pick-up stick

Temple

Ski shuttle

Rug or rag shuttle

Boat shuttlle

Bobbin

Quill

Stick shuttle

made of reeds, not steel (thus the name), and still are in some parts of the world.

A *warping mill* is a device for measuring warp. It comes in both vertical and horizontal models. The difference between warping boards or pegs and mills is that instead of your arm going back and forth, *they* go around, saving your arm this motion. (They are especially good if you have joint problems.) They are faster and more efficient, but take up more space and cost more. If you are measuring warps of eight yards or more most of the time, they are well worth the investment.

A *pick-up stick* is used for picking up individual warp threads for special patterning; it's also good for clearing a sticky shed and as a magic wand when one is called for.

A *temple* (or stretcher) can be used to keep the weaving width constant. They can be used on pieces from lightweight table linens to the heaviest of rugs.

Shuttles come in a variety of shapes, each designed for handling a different kind of weft more easily. Ski shuttles and rug, or rag, shuttles are used for holding heavy yarns. Boat shuttles are faster to use with medium to fine wefts, as the yarn is wrapped on a bobbin or quill (looks like a short straw) and then feeds out automatically as the shuttle glides through the shed. Boat shuttles are more expensive, and require bobbins and a bobbin winder. A couple of boat shuttles and a dozen bobbins will keep you going for a long time. If you use only heavy yarn or rags, don't bother with a boat shuttle because it can't hold as much heavy yarn as a ski or rag shuttle; you'll need to change bobbins too often. Stick shuttles are the easiest to make and the cheapest to buy and are the most awkward to use. They come in many styles and lengths.

A **threading hook,** or heddle hook, is used for drawing (pulling) the warp threads through the heddles. It can be used to sley the reed as well, though it is slightly awkward for this purpose because of its length.

Sley hooks, or reed hooks, are short, flat hooks used for drawing the warp threads through the dents (slots) in the reed (called "sleying the reed").

A **sectional warp beam** has pegs at 1- or 2-inch intervals. For weavers putting on very long warps all of the time, it is a time-saver. To use one as intended, you also need a spool rack, spool winder, spools, a tension box and yardage counter. We won't cover sectional warping in this course but you can find out about it in other books. Ask your shopkeeper for information.

A **tension box** creates tension on warp going from spool rack to sectional warp beam.

A **spool rack** holds spools for sectional or paddle warping.

A **paddle** is used to measure many warp threads at once, saving time over measuring one end at a time.

A **raddle** is used when warping from back to front. It is the tool used to separate and spread the warp to the correct width when rolling it onto the warp beam. It is a board as long as the loom is wide with pegs (or nails) at 1-inch intervals. Many weavers make their own using finishing nails for pegs.

Tensioning device. Frame for holding lease sticks that attaches to either front or back beam. Designed to help put even tension on all warp threads during beaming process. (Not shown.)

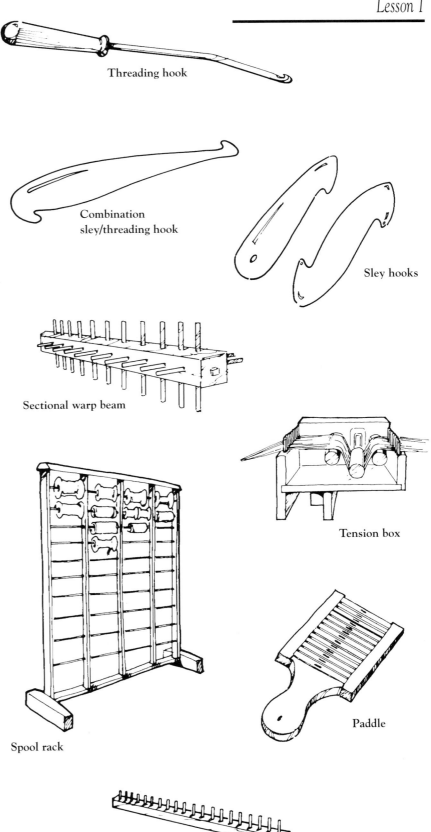

Threading hook

Combination sley/threading hook

Sley hooks

Sectional warp beam

Tension box

Spool rack

Paddle

Raddle

Weaving vocabulary

Balanced weave—a fabric in which the number of warp threads per inch is the same as the number of weft threads per inch. It can be loose or tight as long as the count is the same.

Beaming the warp—rolling the warp onto the warp beam at the back of the loom.

Cross, lease—the figure eight made at one end (or both) of the warp when measuring. It is used to prevent tangles later.

Dent—a slot in the reed; a 12-dent reed has 12 dents per inch.

Draft—a map of the pattern to be woven. A full draft is made up of four parts: threading, tie-up, treadling, and draw-down. Drafts are the international language of weavers. They tell you how to weave fabric with shaft-controlled weave structures.

Draw-in—the pulling in of selvedges while weaving; usually 1 to 2 inches.

Dressing the loom—warping the loom.

e.p.i.—ends per inch, the number of warp threads in an inch measured across the width of the warp.

Fell—the front/forward edge of your weaving, the edge made by your most recent weft shot.

Filler—weft.

Fiber—raw material, animal, vegetable, mineral, or synthetic, made into yarn.

Fiber content—important to know for predicting how a yarn or fabric will behave and how to care for it. Try natural fibers such as wool, cotton, linen, silk, etc., each of which has its own wonderful characteristics (see pages 204-206).

Finishing—final treatment of the woven fabric, including washing, brushing, etc.; also includes techniques such as fringes knots, and hems used to secure the weft in place.

Lease sticks—flat (or sometimes round) sticks that come with the loom, usually as long as the loom is wide. They are used in some methods of warping for holding the cross or creating extra friction during beaming.

Loom waste—not the fur balls that accumulate under the loom, but the parts of the warp that tie on to the loom at front and back and never get woven.

p.p.i.—picks per inch, wefts per inch, just as e.p.i. is warp ends per inch.

Pick, shot—one pass of weft, often called a weft shot.

Ply, plied—when yarn is spun, it is twisted into a single strand. A plied yarn has two or more strands twisted together; two single strands, or singles, plied together are called a two-ply yarn, three singles a three-ply yarn, etc. A single-strand yarn is often called a single ply even though it was never plied.

Problems—a word often used for opportunities to invent creative solutions or learn more. Whatever you call them, you'll have them, even when you reach that stage called "advanced". The only way to avoid them is to never try anything new.

Reed—the steel piece that fits into the beater of the loom. Reeds commonly have 4, 5, 6, 8, 10, 12, 15, or 20 dents per inch. Other sizes can be obtained if you need them. They determine how close together your warp threads will be, the sett. The reed and beater together help you to push the weft into place.

Selvedge—the side edges of a fabric where the weft passes around the outermost warps. Also spelled selvage or selvege.

Set, sett—e.p.i. Set is the verb, sett the noun. The warp was set at 10 e.p.i. The warp sett was 10 e.p.i.

Shed—the space created between upper and lower warp threads when shafts are raised and/ or lowered. The shuttle carrying the weft goes through the shed.

Shot—see pick.

Sley—to pass the warp through the reed.

Sley hook—a short hook designed for quick threading/sleying of the warp through the reed.

Take-up—the curving of warp over and under weft and weft over and under warp, and consequent shortening, narrowing, and thickening of the fabric.

Threading hook—a long, skinny hook designed for threading the warp through the heddles.

Warp—the yarn attached to the loom, held under tension during weaving.

Warp end—one entire warp thread (not just the end of the thread).

Web—woven fabric, more often used to refer to fabric still on the loom.

Weft—the thread that's woven from side to side, over and under the warp threads.

Yarn, thread—mostly used interchangeably here; I think of thread as thinner, yarn fatter.

Your First Piece

The value of making samples

Choosing yarn for your sample

Step-by-step warping

Warping from front to back

Warping from back to front

Deborah Chandler's hybrid method

What to have students weave for a first piece is a matter of great philosophical debate among teachers. "Something beautiful and inspiring to get them confident and enthusiastic, and if they don't really learn anything that's okay for now," is at one end of the spectrum. At the other end is, "Now that you've woven this tapestry you must unweave it, just so you'll know that a great weaving takes a lot of learning and can't happen the first time." I fall somewhere between these two.

The value of making samples

I encourage samples. Of course, I want you to be inspired and encouraged by your first weaving experience; if you're not, it's not likely that you'll go on to a second. But I believe that you came to class not just to weave, but to learn how to weave; there is a critical difference between the two. I want you to know what you're doing, and I think you do, too, or you wouldn't have bought this book. So, while I want your first piece to be wonderful, I also want it to teach you a lot. More

than anything, I want it to teach you that learning to weave is easy and fun, and that you can weave nice pieces immediately.

Like most people, when I first started weaving I wanted to weave real things, things I would like to own and use and show off. I had never had any weaving instruction. Consequently, I had no understanding of yarn properties as they relate to weave structures, color combinations and what they do, what the loom was capable of, and much more. I embarked on project after project with no foundation, and was disappointed by most of what I created because they were all either ugly (experimental) or boring (safe). Two years later, I took my first class and promptly started trying to weave real things again, feeling confident in my newfound knowledge. More ugly pieces, a few okay ones—again, the experimental versus the safe.

Clearly, I had to learn what was going on so I could begin to understand what was going wrong. I reasoned that weaving samples, pieces roughly 6 inches by 12 inches or longer, would cost me less than weaving bigger pieces and allow me to make my discoveries more quickly. I'd be saving both time and money. In the event that one ever came out well—it was bound to sooner or later—I'd have a basis for doing something larger.

So I started. And I learned.

I wove samples for a long time before I realized that I was beginning to settle down into successfully weaving "real things". The sample stage lasted a long time for me because I enjoyed it, got really excited about discovering what weaving was. There could be no disappointments because there were no expectations. I was learning how weaving worked, making up and solving puzzles, and it was loads of fun. I didn't expect that. I even remember hearing one woman tell me she liked to weave samples and my thinking she must be crazy—who'd want to waste time doing that? So I encourage, recommend, and urge that you weave samples.

Recently, I heard another teacher's wonderful reason for sampling. Kathryn Wertenberger points out that you can have a good idea which you try out on a sample, but while you're weaving it something new occurs to you and you end up with something even better than you were going to have originally. There's a carrot on a stick for you!

A sample as a learning device

A sample doesn't need to be a "thing"; it is a learning device. If you have set out to learn something, and you do, then the piece has fulfilled its function. If it should also happen to become a scarf or table runner, then that's a bonus. What you learn may be a positive—this I want to do again. Or it may be the reverse—now I know something not to do, something that didn't work. Either way you have learned.

By now you won't be surprised when I say your first assignment will be a sample. It will be nice; you'll enjoy it. Its purpose is to help you get used to your loom, get the feel of what's going on, play with some of the possibilities. It's to be large enough so that you get to play and enjoy for a while, but small enough that you'll be done and still want more.

Because the primary goal of this lesson is for you to learn to put a warp on your loom and understand how it all works, for this assignment I'll give specifics for the piece you'll weave. In Lesson 4, I'll discuss plan-

ning, and from then on you'll be designing on your own. So, your sample will be 10 inches wide and two yards long; it will have two colors in the warp in 1-inch-wide stripes, and two colors in the weft. The sett will be 12 e.p.i. (ends per inch). Parts of the finished sample are shown on page 78.

Choosing yarn for your sample

For this sample, I suggest you use a wool yarn because it's the easiest to work with. Its elasticity will help compensate for your inexperience at achieving consistent tension with your warp threads. I'll talk more about this later.

Choose a wool yarn that is plied (has two or more strands twisted together), not too stiff, not too stretchy, and not too fuzzy. A medium-weight yarn about the size shown here and yielding about 1600 yards per pound will work well. (Hold your yarn next to the picture for comparison.) A four-ounce skein of each color should be enough. Avoid standard knitting yarns for now; they have characteristics that require special tricks for successful weaving.

Your warp yarn should be strong enough to hold up during weaving. One method for testing yarn strength is to try to pull the yarn apart with both hands. If it breaks with a "ping", it'll work fine; if it breaks with a "thud", it may not be strong enough.

Check to see if your yarn is the correct weight by wrapping the yarn around a ruler for 1 inch, placing each wrap right next to, but not on top of the previous one. Then divide the number of wraps in 1 inch by two. If this number is 12, then the yarn will work at the 12 warp

Choose a yarn about this size.

Wrapping your yarn for 1 inch around a ruler will give you an idea of how many ends per inch it should be sleyed.

threads per inch that I specified. If the number is much smaller, then your yarn is too fat, and you'll need to choose a skinnier yarn. If the number is much greater than 12, the yarn is too thin.

I've specified two colors so you'll see how they interact and because that's more interesting than using only one. Use any colors you like, but the more contrast there is between them, the more you will see what's going on: black and white are a better choice than blue and black, for example. On the other hand, it is hard to see the interlacement of the threads of very dark colors, so green and white might be better than black and white. I've used black and white for contrast in the photographs.

Yarn handling

When you go shopping for yarn, you'll notice that it is packaged in a number of forms: skeins, balls, pull skeins, cones, tubes. Shape does not indicate quantity; any amount can be packaged in any shape.

Of the five ways of packaging yarn, only skeins (which is how many weaving yarns come) are prone to serious tangling and require special treatment before they can be used. Yarn from balls and pull skeins can be pulled from either the outside or the inside; the inside is preferable because the unit will lie still instead of rolling all over, picking up dust bunnies, and getting tangled up in things. Cones and tubes have cardboard in the center, and so must be pulled from the outside. A cone will stand up on its own; a tube needs to be set onto a nail or dowel to hold it still. If the cardboard has come out, you can treat the cone or tube of yarn as a pull skein, but sometimes they have been wrapped under so much tension that

this won't work: you'll get whole tangly clumps of yarn instead of the single strand you want.

If you're going to own only one piece of equipment (besides a good pair of scissors) make it an umbrella swift (see page 16). Most of us remember scenes of two people making a ball of yarn. One would hold the skein of yarn around outstretched hands while the other wound the ball. An umbrella swift does the job of holding the yarn, and it's ready and waiting at any time, day or night. It's not quite as companionable as a human partner, but what it lacks in conversation it makes up for in efficiency.

Squirrel cages and yarn reels provide the same function, cost more, but have other advantages. Ask your local shop owner about them.

To put a skein on a swift, open up the skein to its full size. Find, but do not yet untie, the ties securing it. Make sure that the yarn going through the ties is straight and doesn't double back; then put the skein around the swift and adjust the swift to the correct size, large enough to hold the skein securely but not too tightly. The ends of the skein will be either tied together or knotted around the skein individually; there may or may not be additional ties. Cut or untie these ends and carefully separate them from the rest of the skein right away. When the skein was made, it had no tangles and the ends were connected last; if you put an end through the bundle you will create the first tangle, and the yarn will not feed freely. Occasionally, a skein will have problems that can be solved only with loving patience. Most, however, will unwind easily and uneventfully as soon as you've pulled the ends free. You can wind a warp directly from a skein with the

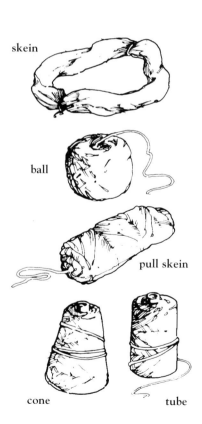

skein

ball

pull skein

cone   tube

Yarn is packaged in many forms.

Yarn

Choose two colors of plied wool yarn, not too stretchy, and not too fuzzy. A medium-weight yarn yielding about 1600 yards per pound will work well. Use contrasting colors.

swift feeding it to you. When you've used all you need, wrap the ends around the skein and tie them together again. Or you can ball the yarn as described below.

The companion tool to the swift is the ball winder (see page 17). This clever device will make a ball of yarn which will sit flat and pull from the center—and do it in a matter of minutes. Ball winders will easily make 4-ounce balls, and many will make larger ones. The instructions for use come with them; however, some don't mention that the plastic core weighs 1 ounce, so if you are trying to make a ball of certain weight, just weigh the core plus yarn, subtract an ounce, and keep going as necessary.

Step-by-step warping

There are as many ways to warp a loom as there are weavers, for everyone has his or her own special tricks. Some weavers use different methods for different warps, different looms, or different moods. There are no absolutes.

All those variations can be lumped into two basic approaches—front to back and back to front. Warping from front to back means that the warp follows a path from the front of the loom to the back; it goes through the reed, then through the heddles, then is wound onto the warp beam, and when it's almost all wound on, the front end is tied to the front apron rod and it's ready to weave.

Warping from back to front accomplishes the same steps but in the opposite order: first the warp is wound onto the warp beam, then the ends that will be in front are threaded through the heddles (from the back toward the front), then they are sleyed through the reed, then tied onto the front apron rod.

Both methods have strong, even fervent advocates. Over the years, though, my own fervor has mellowed and I now can sincerely and from my own experience make a good case for either method, especially for different circumstances. (And I can laugh at how funny we weavers sometimes are in our hysteria about which is the "right" warping method.)

I'll give you instructions for both methods, each in its simplest (yet complete) form. I'll mention slight variations for you to try within the main body of each section, as well as a fairly major alternative within back-to-front warping. Finally, I'll present a third option, a hybrid of the two methods that I have used and that nearly every weaver I have told it to says is totally crazy.

So, what follows is Method A: Warping from front to back, Method B: Warping from back to front, and Method C: Deborah Chandler's Hybrid in short form. Start with Method A, use it three or four times to get over the most awkward stage, then go on to Method B and give it a fair try. I have known weavers who were absolutely dedicated to A and later were much happier with B, and I've met just as many weavers who had the opposite experience. I confess to thinking that those who use both are probably the most sensible, but we have no rules requiring that. Once you're comfortable with both methods, consider my Method C or create your own. What I want to do now is get you on the loom and weaving; later you can develop the way that you like best of all.

There is a lot more to weaving than throwing a shuttle. Your time at the loom may well be only about half of your total project time. Often, especially in the beginning and on small projects, setting up the project takes longer than weaving it off.

Don't be too discouraged by this. The more times you do it, the more adept you'll become and the less time it will take. Some weavers enjoy warping more than weaving. Of course, many others prefer weaving.

Learning and being comfortable with warping the loom puts you on the path to self-sufficiency. Because this procedure is an essential part of weaving and is the foundation of good cloth, I'll spend quite a lot of time on it.

In my first class, I walk my students through the warping process. Here, I hope these photos and sketches will be an adequate substitute for a walkthrough. I suggest that you follow the directions step by step, keeping this book next to you as you work. You'll find that learning by doing is an invaluable approach to understanding warping. All these words will make a lot more sense after you've warped your loom once.

Method A: Warping from front to back

You will need:
- Warping board or something to measure your warp on.
- 4- (or more) shaft table or floor loom.
- 12-dent reed. (If you don't have one, use what you have and choose a yarn that will fit it. Reread "Choosing yarn for your sample" (pages 23–24), and/or page 211 for more information on how to substitute.)
- 240 yards each of two colors of wool yarn (as described on page 23).
- Sley hook or threading hook.
- Scissors.
- Ruler, tape measure, or yardstick.
- Masking tape.
- Warp separator.

SYNOPSIS OF WARPING FROM FRONT TO BACK

Now that you've assembled all the supplies you'll need, it's time to start putting your warp on your loom. These are the steps you'll follow:

1. Measure the warp.
2. Sley the reed.
3. Thread the heddles.
4. Tie onto the back apron rod.
5. Beam the warp.
6. Tie onto the front apron rod.
7. Tie up the treadles.

This short list can be a quick reminder later, and give you some sense of direction now. Don't be dismayed if you feel clumsy and awkward and suddenly have too many thumbs. That's normal; everyone goes through it. It will pass. Later you'll be amazed at and derive great pleasure from your speed and dexterity.

MEASURING THE WARP
Measuring tools

Though you can measure your warp on just about any stationary object, a warping board or warping mill will ease your work considerably. Warping boards are made with rows of pegs along each side, either a yard or half-yard apart. They are easy to use, relatively inexpensive, and nice to have around, as you can hang yarn or your coat on it when it's not being used for its first purpose.

A warping mill is easier on your arm and shoulder, faster to use, takes up more space, and costs more. Warping pegs cost the least, are less convenient to use, but they can be stored in a drawer or loom bench when not in use. If you have none of these, you can turn chairs upside down and use the legs as pegs (anchor the chairs so that they don't creep together as you use them), or

Find two yards on your warping board or other measuring tool. Use a guide string to help you.

drive large nails into your garage wall. I knew a mother-daughter pair who for many years measured their warp around gallon cans of food spaced the proper distance apart on the living room floor; it makes my back ache to think of it, but it worked.

Because it is both common and convenient, I'll discuss the use of the warping board here. First, if you can, find a place on the wall to mount your warping board permanently. It should be well lit and easy to get to. Have someone hold the board at different heights while you move your arms back and forth from peg to peg. You should be able to easily reach and move around the lower and upper pegs. If you don't have the space to install your warping board permanently, find a place where you can prop it up to work comfortably. Sometimes the loom itself has a perfect "resting place" for a warping board.

Guide strings. As your sample warp is to be two yards long, you will need to find a two-yard-long path on your warping board. A good way to do this is to measure a piece of yarn—a guide string—two yards long plus a few extra inches for tying it onto the pegs. Choose a contrasting color of yarn to distinguish it readily from the warp you'll be measuring. Make a path with it on your warping board

until you find just the right pegs for the length of your guide string. The path needs to include several pegs that are close together at one end, as shown across the top in the drawings. Now tie your string to the pegs. You'll take it off after you've used it to measure your warp.

The path your guide string follows will vary according to the size and layout of your warping board, as shown in the two illustrations at right. The three illustrations below show that many paths will work.

Starting to measure

Now that you have determined the path of your warp, tie one of your colors onto the peg on the vertical side where the end of your guide string is. Any knot that holds will do. A slipknot is fast; a square knot is fine, too. Follow the path of your guide string until you reach the next-to-the-last peg. Here you will start making the cross, an essential step in measuring the warp. The cross, or lease, is a figure eight that prevents tangles and keeps the warp ends in order.

Making the cross

This step will be immediately apparent as you do it. The cross is made around the two end pegs of your warp length. Take the warp thread over the next-to-the-last peg,

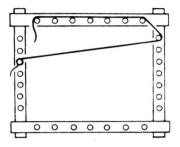

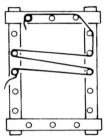

A two-yard guide string on 1-yard-wide warping board (top) and 1/2-yard-wide warping board (bottom).

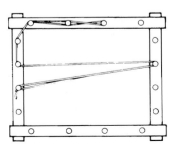
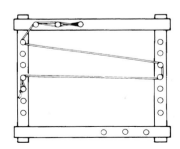
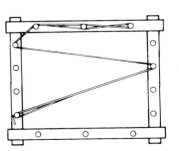

Three examples of three-yard-long warps. Any of these paths will work.

under and around and over the top of the last peg, then under the next-to-the-last peg. Now go back over the top of the third peg and follow the same path of the first warp back to the beginning. From your starting point to the last peg of your cross is one warp end; when you return back to your starting point, you have measured two warp ends.

Go back to your cross for a minute and trace the figure-eight path of your cross with your finger. If you think "figure eight", you'll likely find that making the cross is soon automatic. (For some people,

it is never automatic. If you're one of them, draw arrows on the board in pencil or on tape to remind you where to go.)

Measure all 60 threads of your first color. As you are measuring, try to keep just enough tension on your warp so that it goes around the pegs without drooping but is not so tight that the pegs bend. To make space for more ends, you may find that you need to slide the previously measured ends closer together toward the back of the pegs.

If you are alone and not interrupted, you may be able to count the

<table>
<tr><td>*Tie on the end of one of your colors of yarn and follow your guide string. Make a cross at one end. Measure 60 ends.*</td></tr>
</table>

Making the cross. Go over the next-to-the-last peg, under and around and over the top of the last peg. Then under the second-to-the-last peg, making a figure 8. The cross helps prevent tangles and keeps the warp ends in order.

Photography in this section by Eric Redding.

warp ends as you go. For those people not so secluded, there are other means of keeping track. A counting thread is one. After you've measured ten threads (five one way and five the other), tie a piece of yarn in a contrasting color loosely around them, leaving 6-inch tails. When you've measured another ten ends, use the tails to tie loosely around the next group. Keep doing this, and when you have six groups you know you have sixty warp ends.

If you would rather just count threads periodically, you can count all the threads anywhere along the warp path. Or look at the cross: half the warp is on top, the other half is below. If you count the threads on top of the peg, you need count only half of the warp, then multiply by two for the total number of ends measured.

> *Read to here first, then go back, read it again, and do it.*

Tying the cross

After you've measured all 60 ends of your first color, you need to

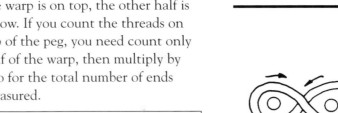

Making the cross.

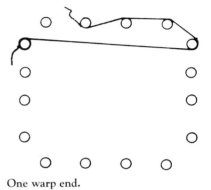

One warp end.

Two warp ends.

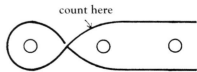

count here

Count warp ends on top of the next-to-the-last peg and multiply by two.

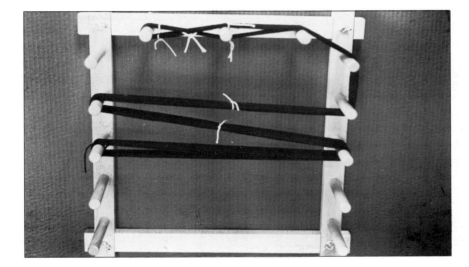

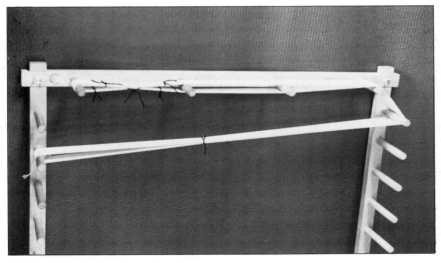

A two-yard warp on 1/2-yard-wide warping board (top) and on a 1-yard-wide warping board (bottom). Cross is tied; choke ties are used to contain the warp.

Warping Front to Back

After 60 ends have been measured, tie off your warp thread at the point where you started measuring. Tie the cross.

Tie the cross in five places. Make sure that one tie goes horizontally *around* the cross so that the cross is held inside. This tie helps to organize the threads and makes it easier to use the cross correctly while sleying the reed.

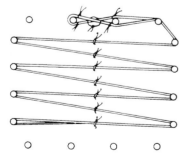

Choke ties help keep long warps from getting tangled.

secure the cross so that it stays intact after you remove the warp from the warping board. Tie the cross in five places, as shown at right. Choose a contrasting color of yarn to make it easy to see so that when it's time to cut it off, you won't cut the warp accidentally. Tie four ties vertically on the warp that goes above and below the pegs on either side of the cross to keep these sections separated for when you need to find them later. The fifth tie protects the cross. Tie it *horizontally* around the cross so that the cross is held inside the tie. The tie yarn will go through the openings on either side of the cross as illustrated. All five ties should be tight enough to keep the yarn contained but loose enough to get a scissor blade in easily.

Removing the warp from the warping board

When the cross is secure, you can take the warp off the board in stages. First, slide the end farthest away from the cross off its peg, holding the warp bundle firmly. Now is the easiest time to cut this end of the warp—one cut with a good pair of scissors will do the job; however, many people prefer to wait until the last possible moment (just before tying the warp onto the front apron rod) before cutting, and then may cut only some of the threads at a time.

Whether you've cut the end or not, tie the whole warp bundle into one large overhand knot near the end of the warp (see photo at the bottom of page 31). Tie it tight enough to be secure but not so tight that it's hard to untie later. The purpose of this knot is to keep these warp ends in alignment during warping. Leave it tied until you are ready to tie those ends onto the front apron rod, the last stage of the process.

Now lift the rest of the warp off the warping board. Because you have only 60 threads and because your warp is only two yards long, it won't tangle much. The ties in the cross and the knot at the other end will keep a short warp pretty well contained. When measuring a long warp or very slippery yarns, it is usually a good idea to put more ties, called choke ties, along the length just to keep your warp secure and in alignment. Some weavers make their choke ties very tight to keep the yarn from slipping. If you decide to do this, I recommend tying a bow for easy removal of the tie. If you'd rather tie a knot, then leave the tie just loose enough to get a scissor blade in easily; it's very frustrating to cut warp while cutting ties.

Chaining the warp, done by itself or in conjunction with choke ties, helps contain the warp and shorten it so that it is easier to handle. A measured warp is often called a warp chain. Chaining a warp is just like chaining in crochet. To begin, make a loop in the end where you tied the overhand knot, and if it's still on the board, remove the warp from the board as you chain. Your hand acts as a crochet hook to make a series of loops which can be easily removed later on (see photos on page 32). Continue to chain the warp until you are a couple of feet from the cross, at which point simply remove your hand from the last loop. The big advantage of warp chaining is that it makes your warp less vulnerable to tangling in transport, whether you're carrying it across the room or across town.

Now your choked and/or chained warp is ready to go to the loom. Repeat the measuring and chaining procedures with your second color; they will probably go a lot faster this time. When both warp chains are ready, it's time to go on to the next step, sleying the reed.

SLEYING THE REED

To sley a reed is simply to pass the warp yarns through the dents (spaces or slots) in it. You could take any measured warp and stick the ends through a reed with your fingers and you'd have sleyed the reed. There are, happily, tools and methods that make sleying go a little faster and the succeeding steps easier. These time and effort savers are what this section is about.

Whether you're using a floor or table loom, the procedure is the same. First, be sure you have the right reed in the beater. For a warp sett of 12 e.p.i., a 12- or 6-dent reed is the easiest to deal with; you'll be sleying either one or two threads per dent, respectively. If you only have

Tie choke ties to contain your warp as needed. Remove the warp from the warping board. Tie an overhand knot in the end opposite the cross. Chain your warp as necessary. In the same way, measure out and chain 60 ends of your second color.

Removing the warp from the warping board

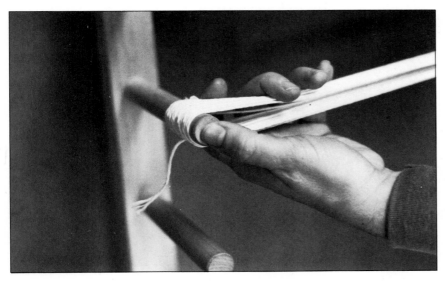

Slide the end furthest away from the cross off its peg, holding it firmly.

Tie an overhand knot in the end of the warp.

Chaining the warp

To start chaining, make a loop at the end of the warp.

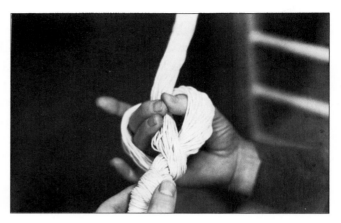

Pull warp from ahead of the loop (working away from the knotted end) through your first loop.

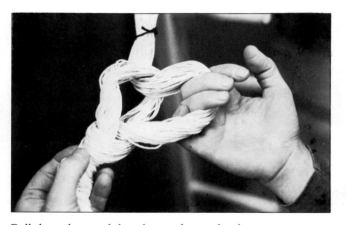

Pull through enough length to make another loop.

Continue looping loops inside of loops, as in crochet, until you reach the cross. Let the cross end hang free, making sure not to pull it through the last loop.

a reed with a different number of dents, you may need to sley a sequence other than a constant one or two threads per dent to obtain a sett of 12 e.p.i. (If you have only a 10-dent reed, use that with one thread per dent. Your fabric will be looser than it would be at 12 e.p.i., but it will still be stable.) For a detailed discussion of reeds and warp setts, see pages 210–212 in Part IV.

With the correct reed installed, tie or clamp the beater into an upright position. Some looms have a pin or other means of holding the beater in a fixed position. If your loom has an overhead beater, it will automatically hang in the best position, but you may want to tie it anyway to keep it from swinging as you work. Position the beater in the notches closest to the front of the loom so that you can reach it easily.

Sley hooks come in a variety of designs and materials, long or short, from plastic to sterling silver. They all work, so find one you're comfortable with. The only significant difference is in length. A threading

hook is much longer than a sley hook because it is designed to thread heddles; many weavers use one for sleying the reed and are happy doing so. I prefer the compactness of a sley hook because I can use it by simply flexing my wrist. If you have both available (they are relatively inexpensive), try each one and see which you prefer.

If you have neither a sley hook nor a threading hook, you have several alternatives. You could use your fingers to poke the yarn through. This works fine with smooth, stiff, thin yarns, but it is tricky with fuzzy or fat ones. You can cut a sley hook out of a plastic lid, or if you have a means to dull the edges, cut a thin piece of tin or aluminum (sharp edges will cut both you and the yarn). A small crochet hook might work, or a reshaped paper clip. Cut a notch in an expired credit card. Anything stiff enough to hold its shape should work.

Now, gather your warp, sley hook, scissors, ruler, masking tape, and whatever else you want to have

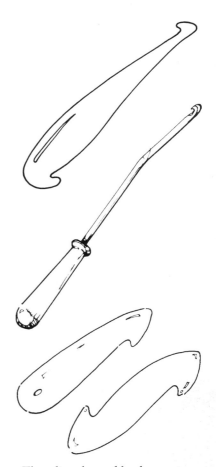

Threading sley and hooks.

Warp chains ready for sleying. Wrap warp securely around the breast beam, leaving just enough warp (four to six inches) forward to sley efficiently. Gather scissors, ruler, and sley hook; tie, clamp, or pin beater into an upright position.

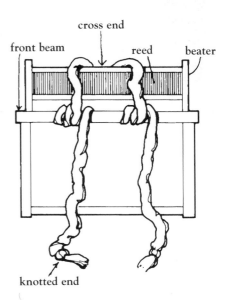

Warp chains ready for sleying.

33

Warping Front to Back

within reach (coffee, Kleenex, tele-phone, this book, etc.) and take them to your loom.

Lay your warp chains across the front beam, approximately centered, with the cross end hanging over the top of the beater and extending 4 to 6 inches past it, toward the castle. Wrap the warp chain around the beam, leaving most of it hanging in front of the loom. Wrap the chains several times or tie them in knots so they can't pull forward. The goal is to be able to pull threads from the cross without the chain shifting.

Where to start sleying

The next step is to decide where in the reed to start sleying. Your weaving will be easier and your warp tension more even if your warp is centered on the loom. A little arith-metic is called for: your warp is going to be 10 inches wide; if your reed is 15 inches wide, then you'll have 5 inches left over. Divide this figure by 2: $5" \div 2 = 2\frac{1}{2}"$. To center your

warp, you'll leave $2\frac{1}{2}$ inches of reed empty on each side. With your ruler, measure $2\frac{1}{2}$ inches in from the end of the reed, and start sleying there. If the reed is 36 inches wide, you'll have 13 inches empty on each side.

$$36" - 10" = 26"; 26" \div 2 = 13"$$

Holding the cross

Beater secured, warp chains se-cured, all tools within reach, starting place found, you are now ready to pick up your cross in preparation for sleying. Take one of the warp bun-dles and drop the cross over your left hand in such a way that the figure eight is held open. (If you are left-handed, put the cross over your right hand and from here on use left when I say "right" and right when I say "left".)

Make a fist around the cross to protect it; you still have the use of your thumb and index finger. Tuck the yarn down to the base of your fingers and palm of your hand and

Cutting the ties off. Be careful not to cut the warp yarn.

Cutting the loops at the end of the warp.

try closing your last three fingers and flexing your first two. It should not be uncomfortable. Weird maybe, but not uncomfortable.

Whether you start sleying from the right or left is up to you and depends on how you hold your left (cross-holding) hand and wrist. You want to avoid dragging your hand across the warps you've already sleyed and possibly pull them out. I prefer to sley from right to left. I think this works for the majority of right-handers, but not all, so see what feels best for you.

With the cross in position in your hand, carefully cut the five ties off the cross and cut the loops at the end of the warp. To determine the order in which to take the threads, look at the cross from the side and observe their Lincoln-log-like stacking. You need to take the top thread off the stack each time, which means the ends will alternate in coming from the left or right of your index finger. To choose, look at the stack right where the threads are crossing, at the center of the X.

Lift the first thread off, quickly closing your hand again to keep the rest of the warp threads of the cross in place. Fold the thread to make a loop at the end and place the loop between your left thumb and index finger. With your right hand, insert the sley hook through the chosen dent in the reed, pointing it from the back toward you. I find it easier if the hook is facing down, so I can pull the yarn down and away all in one motion. Catch the loop of yarn with the hook and pull it through the reed so that the yarn is headed toward the back of the loom. Then take the next warp from the cross, sley it through the next dent, and so forth. Pull each thread through the dent as far as it will go so that it is

taut from where it is wrapped around the beam. Doing this will make the warp lie flatter, and you'll be able to see where you are much better than if the ends are loose and jumbled.

Because you're making a striped warp, first sley all the threads of one color in their correct location: that is, sley 12 ends, skip 12 dents, sley 12 ends, skip 12 dents, and so on. Fill in the spaces with your other color. When that's done, you're through sleying.

If, after you've sleyed the reed, you discover that you measured wrong and the warp is not centered, don't move the threads yet. Many looms have beaters longer than the reed or have open-ended beaters, allowing you to slide the reed back and forth. If yours is one of these, simply slide the reed over. It's the warp that needs to be centered, not the reed. If your reed won't slide, you can move just the edge warp threads from one side to the other, over the top of the rest of the warp. Move the threads in order, one at a time, and it will be fine.

Sleying errors

It is very likely that you'll skip a dent or put two threads in one dent as you're sleying. This is not a catastrophe. Especially this first time, it is a good idea to check each stripe as you complete it. This way, if you have to move a thread, it is easily done—and you can hardly go wrong with the second color, as the spaces are already counted out.

If you discover an empty dent, simply take the next warp off the cross and put it in the empty space; if you've finished sleying when you discover the error, just take the warp from whichever side is closer to the error and put it in the space. It will not be in perfect order, but that

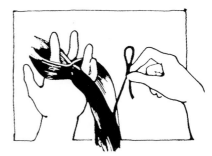

Removing threads from the cross. Lift thread off with right hand; close left hand to protect cross; fold over end of single thread and place between right thumb and index finger in preparation for sleying.

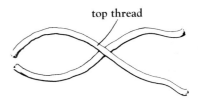

top thread

When selecting the threads from your cross, always take the top thread. To find the top one, look at the stack right were the threads cross each other.

Sleying the reed

Lift the top thread off the stack. Notice that the sley hook is kept in the hand.

Fold the end to make a loop. Insert the sley hook through the chosen dent in the reed, from the back towards you, and catch the loop with the hook. Draw it through the reed.

Sley all ends of one color. Sley 12 ends, skip 12 dents, sley 12 ends, skip 12 dents, etc.

Sley all ends of the second color into empty dents.

doesn't matter. As you beam the warp (roll it onto the back beam), you'll be combing it with your fingers. A few out-of-line threads won't create problems. Similarly, if you find two threads in one dent, simply take out the extra one and sley it where you need one.

The purpose of the cross is to make warping easier. If you are so rigidly attached to its perfection that you end up moving dozens or hundreds of threads just to keep them as they originally were, the cross has done you no favor—it's made more work for you instead of less. Using the cross will keep your warps more organized than tangled, and for that we are grateful. A few threads out of line won't create a tangle, and even a few dozen out of a few hundred won't cause enough of a mess to get excited about. Part of why you're weaving is to handle yarn anyway, and combing out (gently fondling) some minor irregularities just gives you more opportunity to enjoy that pleasure.

As you may have realized, after the ties have been cut off the cross, the only thing keeping it intact is your hand. In the strictest sense, that means you cannot leave your loom until you've finished sleying the bundle in your hand, which always leads to the question, "What if the phone rings?" (Or, more importantly, my child needs me NOW.)

There are any number of answers to this, but your concern is that the cross doesn't disappear. If you are working with a fairly sticky or hairy yarn, you can gently lay the cross down on the beam and it will hold its shape. I keep a roll of masking tape near my loom and put a piece about 4 inches long across the X of the cross if I expect to be gone awhile; then I know it will stay on the beam where I left it. The trick is getting the tape off the yarn without scrambling it; use cheap tape, only slightly sticky, and it's pretty easy. (There are now several brands of removable tape available.)

Other alternatives involve planning ahead. If you have small children or some other activity that may require frequent or instant jumping and running, keep your warp groups to a number that won't take long to sley. I don't get interrupted so I let my groups go up to 18 inches; greater widths are awkward to thread. The number of threads in a group depends on the warp sett. At 6 e.p.i., that's only 108 warp ends, while at 24 e.p.i. it would be 432 threads. If you expect to need to get up, keep your count down, to, say, 50 to 75 threads per group. I knew one young mother who always kept her groups to 10 threads. If you feel the need to stop that often, then I suggest you use lease sticks. It's slower, but you can get up whenever you want.

Using lease sticks

Lease sticks are long, flat sticks that come with the loom, usually two or three of them. Instead of putting your hand in the cross, you slide the sticks through it in the same places the pegs were when you measured it, or that your index and ring fingers would have been had you used your hand. Put all of the warp on the sticks at once, then tie the ends of the sticks together and tie the pair onto the loom, either between the front beam and beater or directly to the front beam.

When the warp is safely on the sticks, with enough warp length extended forward to reach a few inches beyond the beater toward the castle, take the ties off the cross and spread your warp out, cutting the ends and

> *Find where to start sleying. Hold the cross in your left hand, cut off the ties and cut the end. Sley all 60 ends of one color, sleying 12 ends, skipping 12 dents, sleying 12 ends, skipping 12 dents, etc. Repeat for the second color. Check and correct any sleying errors.*

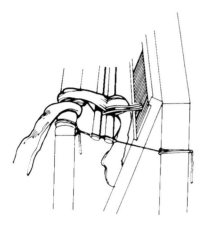

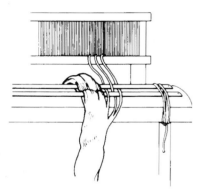

Sleying the reed from lease sticks. Lease sticks can be tied between front beam and beater (top) or onto the front beam (bottom). You can lift the threads out of the sticks or leave them in, whichever you prefer. Eventually, the sticks will need to be removed, but that can wait until the very end of the warping process, if you wish.

loosening it up so that you can pick off individual threads. Sley the reed as you would with the cross in your hand, this time lifting the threads off the sticks and sleying from right to left or vice versa, putting them in the reed in the same order as they are on the sticks.

After the reed has been sleyed, by whichever method, the cross has done its job and is gone. The threads are all lined up in the same order in which they went onto the warping board, and there should be virtually no snarls. Of course, it is possible to warp a loom without using the cross, and if you drop one and lose it, just continue sleying, doing your best to maintain some orderliness. Losing the cross simply means you'll have more combing to do when beaming, rarely a really terrible task, and not bad at all on short or narrow warps.

If you plan to leave your loom for awhile, tie bunches of the warp into slipknots or bows behind the reed to keep it from falling out. Kids, cats, curious adults, falling objects, any number of things can cause the reed to move or the warp to be jostled, and tying the warp ever so slightly can prevent lots of frustration and "if only I had's . . .".

THREADING THE HEDDLES

As you can now begin to see, the warp is making some progress. The ends are pointing in the direction you want them to go, and if you keep that in mind, it may be easier to remember the sequence of events to follow.

Threading the heddles takes longer to describe than it does to do. And as with sleying the reed, each time you do it, it will get a little faster and less awkward. Certain steps in warping are small time-savers, especially as long as you are working at a very conscious level.

Soon many of these steps will become so automatic that they will require no concentration, and by then it's useful to have developed good habits. I recommend that you use this guide for the first couple of times, perhaps taking notes in the margin on your second time through. Then, after you've made eight or ten warps, read through it all again with an eye to picking up those time-savers that didn't register in the beginning when it was all new.

So, to threading. Loosen or untie the warp chain from the front beam and pull the warp forward until it reaches 6 inches past the castle (or the last shaft you'll be threading). Then be sure the chains are tight again because now it's even more important to be able to pull against them.

Release your beater and tip it back so that it's leaning on the castle. Now go to the back of the loom and arrange the loom and your body so that you are sitting as close to the castle as possible. You'll be reaching through the castle to get to your threads, and sitting closer to the heddles contributes substantially to ease and maintaining your stamina.

Reaching the heddles for threading

If you have a table loom, you'll be reaching over or around or through the back. Floor looms come in a variety of designs, and the means of getting close to the castle vary. Some allow you to remove beams; others fold; still others are large enough that you can sit inside them. The drawings here show four of the most common floor loom designs. B stands for back beam, W for warp beam; sometimes one is removed, sometimes the other, sometimes both, sometimes neither. Compare these illustrations with your loom, try the strategies suggested below, and decide what is most comfortable to you.

A: Sit inside; don't remove anything.

B: The whole back end will fold up close to the castle or may drop to the floor. Removal of the back beam (B) may permit better access; try lifting it off. The warp beam (W) is probably fixed and not in the way.

C: Although parts of the back may fold, the majority of the parts won't. It's very likely that the warp beam (W) lifts out easily; the back beam (B) either folds up or lifts off.

D: The best way of working with an X-frame loom depends partly on how large or small it is, how stable it is when folded up, and how long your arms are. On larger looms, the back beam (B) and/or the warp beam (W) may lift out. With the warp beam (W) out and the back beam (B) in, you may be able to sit inside between the back beam and the castle to thread. Some looms are designed so that you leave the back beam and the warp beam in place and instead lift out the shafts and reed, putting them all in a rack on a table, to be replaced after you've finished threading. Another alternative is to fold the loom all or part way, which puts the beams right next to the castle and makes reaching through easy. Some X looms are stable enough that you can do this easily, others will need to be propped against a wall. If you have long arms and a small loom, you can reach over the back beam and thread from the back, but your

back may get tired.

If you will be threading from a sitting position, choose a seat low enough so that your back will be straight. A footstool, milk box, inverted wastebasket, sewing machine cover—try sitting on different objects until you find something practical and comfortable. Some weavers are most comfortable and efficient with their eye level somewhere between the heddle eyes and top heddle bar. If you wear bifocals, it's better to have the shafts lower so you can look down through your glasses; if you wear trifocals, you are faced with a challenge that has no easy solution, as you already know better than I. If you're using a table loom, you may find that standing at a counter or table is more comfortable. It's easier than sitting on the floor, though that's fine for some bodies. Also look for a way to raise the loom's shafts—by weighting the treadles with bricks, pulling the levers, etc. Raising the shafts can supplement sitting low to prevent back aches and improve visibility.

Positioning the heddles

Any loom wider than 20 inches will have some kind of hook(s) connecting the heddle bar to the shaft frame for support. When you are ready to start threading, unhook all the hooks on both the upper and lower heddle bars so that you can slide the heddles around as you need them. Rehook them just before you start to weave. It's a good idea at this time make sure that you have enough heddles on each shaft before you begin to thread. If there will be 15 warps threaded on each shaft, for example, then each shaft will need to hold 15 heddles. This is less important in this narrow project with relatively few threads, but it's a

Prepare your loom for threading. Adjust warp and back beams and shafts for comfort; place table looms at a comfortable height.

A.

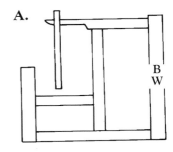

B.

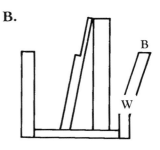

C.

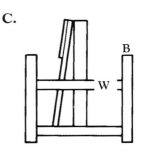

D.

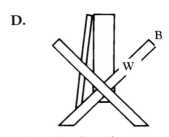

Four basic floor loom designs.

major consideration when you're threading wider pieces or one with many threads. (See pages 212–214 for more on heddles.)

Now, slide all your heddles to your left. (Lefties, do the opposite.) If you know that you have many more heddles than you'll need, you may slide some of the extras back over to the right side of the shafts. In theory, this gives the shafts a better balance because the weight is more evenly distributed, but I've never found on my loom that doing so makes much difference. Occasionally those heddles can come in handy for fixing mistakes, and in general it's a good habit to develop.

There will be times when you are using the full width of the loom but still have many extra heddles. Instead of removing them, just space them out among your warp threads. Thread a dozen or so warps, then pull over and leave some empty heddles, then thread some more warps, then leave some more empty heddles, and so on. This way, your heddles are out of the way without your needing to remove them and replace them later. If you do have to take heddles off, slide them onto a string or wire to keep them lined up; when you return them to a shaft, just slide them off the string onto the heddle bar. (It's a known fact that bundles or bunches of loose heddles contribute to insanity—to mine, anyway.)

Threading

Back to our sample warp. Read the following, up to "Tying on to the back apron rod" (page 44) *before* starting to thread; then reread it as you thread.

From the heddles on the left, pull out one heddle from each shaft (assuming you have a four-shaft loom; if you have more shafts, take a heddle from each of the first four.)

The shaft closest to the beater is shaft 1; the shaft closest to you is shaft 4. To begin threading, pass the yarn that is farthest right in the reed through the heddle on shaft 1. Put the yarn from the second sleyed dent in the reed through the heddle on shaft 2. Thread the third thread onto shaft 3, and the fourth onto shaft 4. Keep going in this manner, threading new groups of four threads on four heddles, until you've threaded 12 threads (an inch of warp width), or three groups of 4. Remember— one thread per heddle and vice versa. This manner of threading is called a straight draw.

You need to be aware that metal heddle eyes have a directional twist. Twist a heddle toward you and then away from you. The eye appears to be more open one way than the other. Threaded correctly, this twist allows a warp threaded through the eye to travel in a straight line from front to back. If threaded the wrong way, the thread will bend and may fray and break. Try threading a heddle from both sides of the eye and you'll see that one way the warp moves in a straight line through the heddle; the other way it has a kink in it. If your heddles are hanging so that it is awkward to thread them easily, turn to page 213 for information on correcting them (which can wait until later if you want to keep going now).

Tying overhand knots

When you have 12 warps threaded, tie them all in an overhand knot with the ends reasonably even. Any unevenness or other extra length not necessary is your first contribution to loom waste: yarn and money thrown away. Tie the knot tightly and as close to the end as you can get it.

After you become even a little

On wider looms, unhook heddle hooks. Check to see that you have enough heddles on each shaft.

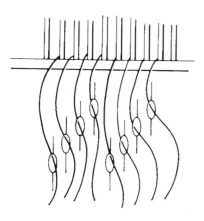

Eight threads threaded in a straight draw.

adept at threading, you'll see that it's faster to separate 12 heddles from the group at once than to pull out four heddles three times. Pulling out these small, separated groups makes it easier to see which heddle to thread next. Otherwise, you must keep looking at the confusion of threaded heddles to see what you've already done. This sounds like a picky matter, but when you're doing it, you'll see the difference.

Developing a threading method

Every weaver has her own techniques and tricks for threading. Look at the illustrations and read the description of how I do it, try it that way once or twice, and then alter your motions to fit your own anatomy and preferences: whatever works best for you is the best way to do it.

Here's how I thread my heddles:

1. I'm sitting low behind the castle of my loom, facing the back of the reed. I pull out my first 12 heddles from the large mass of heddles on the left and slide them to approximately in front of the right end threads in the reed.

2. I reach through the space between the two groups of heddles with my left hand and take hold of the first couple of inches of warp threads hanging from the right side of the reed. I pull them taut against that secure wrapping around the front beam. By holding them taut, I can easily pick off the next appropriate thread with my right fingers, which I will use to thread it through the heddle.

3. I pull the chosen warp thread taut with my right hand; at a point about 3 inches past the heddle I fold the yarn over my index finger.

4. Holding the heddle still with my left thumb and index finger (I've tucked the bunch of warp into the palm of my left hand and hold it there with my last two fingers), my right hand goes back to the heddle and I slide the loop of the warp off my finger and push it through the heddle eye. With the same right fingers, I pull the thread through the heddle, and as I pull it toward me I also pull it to the right, sliding it over (sometimes it needs a little help) to make room to thread the next heddle.

5. Pull until the thread is taut again. That keeps all the warps neatly lined up, and then making the ends even is simple. One of the most important reasons to have your warp chain wrapped tightly around the front beam with only as much length as you need for threading is that the threaded ends will not be able to get uneven. This will save you a lot of time and yarn.

No matter what you are threading or what your warp sett is, always tie your back knots in groups of 1 to 2 inches of reed width (at 12 e.p.i., that is 12–24 warps; at 8 e.p.i., 8–16). If you tie more than this together, the warps on the edges of the group will act as if they are shorter than those in the center, and the result will be a decrease in the amount of warp that you can weave, and possible tension problems at the end.

Instead of tying a knot after threading 12 heddles, you could wait to tie until after you've threaded the entire warp, but there are good reasons for tying as you go. First, and

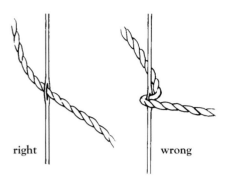

right   wrong

Metal heddles have a directional twist. Thread them so that the warp travels in a straight line from front to back without kinking.

Thread from the right and thread 1, 2, 3, 4, 1, 2, 3, 4, etc., until all warps are threaded. Thread one group of 12 at a time, tying each group in an overhand knot as you go.

Threading the heddles

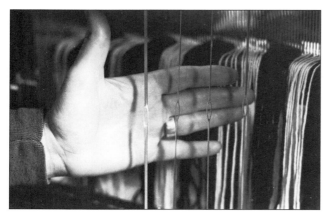

Having slid all heddles to the left (or right, if you're lefthanded), separate out four heddles, one from each shaft.

Hold the heddle steady with one hand; thread with the other one. Thread a fold, not an end.

Catch the warp with the same hand that threaded it. It'll feel awkward at first, but will be much faster later.

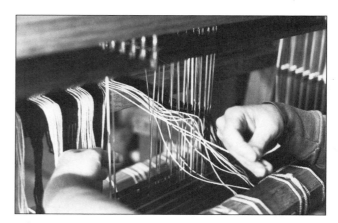

After you've threaded the heddle, slide it out of the way by pulling the warp sideways.

After you've threaded 1 inch of warp ends (12 ends), check for correctness and then tie them in an overhand knot.

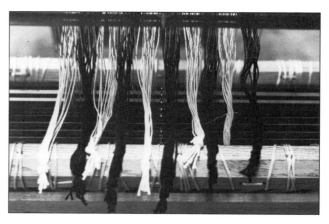

Threading finished.

quite important, as you tie each small bundle, you can check your threading for errors, correcting them early and easily. Second, tying off groups as you go decreases the likelihood of loose threads falling back into the heddles and coming out in the wrong place. This too is very important, for those errant threads will have to be fixed. And finally, it's a small task to even the ends of 12 threads or so, especially compared to lining up hundreds. If you do it one bundle at a time, you won't get sick of doing it. (If your warp is anchored well around the front beam this should be a minor matter.)

Using a Threading Hook

While I don't use a threading hook (or heddle hook) because I believe I can thread faster without one (and I like the feel of the yarn), I once saw a man in a commercial weaving mill using a threading hook so fast that it took me a minute even to see what he was doing. Clearly, technique and practice are the key.

To use a threading hook, reach through the shafts with your left hand and hold the warp taut, as above. But now, instead of lifting a thread off with your right hand, pick the farthest right thread out with your left forefinger and hold it away from the rest of the group with that finger and your thumb, creating a straight line of thread at about a 45° angle to the reed. Put the hook through the heddle from your side toward the thread, catch the thread with the hook (or lay the thread onto the hook) and pull it all the way back through the heddle eye until it is straightened out on your side. You can slide the heddle both out from its group and over to the right with the hook as soon as you have it in the eye. You may need to separate the heddle and/or hold it

still with your left hand first (depending at least partly on what kind of heddles you have). Your left hand has many tasks when threading with a hook; with practice you'll develop a smooth system and dexterity.

Crossed threads

Crossed threads are the most common mistake in warping and can occur in either of two places. (They are easy to fix, and I'll tell you how in a minute.) The first place is between the reed and heddles. To avoid crossing threads here, be sure that you take threads from consecutive dents in the reed, first thread to first heddle, second to second, etc. If you have more than one thread per dent in the reed (on purpose), be sure to thread all threads from the first dent before going on to the second. If you cross threads between the reed and heddles, one thread won't be able to rise when it's supposed to.

The second place to find crossed threads is among the heddles. If, as you threaded, the end of a warp went around another heddle and came out in a different space, the twisted threads will again not allow clear sheds, as with the other type of crossed warps. The difference is that these are harder to see and so can create problems more difficult to track down.

Either type will cause mistakes in your weaving, and the strain of being pulled up and down at the same time may well break the thread. You'll discover crossed warps when you start to weave and something isn't quite right. (Having good light is more important during sleying and threading than at any other time in weaving.) Once you've started weaving, you can locate crossed warps by looking sideways through each shed; crossed warps will be stuck in the middle of the shed.

Threading a heddle.

1. Fold a warp end around your index finger.

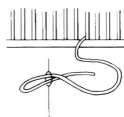

2. Push the fold through the heddle.

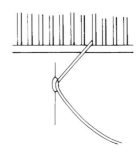

3. Pull the fold all the way through and then pull on it sideways to slide the heddle over to the side.

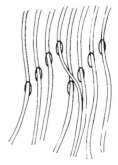

Threads crossed within the heddles. This will have to be fixed, and sooner is easier than later.

43

Warping Front to Back

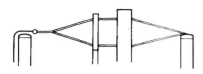

Clean shed, no crossed warps.

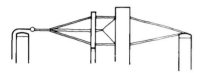

Shed with warps crossed between reed and heddles.

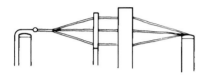

Warps crossed within heddles are harder to find.

Look sideways with the shed open to check for threading errors.

After you've found which threads they are, untie and unthread them, then correct the error, retie the threads, and continue on. It's far better to find these errors as you're warping, as they are much easier to fix early on.

When you've finished threading all of the heddles and tying your warp into small groups, put your loom back into its weaving position. If you folded the back up, extend it out again and put the beams back on. Most of the time-consuming work is done. What's left is very important but relatively speedy.

TYING ONTO THE BACK APRON ROD

At this point, the ends of your warp are hanging behind the heddles in small knotted groups. The next step is to attach these bundles securely to the apron rod; any way that holds is fine. Beyond security, the only concern is waste. As the yarn back here can't be woven, you will want to keep it to a minimum. I'll show you three ways to attach warp to the back apron rod; other weavers can show you more.

With any system, always *pull your apron rod out from the warp beam toward you and then up over the back*

beam toward the castle. When you look at the loom from the side, the warp should go horizontally from the front/breast beam to the back beam.

Every weaver I've ever known has forgotten this at least once, and even years of experience do not make one immune. If you forget to go over the back beam and your warp is going from the warp beam straight up to the heddles, you will get a poor shed at best, or none at all. Fortunately, it's an easy error to fix, requiring at most a screwdriver or wrench. You don't need to untie and retie unless you have a very unusual loom. Instead, simply lift off the back beam (which may be screwed or bolted on), slide it under the warp, and replace the beam with the warp lying on top of it.

Types of aprons and rods

Every loom manufacturer uses a different kind of apron rod and a different means for attaching it. I suspect that long ago, when weaving vocabulary was being developed, looms had cloth aprons attached to both the fabric and warp beams. These aprons were simply large pieces of sturdy cloth with hems at the ends, and slid through the hems were long sticks or rods—thus,

Preparing to tie onto the back apron rod.

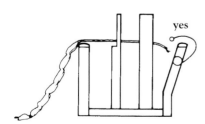
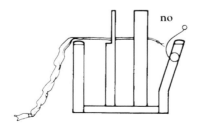
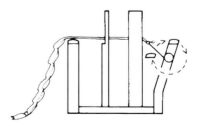

Pull your apron rod up over the back beam as shown at left. If you forget to go over the back beam and have already tied on, you can correct this by simply lifting off the back beam and sliding it under the warp and apron rod. Lift the yarns up with the beam and return it to its original position.

apron rods. These days, some looms still have cloth aprons, some have apron cords, some have webbed straps, any of which work fine as an apron rod holder.

The rods themselves may be of wood or metal, flat or round. I prefer round apron rods because it's so much easier to tie the warp around them. Sometimes I use a method for attaching my warp in which I don't actually tie the warp onto the rod; it's easy in back, but (for me at least) less desirable in front.

If your loom has cloth aprons, use two apron rods instead of one in each apron. Slide the first through the apron hem, then lash a second one to it (through small cuts in the apron) with a strong cord, 3 to 5 inches away. This allows you to tie onto the rod anyplace along its length, rather than needing to work around the fabric; that saves wear and tear on the apron, the yarn, and you.

Methods of tying on

Try all three of the following methods for tying on, one per project, and decide which you prefer. I've provided photos for the first method only; I suggest that you start with this one, the simplest. Drawings are provided for the other two methods. The second is the fastest once you're use to it. The third method is also good for emergencies, as described on page 228. Method I uses the most yarn; methods II and III are good if you need to conserve yarn.

I. Overhand knot method. The overhand knot you tied after you threaded a group of heddles serves as the first knot in this method. The second step is to tie another overhand knot around the apron rod. Pull this new knot tight, with the first knot right up against the new knot to keep it from slipping. (This is important! It may not slip now, but it probably will later as you approach the end of your weaving.)

II. Lark's-head knot method. By attaching cords to your apron rod, you can decrease your loom waste and have a quick way of tying on. First, make loops all the same size with a strong, nonstretchy yarn. Make the same number of loops as you have knotted warp bundles. Attach the loops to the apron rod as shown. To attach your warp, make a lark's head at the other end of the loop and put the knotted end of your warp through it. Pull tight, placing the knot in the warp close to the lark's-head knot.

Tie onto the back apron rod, using one of the methods described here. Bring your apron rod up over the back beam before beginning to tie on.

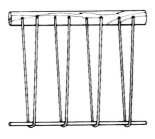

Apron strings.

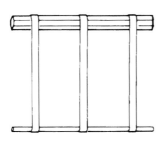

Webbed straps.

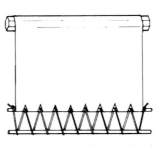

Cloth apron with second rod.

Warping Front to Back

Methods of tying onto the back apron rod

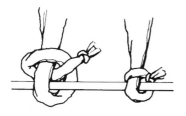

I. Overhand knot method.

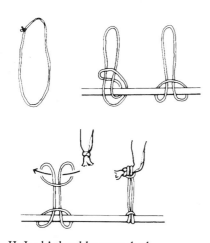

II. Lark's-head knot method.

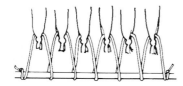

III. Lash cord method.

III. Lash cord method. This method uses a long cord which lashes the warp bundles onto the back apron rod. Start at one side, tie the lash cord onto the apron rod, then thread your cord through a warp bundle, bring it around the apron rod and through the next bundle, and so on, until all warp groups are lashed onto the rod. Tie your lashing cord to the apron rod and adjust your cord until all groups are even. The more even they are, the less waste you'll have. Of these three methods, this one is the only one which can also be used to tie onto the front apron rod.

With the first two methods, it's easiest to start at the center and work outward, or tie both edges first; either way, you'll be supporting the apron rod, making your work easier.

As you tie your warp to the back apron rod, bring it straight back from the reed. If your warp is 20 inches wide in the reed, then it should be 20 inches wide on the apron rod. Don't crowd the warp on the apron rod, as it abrades the yarn and may make your tension uneven.

If you are putting a narrow warp on a wide loom, the strain of the narrow warp will tend to bend or break an apron rod. The solution to this is very simple: slide the supporting apron cord off the apron rod for the width not being used; that is, have the apron cord pulling the rod toward the beam only where the warp is pulling it toward the castle. The strain won't show up until the weaving is almost done, so don't be overly concerned now. Just remember when you see your apron rod bend that there's a note here about it.

BEAMING THE WARP

Beaming your warp properly is without question the most important part of warping, no matter which method you use. How well you do it determines how much you can enjoy weaving the warp off. Your goal is even tension.

As you know, the loom's biggest job is to hold a set of yarns under tension so that it is easy to weave other yarns into it. Different kinds of looms have different mechanisms,

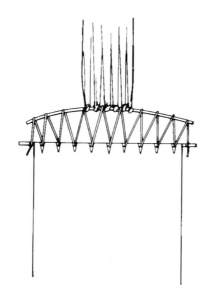

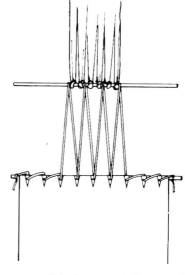

To prevent bent or broken apron rods on narrow warps, slide the outer lash cords off.

Tying the warp on to the back apron rod using the overhand knot method

1. Loop over the apron rod.

2. Bring first knot over top of the warp group.

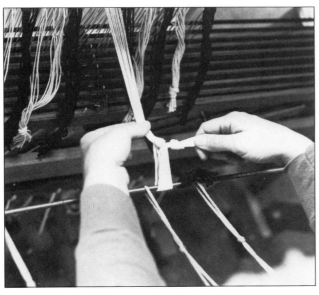

3. Bring knot around and through.

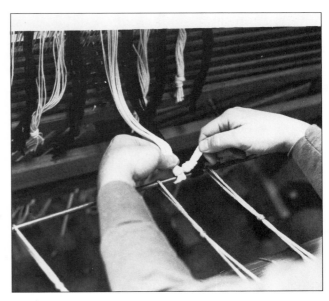

4. Pull the first knot snug against the second knot, and both against the apron rod.

Warping Front to Back

but all looms are warp holders, tension providers. If the warp is tight, the weft packs in easily, beats down fairly closely. That's why it is important to be able to provide a great deal of tension on a tapestry or rug loom. If the overall tension is looser, the weft will not pack in as much, and the lack of resistance results in a softer fabric. Thus, rugs require tight tension, shawls looser.

Now, imagine a warp that is tighter in some places and looser in others. The tighter areas will pack closely; the looser ones will not. The weft cannot possibly stay straight. The tighter warps may break as you tighten the warp enough to have sufficient weaving tension all the way across. The too-loose threads will

create a different set of problems. If they are quite slack, they may not go up when the shaft rises. If this happens, your pattern will have skips. Furthermore, your shuttle will be obstructed by a loose thread hanging halfway in the shed, neither up nor down. And when your shuttle hits the thread, it may well break it.

These are just the simplest of tension problems. See "Troubleshooting" (pages 227–229) for more. Then put your best effort into a good beaming job so you'll experience as few of these frustrations as possible.

It is now time to untie or unwrap your warp chains from the front beam. Unchain part of the length and let the loosened warp relax and fluff up, opening it up to the width

Getting ready to beam

Unwind the warp chains from the front of the loom.

Open up the warp to its full width. Shake and comb it out so that all the warp in front of the reed looks fairly orderly. Pull the beater forward.

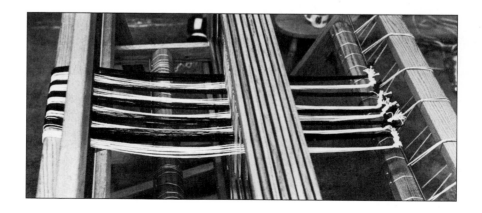

needed to go through the reed. If any tangles are visible (none should be) or the warp is crossed over oddly anywhere, gently shake the chain and comb it out with your fingers so that what is in front of the reed is orderly and parallel. Pull the beater forward until it is resting on the front beam. Go to the side of the loom and *without touching the warp or beater* crank the back beam and begin rolling the warp toward the beam. It will be awhile before your warp actually reaches the beam, as first you'll be rolling on the apron strings or apron.

Determining warp beam direction

On some looms, the warp goes around the outside of the beam and then in toward the loom, while on others the warp goes to the inside first, then around toward the outside.

Both arrangements work just fine; neither is preferable to the other. It is important to determine in which direction your beam goes because if you beam the warp in the wrong direction your brake won't hold and you'll have to redo it all. Try either or both of the following tests. Hold the apron rod; start winding it on using the beam's handle, and then try to pull it away again. If it unrolls, wind it in the other direction. If your loom has a ratchet in back instead of a friction brake, first check to see that the dog, or pawl, is engaged (lying on the ratchet wheel). Turning the beam one way, you'll hear a clicking sound as the pawl falls across each tooth of the wheel. You shouldn't be able to turn it the other direction at all, for this is your brake mechanism. When beaming your warp, listen for the clicking to tell you that you're going the right way. On floor looms, it's better for the brake to disengage while beaming (by stepping on the brake pedal); do so after you've determined the proper direction to turn the beam.

Now for beaming your warp. You'll need to crank the warp beam around, comb or shake out tangles, and place some kind of separator between the layers of warp as they roll onto the beam.

Warp separators

A separator, be it heavy brown paper, corrugated cardboard, wallpaper, venetian blind slats, or warp sticks inserted as the warp is rolled on, keeps the layers of yarn apart. Without a separator, some threads will sink down into the roll and others will not, causing the threads to travel different circumferences. The sinkers will end up shorter when you start weaving and so will become increasingly tighter as you weave. Don't rely on newspaper, plastic bags, or cloth; they are too soft and won't do the job, and newsprint rubs off on yarn. Opened-up paper grocery bags are acceptable and easily available. Be absolutely certain that your separator is wider than your warp so that the edge threads won't fall off. Start inserting the separator when the warp has gone one revolution around the beam, just before the second layer of yarn begins to cover the first layer.

All separator materials get mixed reviews; most commonly agreed to be problem-free are flat sticks such as lath, furring strips, or venetian blind slats. I use corrugated cardboard because it is easiest and works well enough.

Tension during beaming

The question of how to get even tension has a simple answer: don't apply any. Having helpers hang onto

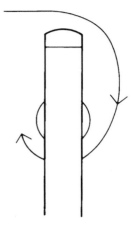

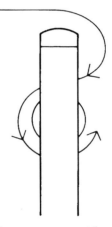

Warp beams may turn either direction to wrap the warp on. Check before beaming to see which way your loom's beam turns.

Be sure the dog or pawl is engaged. If it is, you'll hear a clicking sound as you beam.

Beaming the warp

When beaming, cranking the back beam, *do not touch the warp!* Keep cranking until the beater hits the castle.

When the beater hits the castle, stop beaming and come around to the front of the loom and shake out the warp in front of the reed. Comb it out with your fingers if necessary. Tighten the roll every three revolutions by pulling hard on the warp as shown here. Move the beater back against the breast beam and continue beaming.

Add a separator such as cardboard.

Leave the knots in front of the reed tied until you are ready to tie onto the front apron rod. This will protect your warp ends from accidentally "unsleying" themselves.

Begin rolling on. Don't touch the warp during beaming so that the tension across the warp will be even. Shake and comb out the warp in front of the reed whenever the beater tips back to the castle. After the yarn has reached the warp beam and gone around it so that it's about to wrap onto itself, insert the separator. Once you start the paper or cardboard, it'll keep rolling in on its own. If you're using sticks, insert one just often enough to keep the layers apart—every quarter turn might be enough. Tighten your roll about every three revolutions. Stop beaming when there's just enough warp in front of the reed for tying onto the front apron rod.

the warp is unlikely to give you even tension. Placing a consistent weight on the warp is time-consuming and troublesome, as well as unnecessary. The yarn passing through the reed and heddles encounters enough friction, identical for each thread, to travel evenly.

As you roll the warp onto the beam, therefore, don't touch it at all. Use the beater as a visual gauge. Start cranking with the beater tipped forward. Continue to crank until either the beater comes back to the castle by itself or you've turned the beam two or three revolutions (after inserting the separator).

When the beater tips back to the castle, it is time to shake and comb out the warp again, finding and eliminating any errant snags. Every three revolutions or so, you need to tighten the whole roll. The tension is even, but it's too loose for weaving. If you don't tighten the roll now, it will tighten as you're weaving, a subtle change that will cause uneven beating. To tighten it, grab large handfuls of warp on the left and right sides (with only 10 inches you may be able to grab the whole thing with one hand). Brace yourself against the loom and pull hard until you feel the roll tighten. Then, go back and forth across the entire warp, and in a series of large handfuls, keep pulling until the entire

width is tightened. Pulling warp is like pulling hair—if you pull just one, it will break, but a whole handful is much stronger and can withstand much greater pressure.

When the roll has been tightened, once again comb out the warp with your fingers, gently so you won't create knots, pull the beater forward, and crank the back beam with no hands on the warp or beater. Continue until there is only enough warp left in front of the reed to tie onto the front apron rod. I've found that a good measure is for the ends of the warp to just reach the front beam. The knot you tied in the very beginning is your protection against cranking the warp through the reed while you're not watching. Leave it in until you're ready to tie onto the front apron rod, for a curious visitor could easily pull the beater forward and "unsley" all of your warp. (If your warp does come out of the reed, simply resley it, this time from back to front, taking the threads in the same order that they are threaded in the heddles.)

TYING ON TO THE FRONT APRON ROD

When you tied the warp to the back apron rod, your primary concern was wasting as little yarn as possible, so your knots were designed to be as close to the end of the warp

Tying onto the front apron rod.

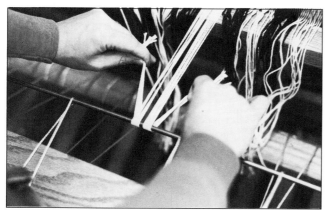

Starting at the center, take about one inch of warp width and bring it around the apron rod, splitting it into two groups.

Tie half of the square knot.

Tie the first half of the square knot all across the width of the warp.

Pat across the warp to check for unevenness.

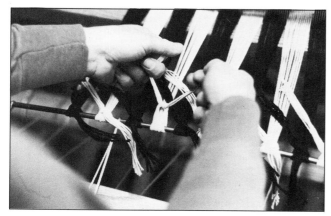

Adjust knots until tension is even. It doesn't need to be tight, just even.

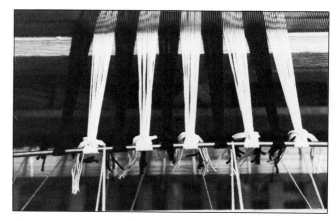

After tension is adjusted, tie the second half of the square knot.

as possible. When tying onto the front apron rod, you still don't want to waste any yarn unnecessarily, but your primary concern will be even tension.

There are several ways to attach warp to the front apron rod; I'll discuss two of them. You'll need to try them out and pick your favorite.

Methods of tying on

Probably the most common method of tying on is to pull one inch width of warp (12 ends in this case) over the rod, split it, and pull up the two groups to be tied together over the warp in the same way you start to tie a shoelace. You will eventually complete it as a square knot, or if you prefer, a bow. For now, tie just the first half of the knot (right over left and then under).

A variation to try is a surgeon's knot. Tie the first half of the knot but make two twists through instead of just one. This holds better and may even eliminate the need for the second half of the square knot.

In either case, start at the center of your warp and tie one inch of warp (12 threads at 12 e.p.i.) around the rod with *the first half of the knot only*. Then tie one or two groups to the left, then to the right, and continue tying half knots from side to side until all your warp is tied on. If you didn't cut the far end of the warp when you took it off the warping board, you may need to cut some of the ends now so that you can separate the groups for tying. The advantage of waiting until now to cut the end of the warp is that once the warp is beamed and under tension, you can cut the end of the warp at exactly the midpoint so that the two sides are of equal length. You may not even need to cut any. At any

rate, your needs and options should be fairly obvious as you look at what you have before you.

Although you can start tying anywhere along the rod, I like starting at the center because this tie supports my apron rod; if I start on one end, the rod is pulled askew and out of balance. After I've tied onto the center, I can then tie the outer edges with no problem. On a wide warp, I may tie the center first and the two ends next for added stability.

Evening the warp tension

After you've tied on all the warp with half a knot, feel the center, the first groups you tied. They are much looser than the rest of the warp, and you can even feel a steady increase in tension as you pat the warp from center to edges. This progression is normal and is why you tied only half a knot. Take hold of the warp ends of your first knot, pull them and their knot forward, away from you so that the warp slides around the apron rod, then pull the ends sideways to tighten the knot. Do the same to the next one, repeating back and forth all the way across. It may take a couple of rounds of adjusting to get all of your sections of warp to have equal tension. As the tension on your warp becomes more consistent, pat the warp with your hand to feel how even it is. It doesn't matter how tight or loose it is; you can adjust that with your ratchet any time. What matters is how *even* the tension is. Experience will teach you how precise you need to be. Don't spend an hour trying to be absolutely perfect, but do spend enough time to get the tension is reasonably even. At this point, tie the second half of the square knot to keep it that way (left over right and then under).

Tying onto the front apron rod

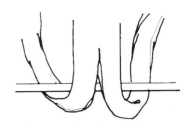

1. Pull a warp bundle over the apron rod, then split it in half.

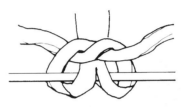

2. Tie the first half of a square knot.

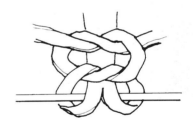

3. Finish tying the square knot after the tension is adjusted.

Warping Front to Back

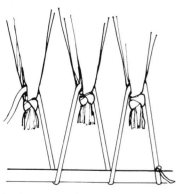

Lashing onto the front apron rod.

In her book *Warping All By Yourself* (Interweave Press, 201 East Fourth St., Loveland, CO 80537), Cay Garrett suggests another way to even up the tension as you tie the front knot. Because the progression of loose to tight is remarkably consistent, start by tying the center knots, then tighten the ratchet a click, tie a few more knots right and left of center, tighten the ratchet another click, etc. How many knots to how many clicks will vary with your tying skills, your yarn, and the size of your ratchet's teeth. It's a good system and one you may prefer to retying and adjusting by hand.

A second way to attach the warp in front is to tie overhand knots in the ends of the warp in one-inch segments all the way across, keeping the lengths as even as possible, then lace those groups to the apron rod with a strong cord, as discussed in tying onto the back beam. If you're trying to squeeze every inch possible out of your warp, this method will save you a few (or more). You must spend time adjusting the lash cord to make sure that the tension on all groups is the same. Their length may not be the same, but their tension must be. I find it easier to even my tension on individual groups tied directly to the rod, but no doubt that's because that's the way I learned. With most aspects of weaving, the way you learn first is the way you'll be most comfortable with, so try both methods while they're still new and decide for yourself which

you like better.

With either method, keep your warp groups small, usually an inch or less and never more than an inch and a half wide. If you tie wider bundles, you will have tension problems and it will take more inches of weaving from the start to get your warp spread out evenly, something you have to do before your "real" fabric begins.

When you're tying your knots in front, your warp ends will not all be exactly the same length, no matter how careful you are. Among other things, variations in the yarn will affect each warp end's stretch. You will discover quickly that your knots will need to be tied according to the shortest ends you have. The ones that are shorter at the front are that way partly because they were longer at the back; wrapping your warp chain around the front beam when you sley and thread should keep this unevenness to a minimum. Generally, the difference in lengths is small and of little concern; however, the more tail that hangs out of your knot, the more yarn you are wasting unless it will be fringe. Your time and calm are valuable too; allow enough length that tying is easy.

If, after you've woven a couple of inches, you find that one section is looser or tighter than the others, simply untie it at the front apron rod and retie it to a more appropriate tension. You can tell when it's even because the inches of woven fabric will be straight instead of crooked.

TYING UP THE TREADLES

On table looms and direct tie-up floor looms, each lever or treadle is permanently attached to one shaft and always operates that shaft. The multiple-tie-up system of most floor looms allows you to lift more than one shaft with a given treadle and aids in helping establish a rhythmical and orderly treadling sequence. Usually, four-shaft looms have six treadles; eight-shaft looms have ten. As you might expect, tie-up systems come in many forms: wires through holes, cords through slots or holes, chains or cords that attach with hooks, or others. If you have a multiple-tie-up system, check your loom instructions to see how yours works. Multiple-tie-up floor looms need to have the treadles tied up before weaving can begin.

Because I want you to really understand the relationship between stepping on a treadle and raising a shaft, for this lesson I'd like you to tie your treadles up as for a direct tie-up loom (tie shaft 1 to one treadle, shaft 2 to the next one, shaft 3 to a third treadle, and shaft 4 to a fourth) and use both of your feet to raise the different combinations of shafts. Ignore the other two treadles.*

Now you're ready to weave!

---

*If you have a counterbalance or countermarch loom: In theory, with a counterbalance loom, shafts will move up or down only in pairs. In fact, however, some will work with one shaft against three. Try doing a direct tie-up and see if you can get a clean shed; that means that one shaft will lower when you step on the treadle, the other three will rise, and you'll be able to see where to put the shuttle between the two layers of threads. You may need to use your other foot to even up the other three treadles/shafts. Counterbalance looms have much treadling personality. If you don't get a clean shed, choose any two treadles (see drawings on page 194), and to one of them tie shafts 1 and 3, to the other one tie shafts 2 and 4 (this will weave tabby, or plain weave). To the other four treadles, tie the following pairs: 1 and 2, 2 and 3, 3 and 4, and 1 and 4. You'll weave twill with these. If you have a countermarch loom, use this same tie-up. While you can tie up one treadle to one shaft as you would for a direct tie-up, you cannot depress two treadles at once.

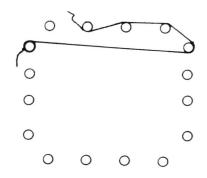

One warp end.

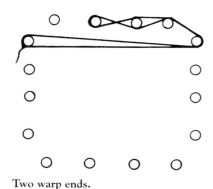

Two warp ends.

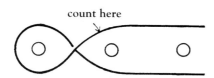

Making the cross.

count here

Count warp ends on top of the next-to-the-last peg and multiply by two.

Method B: Warping from back to front

The end result of warping back to front is the same as that of warping front to back: an evenly-tensioned set of warp ends extending between the front and back of the loom, passing through the reed and heddles, wound firmly onto the warp beam, and tied neatly onto the front apron rod. The steps for achieving this result proceed in a different order and vary in some small but significant ways. If back to front is the method you choose, you'll need to go back and review pages 25 to 27 for all of the preliminaries common to both methods.

You will need:
- Warping board or something to measure your warp on.
- A four- (or more) shaft table or floor loom.
- 12-dent reed. (If you don't have one, use what you have and choose a yarn that will fit it. Reread "Choosing yarn for your sample" (pages 23–24), and/or page 211 for more information on how to substitute.)
- 240 yards each of two colors of wool yarn (as described on page 23).
- Raddle (homemade is fine).
- Sley hook or threading hook (interchangeable in this case).
- Scissors.
- Ruler, tape measure, or yardstick.
- Rubber bands, several small and 2 large.
- Strong string for assorted uses.
- Warp separator.

SYNOPSIS OF WARPING FROM BACK TO FRONT

Here are the steps you'll follow:
1. Measure the warp.
2. Attach it to the back apron rod.
3. Spread the warp in the raddle.
4. Beam the warp.
5. Insert and mount the lease sticks.
6. Thread the heddles.
7. Sley the reed.
8. Tie the warp to the front apron rod.
9. Tie up treadles.

MEASURING THE WARP

Many weavers who warp back to front make a cross at both ends of the warp. The method I'm going to describe uses only one cross, made in the same manner as for warping front to back.

Begin by placing a guide string along a two-yard path on your warping board. Follow the guide string back and forth as you measure your warp, making a cross at one end. This step will be immediately apparent as you do it. The cross is made around the two end pegs of your warp length. Take the warp thread over the next-to-the-last peg, under and around and over the top of the last peg, then under the next-to-the-last peg. Now go back over the top of the third peg and follow the same path of the first warp back to the beginning. From your starting point to the last peg of your cross is one warp end; when you return back to your starting point, you have measured two warp ends.

Go back to your cross for a minute and trace the figure-eight path of your cross with your finger. If you think "figure eight", you'll likely find that making the cross is soon automatic. (For some people, it is never automatic. If you're one of them, draw temporary arrows on the board reminding you where to go.)

Now read from here to "Tying the Cross" (page 58). Then come back, reread, and take action.

Measure 12 threads of your first color, enough for a stripe one inch wide. To get 12 threads you'll go to the end and back twelve times, six trips each way. If you are not distracted while measuring, you may be able to count accurately as you go. Because the threads at the cross are divided in half, you can save time (and cut your chance of error in half) by counting the threads on top of the second peg, as shown in the drawing. At this point, there should be six threads there; multiply by two since just half of your warp is above the peg, and you will know you have 12 threads total.

Now put a counting thread on the warp; this will be used later to lay your threads into the raddle in the correct order. Take a string a foot long or so, fold it in half, and tie the doubled string lightly around the warp about 4 to 6 inches in from the end that does not have the cross. Tie only a half knot as if you were starting to tie your shoelaces. You'll be pulling it out later, and a whole knot is extra work to untie.

You'll use color B for your next stripe. Cut the end of color A an inch or two past the end peg and tie color B to it. It is not critical that the knot be right at the peg; the first couple of inches won't ever reach the weaving anyway, and so the knot will be part of your loom waste.

With color B attached, now measure 12 threads of that color. Then tie the tails of your counting thread around that inch of warp, cut B and tie on A, and measure your third inch. Continue in this way until you've measured a total of 10 inches, five of each color alternately.

As you measure, strive to keep the yarn's tension consistent on the warping board. This factor is important in ensuring success when you are warping from back to front. As you measure, aim to place each thread on the board with enough tension that it's not sloppy but not

so tight as to stretch the yarn a lot or put a lot of strain on the pegs. (A poorly made warping board can bend or even break under the strain of a tightly wound warp.) Work to make the tension on all threads reasonably

Follow the guide string to the end and back 12 times.

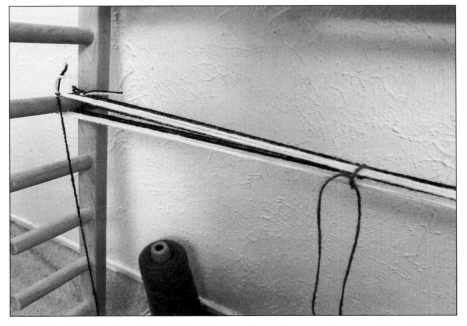

About 4 to 6 inches from the end that does not have the cross, tie a counting string around each section of 12 warp threads.

57

Photography in this section by David Crossley.

Tie the cross in four places.

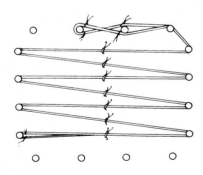

Measured warp with the cross tied in four places, choke ties spaced every yard, and the loop on the last peg tied open in two places.

equal. You can make adjustments later, but the better job you do now, the less you'll have to correct later.

You may find that you can't fit your whole warp on the warping board at one time, if not with this warp then certainly with later ones. The width of your warp, thickness of warp yarn, and length of pegs will be the determining factors. This is normal, not a problem. When you have all the warp that will reasonably fit on the board, tie it off as explained below and start again. Leave the guide string on the board so that you can follow the same path again easily and make each warp bundle the same length.

Read to here first, then go back, read it again, and do it.

Tying the cross

After you've measured 10 inches, 120 threads total, it's time to tie the warp to secure it before taking it to the loom.

The cross will be tied in four places, as shown at left. These ties secure the yarn on either side of the cross and make it easy to find the spaces the pegs are now in when it's time to put lease sticks in them. Choose a contrasting color of yarn or string to help prevent cutting your warp accidentally. Tie the ties tightly enough to keep the yarn contained, loosely enough that the yarn and two of your fingers fit inside each tie.

With a longer warp, it's also useful to tie a choke tie around the warp once every yard or two, to keep it safe and secure. With a warp only two yards long this is less critical, but put one on in the middle of the warp this time just for practice; it will help even if it's not essential. Because this

tie is to keep the threads together, tie it tightly and use a bow instead of a knot so that you can still remove the tie easily.

It is also necessary to tie open the loop at the other end with two more ties. The back apron rod is going to go through the same loop that the last peg is in now, and if you tie it top and bottom it will be very easy to reopen. Make sure that the counting thread is tied around each bundle of 12 threads. Placing the right number of threads in each slot of the raddle takes a lot longer if the counting thread is not in place.

*Removing the warp
from the warping board*

When all those ties are secure, take the warp off the warping board and carry it to the loom. This is a short enough warp that you can pull it all off the board at once, safely. If you're using a floor loom, you'll use most of the length just reaching from the front to back beam for the first step. When you do have a longer warp, it's a good idea to chain it for added security (see page 32).

ATTACHING THE WARP TO THE BACK APRON ROD

Lift the entire beater out of the loom if that's easy, or take off the top rail and reed and set them aside. Slide all the heddles to the sides of the shafts, leaving the center area clear. Be sure the back beam is fully extended, in its weaving position.

Then take your warp to the loom and wrap it once around the front beam with the cross end hanging off the front, the end with the counting thread going toward the back beam through the shafts, long enough to reach the back apron rod.

Briefly, what comes next is this: you will put one apron rod through the loop at the non-cross end of the

Attaching the warp to the back apron rod

Wrap warp around front beam with the cross end hanging off the front and the end with the counting thread going toward the back beam.

Put an apron rod through the loop at the non-cross end of the warp.

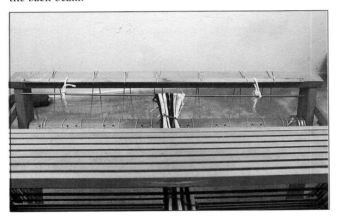

Tie the two apron rods together with about 1/2 inch of space between them.

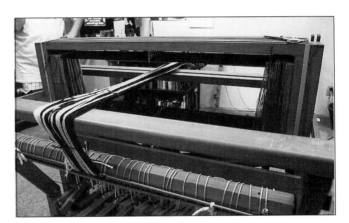

Crank the warp beam until the apron rods are just past the back beam.

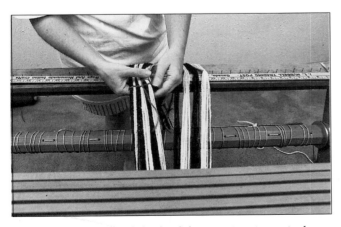

Starting at the open-ended side of the counting tie, untie the first group of 12 threads and lay it in the appropriate slot in the raddle.

To keep threads from jumping out of their slots in the raddle, put rubber bands over the pegs.

warp, attach it (temporarily) to the apron rod that is attached to the loom, and then spread the warp out into the raddle. Next, you'll re-tie the two apron rods together, more securely. I'll discuss these steps again in more detail.

Pull the apron rod that is attached to the loom up over the back beam so that it is hanging inside, toward the castle. Take the second, loose rod and slide it through the loop in your warp. If you have two warp bundles, be sure they are oriented correctly to get the color sequence you want. Slide the rod through both loops. Now tie the two rods to each other.

There are any number of ways you could temporarily connect the two rods—string, tape, rubber bands. I prefer using two loops of string because I want one-half to one inch of space between the two rods so that I can slide the warp around easily while spreading it in the raddle. The weight and tension provided by the rod attached to the loom stabilizes the rod that goes through the warp loop while you're laying the threads into the raddle.

With the two rods connected, crank the warp beam until the rods are just past the back beam. Because the warp is so short, especially if you are working on a floor loom, I had you secure it around the front beam to keep it from whizzing past to the floor behind the loom just from the weight of the apron rods. If one wrap proves to be insufficient, you can wrap it twice around or even tie it on with another cord. How much effort you need to go to will depend on the length and slipperiness of your warp and the distance between the front and back beams of your loom.

(Apparently only North American weavers warp looms alone. In other cultures there are always other people nearby to help. If you have a companion, it's okay to ask for help!)

SPREADING THE WARP IN THE RADDLE

With your warp stable and the rods in place and hanging just past the back beam, center the raddle under the warp on the back beam with the pegs or nails pointing up. Depending on your raddle and beam, you can hold it in place with C-clamps, string, tape, or rubber bands. There won't be a lot of strain on it, but the warp will be sliding past it and you don't want the friction to knock it off. (On some looms the raddle won't sit on the back or front beam. If this is the case, put it in the beater where the reed usually sits or on top of the shafts.)

The pegs of the raddle are one inch apart, just as each section you counted and tied off is one inch width of warp.

Determine what part of the raddle you will use to have your warp centered. Your warp is 10 inches wide. If your raddle is 36 inches long, you'll use the center 10 inches, leaving a total 26 inches empty, or 13 inches on each side. If your raddle is 20 inches long, you'll use the center 10 inches, leaving 10 inches empty, or 5 inches on each side. You might want to write the measurements on the raddle (pencil first) so that it has a built-in ruler.

(length of raddle–warp width) ÷ 2 = length empty on each side

(36"–10") ÷ 2 = 13" on each side

Now you may safely cut the ties off the looped end. With the rod in place, they have done their job.

Starting on the open-ended side of your counting tie, untie the first

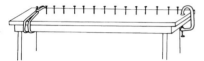

Attach the raddle to your loom with rubber bands or C-clamps, or any other way you can think of.

group of 12 threads (the group you measured last) and lay it in the appropriate slot of the raddle (farthest right or left of center 10 inches). Untie the next section and lay the second group into the second slot, the third into the third. To keep the threads from jumping out of their slots as you work your way across, put a rubber band over the first couple of pegs, over the yarn already laid in. Continue to the end, adding rubber bands for protection as necessary. When you're finished, you may want to run a piece of masking tape across the top, or the rubber bands may be sufficient. Some raddles come with tops, and some of them even slide on gradually, but I've found that sliding the rubber bands all the way down the pegs helps smooth the yarn as it moves on around to the warp beam, which is an added benefit.

As you untied each of those sections you experienced why I said to tie them lightly. Even so, you may have already thought of six other ways to tie off those measured inches. Try them all. Now that you understand the job to be done, you can probably come up with an even easier way to accomplish it.

At this point, the yarn should be spread out across the raddle, with 12 threads (one inch of warp width) in each section, in alternating stripes. The two apron rods are still tied loosely together, at the ends. It's time to adjust your warp on the apron rod so that it's coming straight down from the raddle. When all is lined up well, it's time to tie the two apron rods together more securely.

Find a strong cord (or double or triple a medium-strength one) about twice as long as your warp is wide. At the very end of your weaving the strain on this cord will be terrific.

Tie the cord onto one of the apron rods on one side of your warp, then lace the two rods together across the width of your warp. Tie the string off at the other side. Once the warp is spread out, I find it easiest to lash the two rods right next to each other, with no space between.

Lace the apron rod only for the same width as the warp is wide. If it's laced much wider than it's warped, the rods may bend or even break.

Lash the two apron rods together with a strong cord for the same width as the warp is wide.

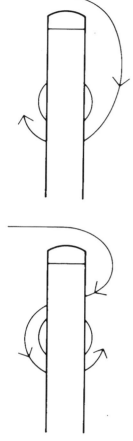

Warp beams may turn either direction to wrap the warp on. Check before beaming to see which way your loom's beam turns.

Be sure the dog or pawl is engaged. If it is, you'll hear a clicking sound as you beam.

With the rods secure, warp attached and spread, it's time to wind the warp around the back beam.

BEAMING THE WARP

Beaming your warp properly is without question the most important part of warping, no matter which method you use. I've discussed this at some length in the section on warping front to back, and I'll repeat myself here in case you skipped that section. How well you do it is a big factor in determining how much you can enjoy weaving the warp off. Your goal is even tension.

As you know, the loom's biggest job is to hold a set of yarns under tension so that it is easy to weave other yarns into it. Different kinds of looms have different mechanisms, but all looms are warp holders, tension providers. If the warp is tight, the weft packs in easily and beats down fairly closely. That's why it is important to be able to provide a great deal of tension on a tapestry or rug loom. If the overall tension is looser, the weft will not pack in as much, and the lack of resistance results in a softer fabric. Thus, rugs require tight tension, shawls looser.

Now, imagine a warp that is tighter in some places and looser in others. The tighter areas will pack closely; the looser ones will not. The weft cannot possibly stay straight. The tighter warps may even break as you tighten the overall warp enough to have sufficient weaving tension.

Too-loose threads will create a different set of problems. If they are quite slack, they may not even go up when the shaft rises. If this happens, your pattern will have skips. Furthermore, your shuttle will be obstructed when a loose thread hangs halfway in the shed, neither up nor down. When your shuttle hits the thread,

it may well break it.

These are just the simplest of tension problems. See "Troubleshooting" (pages 227–229) for more. Then put your best effort into a good beaming job so you'll experience as few of these frustrations as possible.

One other small but critical consideration is the direction in which your warp beam rotates. You've already cranked the apron rods partway toward the warp beam, but read this and then check them again. It's possible to turn the beam the wrong direction, and the result is aggravation. It won't hurt your weaving, though, because you'll have to rewind it before you start to weave.

Determining warp beam direction

On some looms, the warp goes around the outside of the beam and then in toward the loom, while on others the warp goes to the inside first, then around toward the outside.

Both arrangements work just fine, neither is preferable to the other. It is important to determine in which direction your beam goes because if you beam the warp in the wrong direction your brake won't hold and you'll have to redo it all. Try either or both of the following tests. Hold the pair of apron rods; start winding it on using the beam's handle, and then try to pull it away again. If it unrolls, wind it in the other direction. If your loom has a ratchet in back instead of a friction brake, first check to see that the dog, or pawl, is engaged (lying on the ratchet wheel). Turning the beam one way, you'll hear a clicking sound as the pawl falls across each tooth of the wheel. You shouldn't be able to turn it the other direction at all, for this is your brake mechanism. When beaming your warp, listen for the clicking to tell you that you're going the right way. On floor looms, it's better to disengage the brake while beaming (by stepping on the brake pedal); do so after you've determined the proper direction to turn the beam.

Finally, there is the matter of keeping the layers of warp separated from each other as they wrap around the warp beam. While certain warping methods and loom designs eliminate the need for any kind of warp layer separator, for now I urge you to insert something, be it heavy paper, rolled corrugated cardboard, flat sticks, or smooth wallpaper, as the warp is rolled onto the beam to separate the layers. Otherwise, some threads will sink down into the roll and others will not, causing the threads to travel different circumferences. The sinkers will end up shorter when you start weaving and so will become increasingly tighter as you weave. Don't rely on newspaper, plastic bags, or cloth; they are too soft and won't do the job, and newsprint rubs off on yarn. Opened-up paper grocery bags are acceptable and easily available. Be absolutely certain that your separator is wider than your warp so that the edge threads won't fall off.

Let's get on with beaming the warp. If you've wound your warp on the warping board evenly, with consistent tension and no snags, the warp should roll on without your needing to do anything except make sure it's tight enough. If this is your first warp, or even one of your first half dozen, odds are that it will have some inconsistencies. I'll assume here that your warp is not in 100 percent perfect order. As you gain experience, you will be able to omit some of the corrective steps and keep the essentials.

Release your warp from the front so it is free to roll onto the warp beam. Because it's so short this time,

if you're using a floor loom you may need to hold onto the warp to keep it from falling through too fast. (Or ask a friend to.)

Go to the side of your loom and start cranking the warp beam. The raddle will spread the warp to its proper width, the width it will be

Just before the warp makes the first revolution around the warp beam (top), insert a separator such as rolled corrugated cardboard (bottom) to keep the layers of warp from catching on each other.

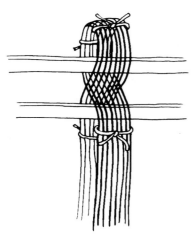

Insert lease sticks into spaces on either side of the cross.

when you weave it. As the tie in the middle of the warp approaches the raddle, remove it—right away, in this case. Generally those ties need to be removed early enough that they put no extra strain on the edge warps, so do so before the warp reaches the castle or even the front beam, depending on the size of your loom.

It's a good idea to shake and snap the warp periodically to open the bundle and help it spread out. If as the warp is moving back, you see any loops or snags or other evidence of threads of different lengths approaching the raddle, you will need to correct them. The threads need to be as even as possible in every way. When you do see a loop or whatever, first snap that section with some vigor. Often a little brisk jerking will solve the problem. If it doesn't, comb the sections lightly with your fingers. Do whatever it takes; this is the most important part of the beaming process.

Rolling the warp on evenly is your first priority. The roll also needs to be tightly wound. If it's not, then it will tighten as you weave—each beat of the beater will tighten it a little, so that the tension will be different for every weft shot and your fabric will be very inconsistent (that is, sloppy). After you've rolled on two or three revolutions, take hold of the whole warp and pull it hard. You need to tighten the roll and you won't break the warp threads—so tug and trust (a valuable life lesson I learned from a wonderful weaver in Ohio).

While you *will* be removing the ties that bind the warp midway to let it spread out into the raddle, *do not remove* the cross ties. When you've wound enough that the cross end of the warp is just in front of the castle, it's time for the next step.

INSERTING AND MOUNTING LEASE STICKS

Now for the step that for years was the hardest part of warping from back to front for me, but which is now, thanks to Sharon Alderman, the easiest part: tying up the lease sticks.

Tie two loops around the top rail of the last shaft, just long enough to reach down to about the level of the heddle eyes. Those loops are to hold your lease sticks. Slide them apart so there's one on each side of the shaft, right and left.

If you have a new loom, it probably came with two or three flat sticks as long as the loom is wide. Those are your lease sticks. If you don't have any, use any lightweight sticks or rods that are longer than your warp is wide (yardsticks or rulers work well). If you can, make holes in the ends for tying them together.

Insert your lease sticks through the spaces in front of and behind the cross at the end of your warp. Tie the ends of the sticks together to keep them from slipping out. Then slide the pair of sticks into the loops you just tied to the last shaft. The lease sticks should be hanging horizontally behind the last shaft. You can now safely cut the ties off the cross.

Now adjust the cross on the sticks so that the warp is taut as it comes from the back beam through the lease sticks and to the front. Sitting in front of your loom, take hold of the first stripe of warp (on either the right or left side) and separate it from the larger group. Slide your finger to the loop at the end (which has not been cut, is still a loop) and pull on it, top and bottom, back and forth, until that section is coming straight from back to front. Then take the next stripe and do the same thing, and so forth across the warp until it is straightened out, evened up, full width, ready to thread through the heddles. If necessary, roll the warp beam forward or back so that the warp hangs about 8 to 10 inches in front of the first shaft.

THREADING THE HEDDLES

The position of your body is important here. A tired back is the most common physical ailment weavers have, and this can be severe enough to end a weaver's career. Please do what you can to avoid discomfort.

You will be reaching forward, lifting a warp thread forward from the lease sticks and threading it through a heddle eye. The parts of your body most involved will be your arms and eyes—both lined up through the efforts of your back. The straighter you sit, the longer you'll last without pain.

Options for optimal positioning include finding a low chair or stool to sit on, removing the front beam or folding up the whole front of the loom, raising the shafts up to eye level, and raising or lowering the height of the lease sticks. You may discover other options as well. Your height, the length of your arms, and your vision will all affect the way you adjust your loom. Find the combination that is most comfortable for you.

The next consideration is the heddles themselves. Before you attached the warp to the back apron, you pushed all the heddles to the sides out of the way. Now it's time to bring them back.

Positioning the heddles

Any loom wider than 20 inches will have some kind of hook(s) connecting the heddle bar to the shaft frame for support. When you are ready to start threading, unhook all the hooks on both the upper and lower heddle bars so that you can

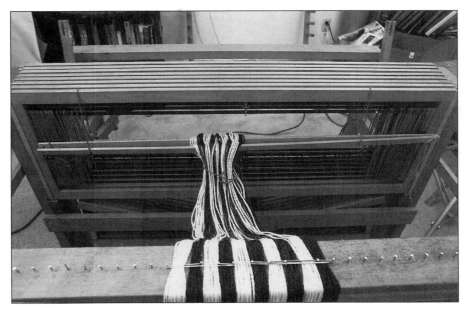

Lease sticks mounted on the loom. Insert the lease sticks into two loops of cord tied around the top rail of the last shaft, just long enough to reach down to about the level of the heddle eyes. Tie the two sticks together at their ends.

Sitting at the front of the loom, take hold of each stripe of warp, one at a time, and pull on it until that section comes straight from the back to the front.

Warping Back to Front

On wider looms, unhook heddle hooks. Check to see that you have enough heddles on each shaft.

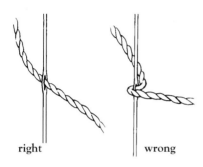

right   wrong

Metal heddles have a directional twist. Thread them so that the warp travels in a straight line from front to back without kinking.

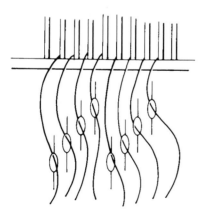

Eight threads threaded in a straight draw.

slide the heddles around as you need them. Rehook them just before you start to weave. It's a good idea at this time to make sure that you have enough heddles on each shaft before you begin to thread. If there will be 15 warps threaded on each shaft, for example, then each shaft will need to hold 15 heddles. This is less important in this narrow project with relatively few threads, but it's a major consideration when you're threading wider pieces or one with many threads. (See pages 212–214 for more on heddles.)

Now, slide all your heddles to your left. (This is written for right-handed people. If you're left-handed, change "left" to "right" and "right" to "left" throughout.) If you know that you have many more heddles than you'll need, you may slide some of the extras back over to the right side of the shafts. In theory, this gives the shafts a better balance because the weight is more evenly distributed, but on many looms, doing so makes no difference. This heddle arrangement does look nice, and occasionally these heddles can come in handy for fixing mistakes or last-minute design changes.

There will be times when you are using the full width of the loom but still have many extra heddles. Instead of removing them, just space them out among your warp threads. Thread a dozen or so warps, then pull over and leave some empty heddles, then thread some more warps, then leave some more empty heddles, and so on. This way, your heddles are out of the way without your needing to remove them and replace them later. If you do have to take heddles off, slide them onto a string or wire to keep them lined up; when you return them to a shaft, just slide them off the string onto the heddle bar.

Metal heddles have a directional twist. Twist a heddle toward you and then away from you. The eye appears to be more open one way than the other. The importance of this twist is that it determines if a warp threaded through the eye will travel in a straight line from front to back or not. If the warp has to bend, it may fray and possibly break. Try threading a heddle from both sides of the eye and you'll see that one way the warp moves in a straight line through the heddle; the other way it has a kink in it. If your heddles are hanging so that it is awkward to thread them easily, turn to page 213 for information on correcting them. Note that the direction easiest to thread by hand is opposite of the direction easiest to thread using a threading hook.

Now to thread the warp through your heddles. From the heddles on the left, pull over one on each shaft (assuming you have a four-shaft loom; if you have more shafts, take one from each of the first four shafts). These four heddles represent one repeat of the threading pattern you will use for this sample. You will be threading the heddle on shaft 4 first, using the farthest right thread on the lease sticks. The second thread will go through the heddle on shaft 3. The third thread will go through the heddle on shaft 2, and the fourth thread will go through the heddle on shaft 1. Another way of saying this is "thread 4,3,2,1". The threads should look like the illustration at left. This sequence of threading is called a straight draw.

Pull the right-hand stripe of warp forward from the lease sticks. Pulling the loop toward you, cut it in the exact center so that the top and bottom threads are the same length.

As you lift individual threads

forward from the lease sticks, note that they alternate, coming from above and below the stick closest to you. The cross is holding the threads in the same order in which they went onto the warping board. They have been rolled onto the beam in that order, and you'll now thread them in that order, so there will be no significant crossing of threads or tangles to cause problems while weaving. That's why you put all that effort into making the cross, and the result is well worth it. (If you doubt that, try it sometime without a cross. It can be done, and is done when the cross is accidentally lost.)

Thread the first four of the cut threads as described above. Now repeat that sequence—thread the next four threads through the heddles on shafts 4,3,2,1, one thread per heddle. Then do it a third time. Three groups of four equals 12 threads, or one inch of warp width. Check your threading to be sure that all threads are going straight through the correct heddles and that none got crossed behind other heddles. When you are sure that all are in the right places, tie a slipknot in that bundle of 12, slide the whole group over to the right out of the way, and you're ready to proceed with the next inch.

Tying the slipknot now is important; otherwise, a thread could fall back in among the heddles and come out in the wrong place. That kind of mistake is hard to find and can cause several kinds of problems. (See page 43 for more information.) So check your threading and tie a slipknot after you finish threading each group.

Underlying the threading procedure are two main concerns: accuracy and efficiency/ease/comfort/speed, at least to the point of getting done in a reasonable amount of time. Most important is accuracy. Mistakes

Threading the heddles

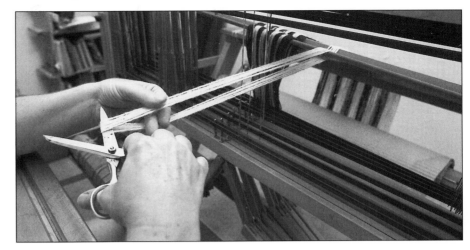

Cut in the exact center of the warp loop in a bundle of 12 warp ends.

Thread the first four threads in a straight draw; 4,3,2,1.

After all 12 threads in the bundle have been threaded through the heddles, check for and correct any errors, and then tie the bundle in a slipknot.

in threading order must be fixed unless you want cloth with obvious and unattractive mistakes in it. These can take a lot of the pleasure out of a finished piece.

Acquiring efficiency, ease, and comfort can make warping considerably more fun for you. I am one of those weavers who really enjoys warping, *especially* threading, because I like the manual dexterity involved. Do I enjoy it more because I've gotten fast and efficient, or did I get fast and efficient because I enjoy it? I watch what I'm doing, and if it seems as though there must be a better way to do something, there usually is, and I find it by experimenting. Enjoying it includes taking care; fixing mistakes is not a big thrill for me.

Here are some more tips to make threading easier and faster and to improve your accuracy:

First and simplest is to pull out an inch's worth of heddles at one time: three from each shaft, 12 altogether. That speeds things up, as you're not starting and stopping as often. It also is your first accuracy monitor. If you count out the heddles you need ahead of time, then

while you're threading you can be observing how many are left on each shaft and thus tell early if you've made an error. When you've completed the group, if you have any extras or are short any heddles, either you counted wrong in the first place or you misthreaded somehow. It is a quick matter now to determine what the error is and fix it; the further your warping proceeds, the more difficult and time-consuming it is to fix threading errors.

You need light. Plenty of it. If you can't see the heddles clearly, you're much more likely to make mistakes. Blind weavers and those with other visual problems work by touch and/or color. You can do that, too, but if you can see, then help yourself to do so. Set up a light so that it will shine down into the shafts. (If you have problems with dyslexia or depth perception, paint your heddle bars or heddles different colors with fingernail polish, one color per shaft. Then thread by color.)

Use the tension that is available by pulling the threads taut. Take a small bundle of threads from in front of the lease sticks (not off them) and

The slipknots prevent threads from falling back among the heddles and coming out in the wrong places.

hold them taut with your left hand. Then pick the farthest right one off with your right hand, pull it toward you, a few inches past the heddles, still taut, and fold it over your index finger. Holding the heddle still with your left thumb and index finger (with the warp bundle tucked into your left palm), pull your finger out as you move your right hand back, and thread the first heddle with the fold in the yarn (usually, that's easier and faster than putting a fuzzy or floppy end through a heddle). If, when you lift the thread out of the bunch in your left hand, you slide your index finger along it toward yourself until it's a few inches past the shafts, then back up to the heddle, you can develop a by-feel routine that becomes automatic. It will feel awkward at first, but with practice will get smoother, I promise.

Now pull the thread through the other side with the same right fingers (this takes practice but is a real time-saver). Poke it in toward you, pull it through toward you, and as you do so pull it over to the right and slide it out of the way. (Sliding works best with flat steel heddles, medium well with wire heddles, and not at all with string heddles. You'll need to slide the string heddles over with more concerted whole-hand or even two-handed effort.)

So, get a good light, sit as straight as you can, hold the threads taut with your left hand and thread the heddles in groups of 12 with your right hand, tie those groups in slip-knots immediately after threading them, and repeat the process until the whole warp is threaded and knotted. Pull your warps straight forward from the back to get them all lined up right again, rehook your heddle bar hooks, and then get up and stretch.

If you want to use a threading hook, read page 43, thinking about lifting threads from the lease sticks instead of the reed. Everything else is the same.

SLEYING THE REED

Time to put your loom back together. Center the reed back in its track and put the top rail back on, or replace the whole beater assembly if it's out. Then tie or pin the beater into an upright position so it is easy to work both in front of and behind it and it will hold still.

Sleying the reed requires reaching over the beater to the heddles and pulling the threads through the reed to the front. Depending on the relative sizes of your loom, your bench or chair, and your body, you may be more comfortable standing than sitting for this part.

Check the length of the warp. Now it needs to reach 8 to 10 inches beyond the reed, and so it probably needs to be released from the back and pulled forward a little way. Step on the brake pedal (if you have a floor loom) or reach back and release the back ratchet (on a table loom) and pull gently on the warp until you have enough to go through the reed and tie in small bundles again. Once you've advanced the warp, pull each group of threads until all are straight and taut once again. Remember the good light you had on the heddles for threading? If it's portable, focus it on the reed now, at different angles until you can see well enough.

Where to start sleying

The next step is to decide where in the reed to start sleying. Your weaving will be easier and your warp tension more even if your warp is centered on the loom. A little arith-

Threading a heddle.

1. Fold a warp end around your index finger.

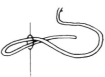

2. Push the fold through the heddle.

3. Pull the fold all the way through and then pull on it sideways to slide the heddle over to the side.

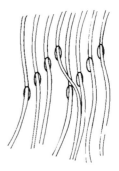

Threads crossed within the heddles. This will have to be fixed, and sooner is easier than later.

Warping Back to Front

An easy sleying method

Take a group of four threads in your left hand and, with the back of your hand facing the sky or tipped to the left, put one thread between each pair of fingers, so that the farthest right thread is between your index finger and thumb.

Make a loop of the first thread around your index finger and use your right hand to pass a sley hook through the appropriate dent in the reed and catch the loop, and then pull the thread through the reed.

metic is called for: your warp is going to be 10 inches wide; if your reed is 15 inches wide, then you'll have 5 inches left over. Divide this figure by 2: 5" ÷ 2 = 2½". To center your warp, you'll leave 2½ inches of reed empty on each side. With your ruler, measure 2½ inches in from the end of the reed, and start sleying there. If the reed is 36 inches wide, you'll have 13 inches empty on each side.

$$36" - 10" = 26"; 26" \div 2 = 13"$$

Right-handed people start on the right side, working toward the left (lefties do the reverse). Reach behind the beater, pick up the first group of threads, and pull out the slipknot. Take the first four threads in your left hand and, with the back of your hand facing the sky or tipped to the left, put one thread between each pair of fingers, in order, so that the farthest right thread is between your index finger and thumb. Notice that the threads are aligned and that it's easy to see which one to take first. With the threads held taut, use your index finger to move the first thread out from the rest, creating a path from the group, around your index finger, to your thumb and back to the group. Hold the section of yarn between your index finger and thumb up behind the reed. With your right hand pass either a sley hook or a threading hook through the farthest right dent you want to thread, going from front to back. Catch the warp thread with the hook and pull it forward through the reed. Keep pulling until the thread has been pulled through and is taut once again. Going this direction, I find it easiest to have the hook facing up and to lay the yarn onto the hook or grab the yarn with the hook. Try it facing up and facing down, and see which you prefer.

When the first thread is all the way through, use your left index finger to lift the second thread away from the group, hold it away and around your index finger as you did the first, and sley it. Sley the third and fourth in the same way. Repeat these steps with the next four threads and then the final four of the first inch, and retie the 12 into another slipknot in front of the reed.

I remember vividly the first time I saw someone lift a thread from a group of warp ends with the thumb of the same hand she was holding the group in. I came mildly unglued, thinking she would wreck her cross, lose control of the bundle of warp. Later, I realized that other people have much more flexible thumbs than I do, and what I could not do at all other people could do with ease. While my thumb doesn't bend much, my index finger does fine, so the description above seems quite easy to me. If for some reason you cannot hold the threads all in one hand and pick one off with the same hand, don't. Use whatever fingers on whichever hand is easiest. Just be sure to feed a loop of yarn, not a loose end, to the hook to grab.

Accuracy in sleying is essential. The three most common errors are to miss a dent (put no threads in it), double-sley (put two threads in a dent), and cross threads (sley dents in the wrong order). Skipping dents or double sleying will create lines in your fabric that may be practically invisible or really glaring, depending on many factors, but they will not cause structural problems. Crossed threads, however, will cause functional problems and will have to be fixed. To correct any of these errors, resley the errant

threads. Sometimes that means only two dents; sometimes it means half the warp.

If you have vision problems, even slight ones, sleying a fine reed can be a nightmare. The following alternatives might prove useful.

Use a larger-dent reed: for instance, double-sley a 6-dent instead of single-sleying a 12. Count dents by clicking your sley hook along them and listening, counting the clicks. Tie a thread in one-inch increments through dents around the top of the reed so that it doesn't interfere with your warp as you're weaving. Don't mark the beater, for reeds slide back and forth and marks on the beater would become meaningless. And always, always, keep your threads taut and straight. Even if your vision is perfect, warps curled around and over and under each other make it nearly impossible to tell which dents have been filled and which dent comes next. When the threads are straight the next open space is far more evident.

When you've sleyed the entire warp, check one more time. Each thread should travel in a straight line through the heddles and reed; none should be crossed anywhere. When all is in order, remove the raddle from the back beam and take the lease sticks out of their loops an out of the warp or secure them to the backbeam to help even out warp tension irregularities.

TYING ONTO THE FRONT APRON ROD

Untie the beater (or pull the pin out) and tip it back so that it's resting against the castle. Pull the front apron rod up so that it wraps in front of and over the front beam and will reach about 1 to 2 inches in front of

Lease sticks can aid in achieving even tension while you weave. If a few warp threads are looser than the rest, the sticks will hold the slack sections back, making the warp in front more even.

Tie the ends of the sticks together, close enough to create some friction on the yarns passing over and under them, but not so close as to make it hard for the yarn slide between them, especially novelty yarns. Next, tie the stick that is closest to the back beam to the back beam, again with a small space between the two. Keep the sticks as far from the castle as possible—lease sticks can creep forward during weaving and interfere with the shed, shrinking it and straining both the warp and the weaver.

If your warp starts out fine but gets uneven as you weave, try inserting one lease stick into each of the two tabby sheds (see * on page 80), or as close to the two tabby sheds as you can get. Weave them in right behind the castle, tie them together as above, then slide them back and secure them to the back beam. You'll see bubbles of warp sliding back too, and generally speaking, those bubbles will stay behind the sticks, giving you a more even warp to weave.

Tie onto the front apron rod using one of the methods described. After all warp is tied on, adjust the tension until it is even. Tie the second half of the square knot if you use the first method.

the beam when held up. Hold a section of warp up to the rod—there is probably more length than you need to tie on. If you want really long fringe, you can leave it as it is, but if you want to weave as much fabric as you can then it is better to shorten it. Crank the warp back a few inches, but not too far—you would not want to unsley all you'd just sleyed. Though the slipknots will prevent that, it's wise to be careful nonetheless; it's a mistake you'd probably only have to make once.

There are several ways to attach warp to the front apron rod; I'll discuss the same two that are described in the section on warping front to back. Try them out and pick your favorite.

Methods of tying on

Probably the most common method of tying on is to pull 1 inch width of warp over the rod, split it, and pull up two groups to be tied together over the warp in the same way you start to tie a shoelace. You will eventually complete it as a square knot, or if you prefer, a bow. For now, tie just the first half of the knot (right over left and then under).

A variation you might like to try is a surgeon's knot. Tie the first half of the knot but make two twists through instead of just one; this often eliminates the need for the second half of the square knot.

In either case, start at the center of your warp, untie the slipknot from a warp bundle, and tie them around the rod with *the first half of the knot only*. Then repeat, tying one or two groups to the left, then to the right, and continue tying one-inch groups of warp in half knots from side to side until all your warp is tied on.

Although you can start tying anywhere along the reed, I like starting at the center because this tie supports my apron rod; if I start on one end, the rod is pulled askew and out of balance. After I've tied onto the center, I can then tie the outer edges with no problem. On a wide warp, I may tie the center first and the two ends next for added stability.

Evening the warp tension

After you've tied on all the warp with half a knot, feel the center, the first groups you tied. They are much looser than the rest of the warp, and you can even feel a steady increase

When all the threads have been sleyed, remove the raddle from the back beam and take the lease sticks out, or take them out of their loops and secure them to the back beam.

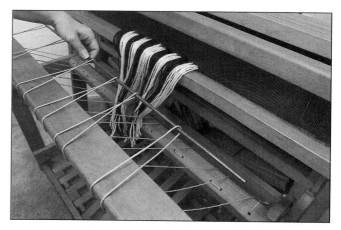

Pull the front apron rod up so that it wraps in front of and over the front beam and reaches about 1 to 2 inches in front of the beam when held up.

in tension as you pat the warp from center to edges. This progression is normal and is why you tied only half a knot. Take hold of the warp ends of your first knot, pull them and their knot forward, away from you, so that the warp slides around the apron rod, then pull the ends sideways to tighten the knot. Do the same to the next one, repeating back and forth all the way across. It may take a couple of rounds of adjusting to get all of your sections of warp to have equal tension. As the tension on your warp becomes more consistent, pat the warp with your hand to feel how even it is. It doesn't matter how tight or loose it is; you can adjust that with your ratchet any time. What matters is how *even* the tension is. Experience will teach you how precise you need to be. Don't spend an hour trying to be absolutely perfect, but do spend enough time that the tension is reasonably even. At this point, tie the second half of the square knot to keep it that way (left over right and then under).

Cay Garrett's method of evening the tension as you go is described on page 54; you might find it worth a try.

A second way to attach the warp

in front is to tie overhand knots in the ends of the warp in one-inch segments all the way across, keeping the lengths as even as possible, then lace those groups to the apron rod with a strong cord. If you're trying to squeeze every inch possible out of your warp, this method will save you a few (or more). You must spend time adjusting the cord to make sure that the tension on all groups is the same. Their length may not be the same, but their tension must be. I find it easier to even my tension on individual groups tied directly to the rod, but no doubt that's because that's the way I learned. With most aspects of weaving, the way you learn first is the way you'll be most comfortable, so try both methods while they're still new and decide for yourself which you like better.

With either method, keep your warp groups small, usually an inch or less, and never more than an inch and a half wide. If you tie wider bundles, you will have tension problems and it will take more weaving from the start to get your warp spread out evenly, something you have to do before your "real" fabric begins.

When you're tying your knots

Tying onto the front apron rod

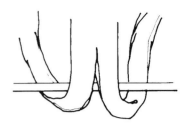

1. Pull a warp bundle over the apron rod, then split it in half.

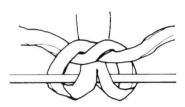

2. Tie the first half of a square knot.

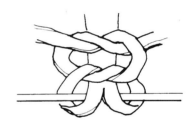

3. Finish tying the square knot after the tension is adjusted.

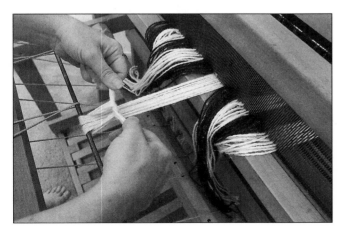

Beginning at the center of the warp, tie onto the front apron rod by pulling one inch width of warp over the rod, split it, and pull up two groups to be tied together with half a square knot (in the same way you would start to tie a shoelace).

After all the warp has been tied with half a square knot, adjust all of the knots until the tension is even across the width. Then tie the second half of the square knot.

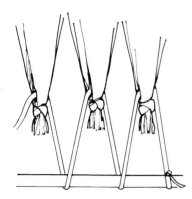

Lashing onto the front apron rod.

in front, your warp ends will not all be exactly the same length. Generally, however, the difference in lengths is small and of little concern. If you find that all of the warp ends on one side of the loom are longer than those on the other, you probably wound too much warp onto the warping board. It's far better to measure the warp in several small bundles than all at once in a single large bundle. Too much warp on the warping board causes the pegs to bend inward just enough to make the warp measured last noticeably shorter than that measured first.

If, after you've woven a couple of inches, you find that one section is looser or tighter than the others, simply untie it from the front apron rod, and retie it so that the weaving is straight.

TYING UP THE TREADLES

This part of the warping process is just the same whatever way you do the job. As with some other parts of the process, I've already described tying up in the section on warping front to back, but will repeat it here so you don't have to flip back and forth.

On table looms and direct tie-up floor looms, each lever or treadle is permanently attached to one shaft and always operates that shaft. The multiple-tie-up system allows you to lift more than one shaft with a given treadle and aids in helping establish a rhythmical and orderly treadling sequence. Usually, four-shaft looms have six treadles; eight-shaft looms have ten. As you might expect, tie-up systems come in many forms: wires through holes, cords through slots or holes, chains or cords that attach with hooks, or others. If you have a multiple-tie-up system, check your loom instructions to see how yours works. Multiple-tie-up floor looms need to have the treadles tied up before weaving can begin.

Since I want you to really understand the relationship between stepping on a treadle and raising a shaft, for this lesson I'd like you to tie your treadles up as for a direct tie-up loom (tie shaft 1 to one treadle, shaft 2 to the next one, shaft 3 to a third treadle, and shaft 4 to a fourth) and use both of your feet to raise the different combinations of shafts.*

Now you're ready to weave!

---

*If you have a counterbalance or countermarch loom: In theory, with a counterbalance loom, shafts will move up or down only in pairs. In fact, however, some will work with one shaft against three. Try doing a direct tie-up and see if you can get a clean shed; that means that one shaft will lower when you step on the treadle, the other three will rise, and you'll be able to see where to put the shuttle between the two layers of threads. You may need to use your other foot to even up the other three treadles/shafts. Counterbalance looms have much treadling personality. If you don't get a clean shed, choose any two treadles (see drawings on page 194), and to one of them tie shafts 1 and 3, to the other one tie shafts 2 and 4 (this will weave tabby, or plain weave). To the other four treadles, tie the following pairs: 1 and 2, 2 and 3, 3 and 4, and 1 and 4. You'll weave twill with these. If you have a countermarch loom, use this same tie-up. While you can tie up one treadle to one shaft as you would for a direct tie-up, you cannot depress two treadles at once.

VARIATION ON WARPING FROM BACK TO FRONT

Probably the most common alternative method of warping from back to front involves more extensive use of the lease sticks. I have described having a cross at the front end of the warp only and inserting the lease sticks after beaming, for threading only. This idea startled me when I first heard it; it was hard to believe that I could beam a warp evenly if it did not have each thread individually tensioned. More traditional in the United States, I think, is the practice of having the cross at the far end of the warp, at the back of the loom, and inserting the lease sticks before winding the warp onto the back beam.

In this variation, a counting thread is tied on at the cross end of the warp. Lease sticks are inserted into the cross when the warp is being attached to the back apron rod and laid into the raddle. Some people tie them in place between the castle and either the front or the back beam, others leave them loose and keep pulling them forward by hand as the warp is moved to the back. Easiest to use is a device, called a warp tensioner, that is a frame with lease sticks built in that mounts on the front or back beam and stays stationary. Regardless of how the lease sticks are attached, the entire warp passes through them on its way around the warp beam. This serves two purposes.

First, the warp is spread more evenly. How valuable this is varies with the yarns, their nature and variety (many warps are made up of mixed yarns).

Second, and more important, the lease sticks help to comb the warp by creating friction, which can be a boon—or a detriment. A very slippery yarn may go on much more reliably if it's run through lease sticks, sometimes even three or four instead of only two. On the other hand, a very bumpy or fragile warp could snag or break from such an obstruction (with two smooth and rounded-edged lease sticks, this is very unlikely, however). The more experience you have with different yarns, the more you'll know when increased friction is a blessing and when it is a curse.

The warp is then threaded, sleyed, and tied as described earlier in this lesson. The major advantage of this variation is that it carries a better guarantee of even tension.

Method C: Deborah Chandler's hybrid method

I was first taught to warp from front to back, which at that time was the less common method. Putting the cross in one's hand instead of on lease sticks was not only revolutionary, it was, to many weavers, downright sacrilegious! Thus began my life (in weaving) as a heretic. Because of that, I've never felt bound by tradition.

The flip side was that for too long—I was young, and just out of the 60s—I automatically resisted anything labeled traditional just because it was so. So I've never learned the difference between rosepath and birdseye, it took a spiritual encounter for me to have any positive ideas about counterbalance looms, and because I couldn't master them on my first attempt, I had nothing but bad words for lease sticks.

Nearly ten years later, I decided it was time to give warping from back to front a fair try. At about the same time, I took on a job as a contract production weaver, turning out many yards of loopy goopy fancy fabric woven on warps of mixed yarns that were the best reason in the world to warp from back to front: so all those loops and bumps and fuzzies wouldn't have to be dragged through the heddle eyes to be beamed, kicking and screaming all the way.

I made a vow to warp from back to front on every warp I wove that winter and spring, to really get the hang of it. With each warp, I tried something a little different, worked out one more bug. By the time I was done, I had devised a system that I really liked, for it gave me everything I wanted and none of the headaches.

I love sleying the reed—off my hand and in general. It's one of the few times in the entire weaving process that I get to actually handle the yarn. I wind the warp without using a paddle, for I get a charge out of touching every inch of the yarn that will be in my weaving. When sleying the reed from the front, I have a whole fist full of yarn. That's better than chocolate! Threading with my fingers instead of with a threading hook gives me more fuzzy touch. Once I've completed these steps, most of the rest is handling the wood of the crank, the shuttles, the beater—nice, but not yarn. So when I started warping from back to front, I had a terrible lonely feeling—no more holding the cross, no more fist full of yarn. Beyond that, for me, the mechanical action of sleying the reed in either direction is just plain fun.

For my rather unusual high-touch, hybrid method of warping, here's what I do:

1. Measure the warp, cross at one end.
2. Approach the loom as if I were warping from front to back; wrap the warp around the front beam with just enough left loose to sley the reed.
3. Sley the reed from my hand.
4. With the heddles pushed out of the way, tie onto the back apron rod.
5. Beam the warp. The reed serves as the raddle and lease sticks.
6. With only a little warp left, carefully take the reed out of the beater and lay it across sticks placed to hold it parallel to and right behind the castle. The sticks are parallel to the sides of the loom and may rest on the front and back beams.
7. The reed still acts as the lease sticks, offering the warp in the proper order. Lifting the threads out of the reed one by one, thread the heddles from back to front. When the heddles are all threaded, the reed is empty.
8. Put the reed back in the beater. Sley it again.
9. Tie the warp onto the front apron rod.

Note: no raddle, no lease sticks, and no undue drag on bumpy yarns. Sometimes I've done the first rough sleying using a 4-dent reed with several threads in each dent. This allows me to pass the loops at the back end of the warp through the reed without cutting them, so I can then pass a stick through them to attach to the back apron rod instead of having to tie knots. This is a faster way to secure the warp at the back, and it also cuts down on loom waste. Then I've switched to the appropriate reed for the final sleying.

The back-to-front method described on pages 56–75 is similar to this one in its simplicity and is definitely much faster—unless you have a lot of different yarns in your warp with changes occurring frequently. For that kind of mixed warp, measuring all the ends you need of each kind of yarn at once and mixing them in the reed as you warp front to back can be the quickest and most efficient way to work. My hybrid method has advantages of both, if you don't mind sleying the reed twice.

The more I weave, and therefore the more I warp, the more I learn. And the more students and other weavers I meet, the more I learn from them.

The hybrid method described here is one I developed nearly ten years ago, and have rarely used since I quit weaving those highly textured 30-yard production warps. Now, finally, I'm smart enough to choose the most appropriate warping method or variation for each project. How sensible!

Please realize that there is a difference between choosing different warping methods for different warps and using different methods without any rhyme or reason. I had a very right-brained student once who was a genius with color but who probably hadn't warped the loom the same way twice in 30 years—because she had no grasp of the logic of it. Talk about creativity! This is not what I'm recommending. In fact, I suggest you choose either Method A or Method B and use it repeatedly until you feel really comfortable with it. Then try the other, and use it long enough to feel on solid ground. Then go back and forth as seems appropriate, or use some hybrid method. And keep notes. I've found myself halfway through warping my loom before realizing it would have been better to use a different method. But in most cases, the method you choose is not critical. Most weavers, like me, warp the same way on every warp for years. It's up to you how many tools you put in your tool box.

So, now, at last, it's time to weave!

Weaving

Your first weaving assignment

Weaving a header

Winding your shuttle

Selvedges

Sequences of the weaving process

Crossed warps, threading errors, and
broken warp threads

Taking your sample off the loom

Finishing your fabric

Learning from yourself, record keeping, self-evaluation

Sample weaving with 1-inch-wide black and white warp stripes. At left is plain
weave; at right is twill. Warp sett is 12 e.p.i.

Your first weaving assignment

And now, to weaving! With this
sample, I want you to get used to
your loom and how it operates. To
do that, I suggest the following: first
weave plain weave (also called
tabby) by raising shafts 1 and 3
together, creating a shed for the first
weft shot, and then raising shafts 2
and 4 together, creating a shed for
the second weft shot, repeating this
sequence over and over. Notice that
in plain weave the weft travels over
one warp, under the next, over the
next, under the next, etc. (It is the
most basic of weaves.)

Using the same yarn for weft as
you did for warp, try three different
beats, that is, packing the weft in at
three different densities. For the
first, try to get a balanced weave,
one in which the number of weft
shots or picks per inch (p.p.i.) equals
the number of warp ends per inch
(e.p.i.). Use a ruler to measure an
inch and count how many picks you
packed in. After weaving 3 inches of
balanced weave, weave another 3
inches in which you beat very hard
(more p.p.i. than e.p.i.), and then
weave 3 inches with a very loose
beat (fewer p.p.i. than e.p.i.). Use
only one color for each 3-inch section. Alternate colors with each
block if you like.

After this 9 inches of plain
weave, repeat the three methods of
beating while weaving a 2/2 twill. A
2/2 twill is a weave structure in
which two shafts are up and two are
down in every weft shot, in a
sequence such that a diagonal line is
created. To weave a 2/2 twill, raise
shafts 1 and 2 together for the first
shot, 2 and 3 for the second, 3 and 4
for the third, and finally 4 and 1 for
the fourth. Repeat these four combi-

nations. You'll notice now that your weft travels over two warps and then under two, then over two, under two, etc., and that with each successive weft pick the weft moves sideways one thread, creating a diagonal.

Because the warp and weft threads intersect less in a twill than in plain weave, you'll find that your weft tends to pack in more easily. So for a balanced twill, beat lightly and count your weft shots per inch.

After you've woven these 18 inches, play around. Try more of what you liked, change colors of yarns, lift different combinations of shafts (in other words, change your treadling sequence), do anything else you can think of. Weave as far as you can, then untie everything and take it off the loom so that you can measure your loom waste and take-up.

Here's a summary of your assignment, but before you begin, please read through the rest of this section on weaving.

Sample I

10" × 2 yd, 2 colors of wool
Weave plain weave for 9 inches:
3 inches beating for balanced weave,
3 inches beating for weft
    predominant (harder beat),
3 inches beating for warp predomi-
    nant (softer beat).
Weave 2/2 twill for 9 inches:
3 inches balanced,
3 inches harder,
3 inches softer.
Play around.

Just a note on grammar. "Weave" is an irregular verb, so please don't say, "I weaved a scarf." It hurts even to write it. I weave, I wove, I have woven, I will weave. I am a weaver. (Whether it's comfortable to call oneself a weaver is

another matter.) Another point: you are a weaver or you weave; you don't "do weaving".

The mechanics of weaving are the easiest part of the whole process: open the shed, throw the shuttle, beat, repeat. (Of course, there are a few details beyond this, some finesse to develop.) Let's review the basic steps so that everything is clear.

The shed is the space created between the upper and lower warp threads when you raise or lower some of your shafts. You can throw a boat shuttle through the shed; a stick shuttle won't flow as smoothly across, so you probably will pass or hand it through the shed. Beating means using the beater to push the weft shot into place. If it's a tight weave, then thinking of it as beating is good. If you are weaving a loose fabric such as a shawl, "beating" has too much force; thinking in terms of gently pushing is more appropriate.

Weaving a header

Before you start weaving, you can see that your warp is not parallel in front of the reed, that from the knots on the apron rod to the reed the warp forms a series of Vs. Your first job is to get the warp ends in the Vs to lie parallel. There are several ways to do this, and all use the same principle.

As you weave, the warp will eventually straighten out, but because the weaving doesn't look good until this has occurred, you want to reach this point as soon as possible. Many weavers start by weaving a "header" using a fatter weft. It can be heavy yarn, old stockings, rags, toilet paper, or even flat sticks, for it is not considered part of the weaving and is pulled out when the piece comes off the loom.

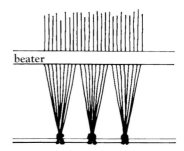

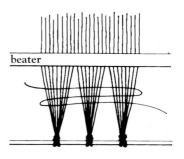

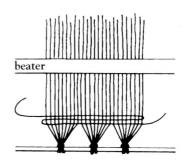

Weaving a header. Here, three weft shots are woven before beating them in. This closes the Vs so that all the warps lie parallel.

Winding a stick shuttle using the figure-8 method. Both sides of the shuttle may be filled.

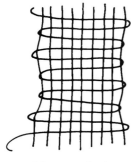

Uneven selvedges.

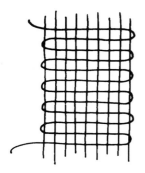

Nice, even selvedges.

Whether you are using a special weft as your header or starting with your planned weft, the fastest way to achieve parallel warp threads is to put three weft shots into alternating tabby sheds* without beating in between, then beat all three together. Repeat the sequence and the threads of almost any warp will become parallel, even with a very skinny weft. If they're not even after three repeats of the sequence, check the width of your knotted groups; if each group is much more than an inch wide in the reed, it will take many more weft shots to get it aligned.

An added benefit of beating the first three shots together instead of individually is that it does a nice job of fine-tuning your tension. Looser warps will pucker or loop in front of the weft and be held there by the three shots. The result is that the warp still to be woven is now very even. The effectiveness of this varies with the yarn being used; it works better for stickier or hairier yarn, less so for more slippery yarn.

Winding your shuttle

Before you begin weaving, you'll need to put some weft yarn on a shuttle. Any shuttle, whether commercial or homemade, will work, but some shuttles are more efficient or work better for different types of weaving. Boat shuttles are faster and

*Alternating tabby sheds is a new phrase. Tabby and plain weave are different words for the same thing. Plain weave (tabby) is woven by raising shafts 1 and 3 together and then shafts 2 and 4 together. The treadling (shaft combinations) given for this assignment is two pairs alternating; thus alternating tabby sheds are 1 and 3 versus 2 and 4. Although this works for the threading you've just done, 1, 2, 3, 4, on a different threading, you might need to do a different treadling to get tabby. I'll talk about this later when the occasion arises.

more expensive; stick shuttles are slower and less expensive.

If you'll be using a boat shuttle, you'll need to wind the bobbin that fits inside it. If you don't have a bobbin, you can use cut-down straws or rolled-up paper—anything on which you can wind yarn. A bobbin winder, either hand or electric, is an invaluable time-saver.

There are many different ways to wind bobbins. One popular technique is to build up yarn on the outside edges of the bobbin, then build up the center. Another method, the one I prefer, is to wind back and forth all the way across the full width of the bobbin as a spool of sewing thread or kite string is wound; the thread seems to feed off the bobbin more smoothly.

A stick shuttle must be wound by hand. About any way you do it will work, though the figure-8 method shown at left allows you to put more yarn on at one time without the shuttle becoming too bulky to pass through the shed easily.

Selvedges

When you actually begin weaving your piece, one of the first questions you'll have will be about your selvedges (sides) and how much weft to leave in the shed and on the side. The goal is to have selvedges that are parallel and reasonably smooth. This takes practice, and just what you need to do to achieve it varies with every piece, so don't let wobbly edges discourage you. While different yarns and different patterns have their own peculiarities, there are some common factors useful to know.

When the shed is open and the weft is passed through, consider the old rule that the shortest distance between two points is a straight line. For a 10-inch-wide warp, therefore, a 10-inch piece of weft would be long enough to reach from side to side. When the shed is closed, however, the weft will take up—it must curve under the warps that were raised and over those that were in the lower position; thus, a longer piece of weft is needed.

Allowing for the right amount of extra weft has everything to do with how straight your selvedges are and how much they will draw in on the sides. The weft needed to travel the extra over-under distance must come from somewhere, and the only available place is the edges. The take-up will pull equally from the two sides, or try to. On one side, there will be plenty of yarn to draw from as it is simply pulling more from the shuttle (if the shed is still open). On the other side, away from the shuttle, it will pull just as much, and in the process will draw the edge warp(s) in with it. That is where draw-in comes from.

Minimizing draw-in

To keep draw-in to a minimum and to keep it consistent, you'll need to leave more weft in the shed than would at first seem necessary. When you weave, instead of having your weft travel straight across the warp, make an angle or curve or some other nonhorizontal trail, as shown below.

If, however, you leave excess weft on the edge, as opposed to within the width, the packing in of the weft shot will create a loop or bubble on that side, resulting in a loose or sloppy-looking selvedge. To prevent those bubbles and loops, pull the weft close to the selvedge thread and leave the excess arc farther in. Practice everything you can think of, remembering you are now developing habits that will stay with you.

You should know that almost every weaver has one better selvedge and one not as good, but you can nurture habits in yourself to get them as consistent as possible. Watch yourself and see what you're doing differently with your right and left hands, and work from there.

One way to have very even straight selvedges is to pull your weft tight and go for a maximum amount of draw-in. I've seen this done and sometimes it works. However, if you are using a firm yarn, the strain on the pulled edges can break the edge warp threads. On the other hand, if you are using a soft yarn it may stretch. If one selvedge pulls in more

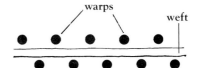

Open shed with weft going straight through.

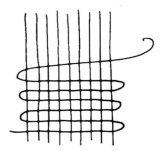

Closed shed with weft going over and under warps.

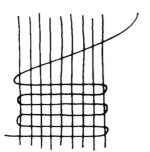 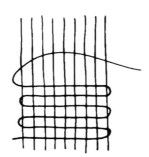 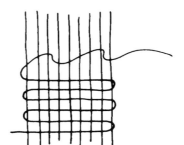 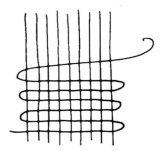

To minimize draw-in allow extra weft in the shed. Angling or curving as shown here are ways to add length to the weft in the shed. If you leave loops on the sides, your finished piece will have loops on the sides.

Weaving

Color play and treadling variations can produce exciting results, as seen in this weft-faced pillow. Here, cotton carpet warp is set 8 ends per inch (e.p.i.), and is completely covered by the weft. The threading is a point twill (threaded 1, 2, 3, 4, 3, 2, 1, 4, repeat), woven on opposites (see page 150 for more on this). By using different color and treadling sequences, all kinds of patterns are possible. In this example, the use of rich purple, pink and red, with zingy specks of yellow, produce an electric effect. You might explore neutral, pastel, or close-in-hue color schemes for equally interesting results. Though complicated in appearance, this pillow is really quite easy to weave. Let your inspiration guide you! *Woven by Yvonne Stahl.*

This overshot runner was done in a beginning weaving class. It is a good example of how a class sample can serve a functional purpose. The simple plain-weave border is a nice contrast to the heavily patterned body of the runner; both the royal blue background and the red pattern weft play equally important roles in the overall design. In overshot, you can generally plan on your pattern weft yarn being twice as large as your background weft in order for it to show up effectively; a steady, even beat is important to achieve a balanced pattern. This pattern is Mary Ann Ostrander, on page 146 of *A Handweaver's Pattern Book* by Marguerite Davison. *Woven by Audrey Kick.*

than the other, one side of your weaving will end up longer than the other side (a trapezoid), one of the few problems in weaving that is virtually impossible to repair.

A temple or stretcher is a tool that is designed to keep selvedges straight, an adjustable tension bar with teeth on both ends that sink into your weaving (without hurting it) and hold it to a fixed width. You place it in the web (cloth) that was just woven, weave a few inches, then lift it off and move it forward, always keeping it within a couple of inches of the fell (front edge, last weft shot). Some weavers use a temple all of the time, for every kind of project; others never use one.

While the tendency when you first start to weave is to pull at the selvedges, resisting the urge will lead to developing a smoother weaving rhythm, especially if you are using a boat shuttle. An even weaving rhythm does a lot for selvedges, as well as makes your weaving progress more rapidly. Practice, though, is probably the main factor in achieving good, even selvedges (if you're practicing good habits).

Special selvedge considerations

Twills have a special selvedge oddity that plain weave doesn't have. When weaving plain weave, you are raising every other thread every other time, so your edge threads go up, down, up, down, forever. With a twill, because of the treadling order, a shaft will stay up for two shots, then down for two. Depending on the direction your shuttle is going, and which side it is on when you change sheds, the edge threads may or may not be caught by the weft. If they are not, then you'll

have a warp float on the side, perhaps for a short distance, perhaps for the entire length of the piece. There are a variety of ways to deal with this; choose the one(s) that works best for you.

The easiest way to avoid edge warp floats on twill fabrics is to simply change the direction of the shuttle. To do this, either cut the weft and start again from the other side or skip one shed in the treadling sequence; for example, instead of 1 and 2, 2 and 3, 3 and 4, 4 and 1, treadle 1 and 2, 3 and 4, 4 and 1. Skipping a shed will cause a skip in your pattern, so you may not want to do this. Try it just to see what it looks like, then if you don't like it, unweave it (reverse your treadling and pull the weft out).

Sometimes changing the direction of the shuttle only changes which side has an uncaught warp; no solution at all. Instead, you can manipulate the shuttle around the edge warp thread, simply going over or under it by hand instead of entering the shed as you normally do. This can be a strain on the warp and is tedious if kept up for very long, but it works well for short distances.

If you know that warp floats at the selvedge will be a recurring problem in a piece, you can use a floating selvedge. I'll tell you about this when we discuss twills (pages 113–114).

Finally, you can apply the following formula to minimize the occurrence of this unwoven edge thread. This works only if your threading begins on shaft 1 and ends on shaft 4 (or vice versa). When weaving a 2/2 twill, if you first treadle 1 and 2, start your shuttle from the opposite side; that is, if the right most thread is on shaft 1, start the shuttle from the left, or if the left

1	2			
	2	3		
		3	4	**shaft 4 is up for two consecutive rows**
1			4	
1	2			**shaft 4 is down for two consecutive rows**
	2	3		
		3	4	
1			4	

Twill treadling order. Here, a shaft stays up for two shots, then down for two.

selvedge thread is on shaft 1, start the shuttle from the right.

Whether you need to use any of the above solutions depends on whether an uncaught warp is a problem. This depends on the project. Practicing these methods in a sample can be valuable, but it doesn't really matter to the sample whether the edge thread is caught or not. Likewise, if you are making something whose edges will eventually be cut off or sewn up, then again this doesn't matter. If one thread *never* catches, eliminate it and your piece will be one thread narrower. If the selvedges will be forever visible, as in a table runner, vest front, or wall hanging, then you do need to choose a way to make your selvedges look nice.

Sequences of the weaving process

The actual sequence of events in weaving anything includes changing the shed, throwing the shuttle, and beating the weft in, but there's the question of order; whether to beat with the shed still open, after closing it, or after changing to the next shed. In weaving tabby, for instance, after you've thrown the shuttle through the 1 and 3 shed, do you beat with shafts 1 and 3 still raised, after you've lowered them and have no shafts raised, or after you've raised shafts 2 and 4? Each choice has its merits, and each weaver a preference. It's a good idea to vary your strategy according to what you are weaving and the yarns you are using; some yarns are more fragile than others and that makes a difference in how they need to be handled.

The argument for beating with the same shed still open is that when the shed remains open, any addition-al weft needed to accommodate take-up is easily pulled from the shuttle end of the weft shot, which reduces draw-in. Changing the shed with the beater still forward creates less friction on the warp yarn since it's passing through air, not rubbing on the reed, which is much safer for a delicate or hairy yarn.

The case for beating after the shed has been closed or changed is made most often for rug weaving, though it applies to other weaving as well. With the shed changed, the weft is locked into place; after it's beaten in, it will not slide back out or shift.

Either sequence can permit a consistent beat, an even density. You are responsible for beating consistently, and if you are consistent, the fabric will be.

When weaving on a floor loom with a boat shuttle, you'll develop a rhythm that is so smooth and flowing that the beat/change sequence is almost imperceptible, both things happening almost simultaneously.

Advancing the warp

As your weaving progresses, you'll notice your shed getting smaller and smaller. This is due to two things: the shortening of the distance between the fell of your fabric and the heddle eyes, where the opening is largest, and to the increase in warp tension that occurs from take-up as you weave, making it harder to open the shed. How far you can weave depends on your loom; in most cases, this will be somewhere between 2 and 6 inches. When the shed has become so small that it is difficult to get the shuttle through, or even an inch or so before that, it's time to advance your warp. (Weavers seeking great consistency

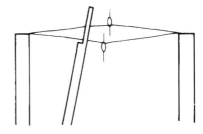

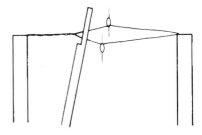

As the fell of your fabric gets closer and closer to the reed, you will find your shed getting smaller and smaller. When you can't get your shuttle through it easily, it is time to advance the warp.

Plaids lend themselves well to all kinds of things: shawls, tablecloths, towels, vests, caps, scarves. Think of weaving plaids in plain weave or twill, knowing that each weave structure will produce a different result. This plain-weave scarf and matching twill hat demonstrate how combining weave structures on one warp can produce varied, coordinated results. There's room for lots of experimenting here. *Woven by Yvonne Stahl.*

Placemats are an all-time favorite project of weavers. This set is woven of durable cotton and will take lots of everyday wear and tear. One-inch-wide stripes of white and brown alternate in the warp; this sequence is repeated exactly in the weft for a checkered mat. Warp sett is 12 ends per inch; 12 weft shots per inch are woven in for a balanced and square pattern. To get fringe on the sides, run two or three more warp threads an inch or so away from the selvedge thread, creating a new "for fringe only" selvedge. Later cut them off, leaving a fringe of weft. Experiment with color; try mats of blue and green, red and white, gray and pink, brown and beige. Explore! *Woven by Bethany Thomas.*

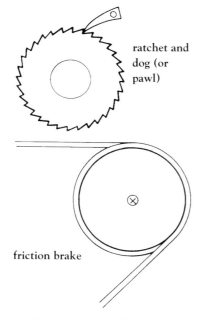

ratchet and dog (or pawl)

friction brake

A ratchet brake can hold only at intervals, in a tooth of the ratchet. On a friction brake, a cable or wire clamps down and holds tight. It can be loosened a little for slight tension release. It can hold tight at any point around the drum.

advance their warp quite frequently, for as the fell advances the angle of the beater changes, causing a different beat if the weaver doesn't compensate for the changes.)

If your loom has ratchets front and back, release the front ratchet first to relax the warp tension, then release the back ratchet to be able to advance the warp. On a table loom, this is done by hand. On a floor loom, stepping on the brake pedal (usually to the right of your treadles) will release the back ratchet.

If your loom has a friction brake, lightly tap the brake pedal with your foot until the brake releases a little bit. Never release a tight tension all at once (with either type of brake) because the sudden release will cause your warp beam to spin and unwind a lot of warp, necessitating rewinding. If you have a brand-new loom, the friction brake may require some adjusting and breaking in to decrease stiffness. Try releasing it over and over, being careful never to bend the cable that wraps around the drum. If this cable should get bent, it will never hold tight again nor release reliably. (You can buy a replacement from the loom dealer or manufacturer.)

After disengaging the back brake, whichever type it is, keep it released and crank your warp toward the cloth beam, again listening for the clicking of the dog, on the front ratchet this time. There should be a handle or crank attached to the cloth beam for rotating it forward. When your fabric is almost far enough forward to get a good shed, reengage the back brake (take your foot off the brake pedal or manually flip the dog back on the ratchet). Then crank the cloth beam forward enough to tighten your warp tension enough to resume weaving. On table looms, the ratchet is released and

the warp advanced by hand.

Advancing the warp too far is a common problem, the result being that either your beater will hit the front beam before it hits the fell or the angle of the beater will be such that it won't beat the weft in well. If you have advanced your warp too far, simply reverse the process, rolling the warp toward the back again. Release the front brake, crank the back beam so the warp rolls onto the back again, then tighten it from the front.

Using lease sticks to help while weaving

If you warped from back to front, your pair of lease sticks have been sitting in the warp by the back beam since you finished warping the loom. If you warped from front to back, you've not used them yet (but you may want to put them in after reading this section).

If they are in place, up to now you likely have been nearly unaware of their presence, but as you advance your warp, they will advance with it, moving closer to the shafts. Just as your woven cloth getting closer to the shafts will decrease the size of your shed, so will the lease sticks getting close do the same. However, they can serve a useful purpose.

Let's say you've woven and advanced the warp to the point where the lease sticks are up to the castle. Let's further suppose that the threads coming off the back beam are not perfectly even, a few being looser than the rest. As you slide the lease sticks back, you can effectively comb those loose threads back as well, so that the loops of looser thread are now (or still) behind the sticks, making the tension in front of the sticks more even, more consistent. This scenario can take place with smooth or bumpy yarns, in a wide variety of situations. Some weavers always keep lease sticks in their warp; others never use them. Certainly, if your warp has gone on well and your tension is even, then you probably don't need the sticks at all, and you can just take them out and forget about them.

If you have lease sticks in the warp, the distance between the front and back beams of your loom will determine how often you need to slide them back. On a table or other small loom, you may need to move them every time you advance your warp; on a very large floor loom, you may only need to move the lease sticks once every three or four advances.

Don't leave the lease sticks near the castle while you are weaving. To do so will diminish your shed, which is annoying to you and hard on the yarn. When the shed is opened, the sticks will hold the layers of warp together at the same time that the heddles pull up on individual threads, straining and possibly even breaking them. The sticks should always be at least as far from the shafts as is your most recent weft shot.

Another option is to tie the lease sticks to the back beam so that as the warp advances the sticks automatically comb the warp, holding the snaggles behind. The obvious advantage of this is that you don't have to keep fooling with them; they take care of themselves. The disadvantage is that if the warp is fragile, it might be safer to be combing those threads intentionally, paying careful attention to each one, treating them all as gently as necessary. Another advantage could be that if your loom is wide, your lease sticks long, and your warp narrow, having the sticks tied up at the ends can eliminate any potential flopping around that could damage your tension on edge threads. (If your lease sticks are long and flop-

ping but you prefer not to tie them, replace them with shorter ones.)

If you warped the loom from front to back and have decided to put a pair of lease sticks in, simply open your first tabby shed, raising shafts 1 and 3, and "weave" a lease stick in behind the castle. Close the shed, then raise shafts 2 and 4 and weave in the other lease stick, also behind the castle, but in front of the first stick. Tie the ends of the sticks together so they don't fall out, and slide them back to, but not beyond, the back beam.

Ending and starting weft

What to do when you end one weft and start another depends on so many variables that the only firm rule is *don't* knot them together. Knots cause bumps that are present forever, and they are both unattractive and unnecessary.

These illustrations show you six options.
A. Overlap anywhere, 1 to 2 inches.
B. Tuck ends in on opposite selvedges; this changes direction shuttle is going, which may or may not matter.
C. Leave ends hanging out while weaving, cut back to selvedge or sew them in after piece has been washed and shrunk.
D. Tuck ends in on the same side; this may cause excessive buildup on one side, especially if you're using a fat weft yarn.
E. Like A, only more finicky. Before starting the new weft, split both ends in half (unply the yarn and cut off half the plies) so that when the two overlap they are together the same size as the yarn was originally.
F. Like E, only *more* finicky. If an abrupt color change is critical, end the first weft on a selvedge,

Ways to end and start weft.

A. Overlap 1 to 2 inches.

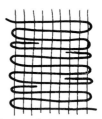

B. Tuck ends in on opposite selvedges.

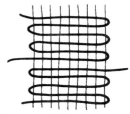

C. Leave ends hanging out and cut them back to selvedge or sew them in after piece has been washed and shrunk.

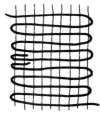

D. Tuck ends in on the same side.

E. Unply the old and new yarns and overlap half of each.

Weaving

As you gain more experience and confidence in your weaving abilities, before long there's a good chance you'll want to try weaving some fine threads. At left is a simple, plain-weave finger-tip towel with pale green overshot borders. The warp is a white cotton set 24 ends per inch; the weft is a natural beige linen packed in for a balanced weave at 24 picks, or shots, per inch. Shiny perle cotton, used for the borders, is a nice contrast to the mat finish of the background yarns.

The napkin at right is woven of fine linen. It has lace borders on all four sides which give liveliness to the plain-weave background. Hemstitched edges add to the heirloom quality of this piece. These two fabrics are especially appealing for their simplicity. If you're not yet ready for fine threads, try these ideas out in heavier yarns for placemats or table runners. When you do try fine threads, you'll be pleased at the joy of weaving fine fabric and surprised that the weaving progresses more rapidly than you supposed it would. *Towel woven by Yvonne Stahl; napkin woven by Helen Irwin.*

Simple plain weave and a cotton novelty yarn work well together to make the shawl and matching purse cover shown here. The warp is a bleached white, 5/2 perle cotton; the weft is a natural cotton bouclé. When woven, the two yarns produce a fabric with a pleasing texture and a lot of drape. In planning, keep in mind what you want your finished product to look and feel like, and then choose your yarn, sett, and beat accordingly. The choices made for this ensemble give it a special appeal, both visual and tactile, for cool summer evening wear. Think of some of the yarn and texture choices you might make for a fall or winter version. *Woven by Katie Potter.*

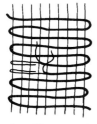

F. Unply the old yarn and overlap it on itself at the selvedge. Do the same with the new yarn.

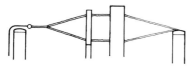

Clean shed; no crossed warps.

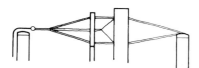

Shed with warps crossed between reed and heddles.

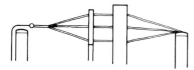

Warps crossed within heddles are harder to find.

Look sideways with each of the tabby sheds (shafts 1 + 3 and shafts 2 + 4) open to check for threading errors.

splitting the yarn back to an inch or so before the selvedge. With scissors, carefully cut off one ply. Take the other ply (plies) to the selvedge, wrap it (them) around the edge warp, and then back to where you made the cut, all in the same shed. Because the split yarn is less than the original diameter, the overlap area is the same thickness as the original weft. Start the new weft in a similar manner. (You can start the new weft at either selvedge because this method creates no excess thickness.) This method is *slow*, but beautiful in its invisibility.

Any of these overlap methods will work. There are times when one or another will be preferable, depending on thickness and color of yarn, how loosely or tightly the fabric is being woven, whether the selvedges will show in the finished piece or be sewn into hems, or how often you are changing wefts, among other factors.

As you weave more and more, you'll discover and develop numerous tricks of your own. The basic process—opening the shed, throwing the shuttle, beating—is that simple. What makes your weaving yours is the little extras you'll add. Every weaving book will have a few special tricks that the author has found to be useful, and tips from readers in weaving magazines offer many more. There is no aspect of weaving that can be done only one way, so never feel restricted or required to do something that doesn't feel right to you. If you don't like it, try something else, and if you can't think of an alternative (as is to be expected in the beginning), ask other weavers what they do. Eventually you'll develop a style that is uniquely your

own and helps you to enjoy weaving as much as you hoped you would when you first dreamt of it.

Crossed warps, threading errors, and broken warp threads

The section on troubleshooting in Part IV is a quick, at-a-glance reference for problems, with probable causes and solutions. You'll find it a handy resource as you do more weaving. For now, I'll mention just a few things which could go wrong (at any time) and what you can do about them. Nearly all problems have solutions.

You learned how to check for crossed warps in Lesson 2. After you've woven an inch or so is a good time to check for them again. Open the shed and look through it from the side. It should be clean, with no warp threads cutting across it or hanging down into it. Look for crossed warp threads between the reed and heddles or among the heddles. To fix crossed warps, simply untie the group of warps which contains the crossed ends, pull the crossed ones out of the weaving, through the reed to where they are crossed, and uncross them. Then rethread them in the correct order, resley, and retie onto the front apron rod. If many threads are twisted in the heddles or crossed between the reed and heddles, you might not even get a shed. (See pages 227–228 for other possible causes of not getting a shed.) If a warp end or section of ends lacks tension in one place, simply untie the group of warps which contains the loose end(s), tighten, and retie.

You may also notice threading errors when you look at your first few inches of weaving. If two adjoining warp ends are weaving together, that is, going over and under the same wefts at the same time, you've either threaded these two warps on the same shaft or missed a heddle between them (for example, threaded 1,3,4 instead of 1,2,3,4). Sometimes you may want this, but if it looks like a mistake because it only happens once, then it is a threading error and needs to be corrected. (Keep reading.)

If a warp end isn't being caught by the weft at all, it may not have been threaded in a heddle. If this is the case, you probably noticed it when you looked through your shed sideways and saw a thread hanging down.

Other errors are noticeable because a thread is out of sequence and not making the pattern it should; for example, a straight diagonal line, as in a straight twill, will have a jog in it. If the jog occurs vertically, it is a threading error; if it occurs along a horizontal line, it's a treadling error.

To correct a threading error, first trace the thread or threads in question to the heddles. With luck, you threaded only one group of heddles incorrectly (for example, 1,3,4,2 instead of 1,2,3,4), and all you need to do is rethread this group. Untie the group of warp threads in error, pull them out of the weaving, through the reed and the heddles, and rethread and resley them in the correct order, and then retie them to the front apron rod.

You may find that the problem comes from having two adjacent threads threaded on the same shaft (for example, 1,3,3,4). If this is the case, and if there isn't a spare heddle where you need it, relax. This is an easy one to fix. Simply take an unused metal heddle from either side (this trick won't work with string

heddles), using wire cutters (*not* your scissors!), cut the sides of the top and bottom slots where the heddle attaches to the heddle bars, remove it from the heddle bars, and then slide it onto the bars in the place where you need it. Save this repair heddle to reuse when you need it on other projects; when the metal fatigues after many uses, just replace it with another heddle.

If you have string heddles, or if you need another heddle and have no metal ones available to cut and move, you'll need to make your own string heddle. This is a common situation so learning how to make a string heddle is worthwhile, and it's easy. Cut a piece of string or smooth yarn about twice as long as one of your heddles plus a couple of inches. Locate the shaft and the point on the heddle bar where you need the replacement heddle. Fold the string in half, with the middle going under the bottom heddle bar and the two lengths coming up, one on each side. Tie an overhand knot even with the bottom of the other heddle eyes, then another knot even with the top of the eyes, then tie the string off over the top heddle bar. Then thread the errant thread through it, resley it, and tie it on in front again.

At some point in your weaving career, a warp thread will break. This is not a terrible problem and can be easily remedied. Warp ends break for various reasons—a thin spot in the thread giving way, a knot in the thread breaking as it goes through a heddle eye or reed when you advance the warp or beat, uneven tension, abrasion of a yarn that is too fat for the reed, or too much draw-in, among others.

Should a warp thread break, simply measure another warp thread that is long enough to reach from the

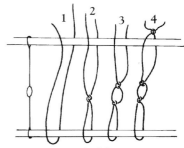

Making a string heddle.
1. Cut a piece of string about twice as long as one of your heddles, and fold it in half around the bottom heddle bar.
2. Tie an overhand knot even with the bottom of the other heddle eyes.
3. Tie another knot even with the top of the heddle eyes.
4. Tie the string off over the top heddle bar.

You can have a lot of fun playing with twills; you can combine twill threadings, vary treadlings, and explore color. Another variation worth experimentation is scale. Here, three brown wool yarns are used as one for warp (you could also use one very heavy yarn) and they are crossed with a doubled weft for a straight-forward, bold design. The squatty looking rows separating the rows of large diamonds result from using the weft singly in these areas. The warp sett for this piece is 10 ends per inch; think of what would happen to the scale of your design if this threading were set 15 ends per inch, 20 ends per inch, or 40 ends per inch (you'd need to change your yarn size, too). *Woven by Louise Bradley.*

Mixing yarns and colors in the warp can produce subtle and rich fabrics, as in the shawl shown here. A single weft, similar in color, serves to further blend the warp colors and textures together. Because some yarns are stretchier than others, wide stripes can potentially cause tension problems in weaving because some yarns will stretch, or give, more under tension. If you're not sure about whether certain yarns or stripe widths will work together, do a sample first. A scarf, because it is small, is a good project for your first mixed warp. Though this technique is appealing in itself, it is also a good way to use bits and pieces of leftover yarns. *Woven by Maggie Putnam.*

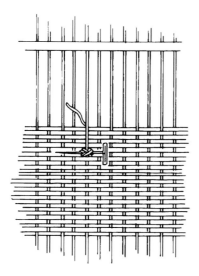

Tying a broken warp end. Place a T-pin in your fabric in line from where your replacement warp comes from the reed. Anchor your replacement warp by making a figure-8 around the T-pin. Depending on how long your warp is (and how much of your warp yarn you have left over in the back), you can either tie the new warp to the old one or hang the new one off the back of the loom with its own weighting device (heavy enough to keep it at the same tension as the rest of the warp). Fishing sinkers, plastic film cans filled with coins or stones, spare scissors or shuttles, and just about anything else can be used as a weight.

front edge of your weaving to the last shaft, plus about 15 inches. Pull the front end of the broken warp toward your fabric and leave the end hanging. Pull the back end out of the heddles and reed and let it hang in back for a moment. Then sley your new end through the reed, thread it through the heddle, and tie it to the back part of the broken one with a bow. Tie it so that you have about 12 inches of the new thread left hanging. Now, go around to the front of your loom and take up any slack on this replacement warp. Place a T-pin in the woven fabric an inch or so from the fell of the fabric, in line with where your replacement warp comes from the reed. Adjust the tension on this replacement warp so that it matches that of the rest of your warp, and then anchor it by making several figure-8s around the pin. This pin stays in place until the weaving holds the new warp in place.

Once the new warp is pinned and tied in place, continue weaving. When the bow reaches the heddle eyes, untie and retie it further back. Keep doing that until the 12 inches of new thread is used up, by which time you'll have 12 inches of the original thread available. Then, untie the bow, pull the new thread out of the heddle and reed, rethread and resley the original thread, and pin it to the fabric. At this point, you're back in business with the original warp thread. (This will make more sense as you're doing it, I promise.)

After the fabric is off the loom, but before you wash it, use a blunt-end yarn needle to sew in the ends of both the old and new warps, overlapping them an inch or two at both ends of the replacement warp.

You'll find that as you get more accustomed to weaving and how your woven fabrics look, your eye will be

alert for these kinds of errors, most of which are relatively easily remedied.

Taking your sample off the loom

You can tell you're almost done when you see the back apron rod approaching the castle. Just as the shed got smaller when the fell of the cloth neared the heddles, so will the shed shrink when the back knots approach the heddles from the other side. How far to weave depends entirely on you and the project. If you are weaving the last half of the last placemat, then you'll want to weave until it's done. If you are weaving a long scarf and you're short on time, you may quit as soon as the shed begins to be less than ideal. If you are meticulous and thrifty, you will probably weave until the shuttle won't go through anymore; you can buy or make some very thin shuttles for those last few inches or use a 5- to 6-inch-long yarn needle. If the piece is a sample and you've already learned what you set out to discover, you may quit long before the end of the warp. Each piece and each day call for a different answer to the question "How far should I weave?"

When you take the warp off the loom, the tension will of course relax, and along with this, your last few weft shots will tend to slide out. There are many ways to deal with this eventuality, and which one to choose will depend on what you're doing. Here are three possibilities:

If you've been weaving a piece that will require no finishing when it come off the loom, say a table runner, then you may choose to secure the weft by hemstitching. You'll probably want to hemstitch both ends, and because hemstitching is most easily done while the warp is still under tension on the loom, you'll need to plan ahead. After you've woven the first 3 or 4 inches of your project, hemstitch the front end. When the weaving is all done, hemstitch the other end. For more on finishes and finishing see Finishes, page 222.

If you want to use the warp ends to create a fancy fringe, you'll want the weft to stay in place until you are ready to work with them. One good way to ensure that it does is to weave a header at the end of the warp, as you did at the beginning of the warp, using a contrasting weft. The header may ravel, but your project weft stays in place.

Tying overhand knots is a popular and easy way to make a fringe, and they can be tied as you take the warp off the loom. Beginning at one selvedge, simply cut a small group of warps behind the heddles, pull them out of the heddles and reed, and tie them into an overhand knot. Repeat the process across the width of the warp. How many warp threads you include in each group will depend on your yarn and sett, and what you want your fringe to look like.

Finally, if you are weaving yardage—a large piece of fabric—a few weft shots loosening up won't be of much consequence. If the yarn is at all fuzzy or textured, the weft will probably stay locked in place pretty well anyway. For this kind of project, you don't need to bother with any special end treatment. Just take the fabric off the loom and machine zigzag across the ends, if necessary, to secure the weft.

Removing a weaving from the loom is remarkably simple and magnificently gratifying. While weaving, you could never see more than 6 to 8 inches of the piece at a time without unrolling it from the cloth beam (which you can do, by the way). Now you finally get to see the whole thing, and the longer the piece is, the more exciting it is.

First, reach behind the heddles and cut the warp as far back as you can. If you've used lark's-head knots or a lash cord, be sure to cut the warp, not the loops or cord. If you wish to measure take-up or loom waste, then untie some of the knots and pull the warp out intact. Untying the knots is time-consuming, so untie and measure just a sampling of knots for measuring, and cut the rest.

Next, pull the warp forward, out of the heddles and reed, release the front ratchet, and unroll the whole piece from the cloth beam. To remove the weaving from the front apron rod, you may be better off to untie the knots than to cut them because the weaving usually starts so close to the front apron rod that there isn't any fringe to work with, and consequently a far greater danger of raveling weft.

If your front apron rod is tied to the loom and won't come free, you'll have to untie the knots to get the weaving off the loom. If your rod is lashed on and able to slide away from the apron cords, you don't need to untie the knots. Just grab one end of the rod firmly with your stronger hand, use the other hand as a knot-stopper, and slide the rod out of all that is tied to it.

That's it: the fabric is off the loom. After a few minutes (or days) of enjoying the pleasure of viewing your weaving, it's time to proceed with the next step, finishing the fabric.

Finishing your fabric

Entire books have been written on this subject, and I'll just touch

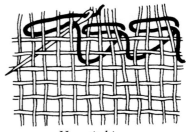

Hemstitching.

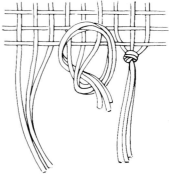

Overhand knots.

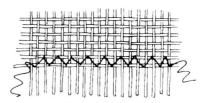

Machine zigzag.

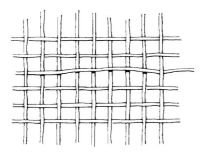

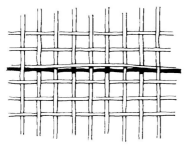

To repair errors, stitch in a new piece of yarn where the thread was supposed to be. Stitch along the original thread on both sides of the error. Cut the old one off where it was floating in error.

lightly on it. The most important point is that 99 percent of the time a piece of fabric (including wool) is not finished until it has been washed. Fixing errors is far more easily and successfully done before the piece is washed, so do that first.

Repairing errors

Nearly any mistake you make can be fixed—a weaving error is not a crisis; however, should you notice an error while weaving, it's usually easier to fix it while the warp is under tension than after you've taken the fabric off the loom. You can either unweave your errant pick or, if you've woven quite a bit before noticing the error, needle-weave a piece of matching thread over the mistake.

Blunt-end yarn needles (long and short) come in handy for repairing weaving errors. When you find a thread that skips over or under some threads that it wasn't supposed to, warp or weft, thread your needle with a new piece of the same yarn and stitch into the fabric where the thread was supposed to go. Stitch along the original thread before and after the error for a little way. After you remove your piece from the loom, simply cut the old thread off where it was floating in error; the overlapped area will keep everything secure.

If the piece is off the loom and the error is in the warp near the end of the fabric, you may want to use the original thread to make its own repair instead of a new one. In this case, pull the warp (or warps) out of the weft to just beyond the error and then needle-weave the end(s) back into the fabric in the correct sequence.

When a piece of fabric comes off the loom, it will relax and be softer to the touch, more flexible. With the tension released, the yarns can begin to bend and curve around each

other; with some patterns the fabric can take on an entirely different appearance. However, until the fabric is washed, it will look more like just a lot of threads than a homogeneous cloth. When the piece is washed, all of the yarns will find their true relationship to each other and will no longer be as likely to shift. That settling will make most repairs/reweaving practically invisible.

Washing to finish your fabric

While washing a fabric may also clean it, the main purpose is to finish it. Different fibers require different handling in washing, and different project characteristics should be factored into which washing method you choose. Above all, use care and common sense, and perhaps some further research. With wool, overhandling and extreme temperature changes are the most common causes of ruined fabrics. Use warm water, shampoo, soap, or gentle detergent, and squeeze, don't wring. It's okay to use the spin cycle of your washing machine to remove excess water, but avoid agitation—unless you want your wool fabric to felt. Lay your fabric flat to dry; the weight of the water will tend to pull it out of shape if you hang it up to dry. If the piece is very large, wash it gently by hand (or feet) in the bathtub. Don't substitute dry cleaning for hand finishing—it's shifting, fulling, you're after, not cleaning.

Much of what you need to know about finishing comes with an understanding of yarns, how they're made, and how certain fibers behave. The previous paragraph is full of wool warnings, and is probably over-cautious for cottons. Read the section on yarns when you want to know more, and especially, learn from your own experience. Given exactly the same assignment and materials, no two people will produce identical results. Therefore, each of us needs to learn what is unique to each yarn and to our own use of it.

Learning from yourself, record keeping, self-evaluation

You don't have to keep records if you don't want to, any more than you have to weave samples or do anything else. I know two weavers who have detailed records of every warp they've ever put on; I know many more who have none. I keep records fairly sporadically, doing very well for a while and then forgetting for a while. There are valuable reasons for keeping records, however, and these reasons are why I continually try to keep them.

First of all, you have to do some figuring in advance anyway, so why not do it in a notebook reserved for just this purpose? It's better than keeping notes on scrap paper because you'll be less likely to lose them. You'll soon develop a system that works efficiently for you, one that you'll be able to refer to easily.

While you're working on a project, you'll need to check your notes to find out how many warp ends you need, how long, what colors, where they go, what the threading order is, and how you want to weave it. Your planning calculations make up the first part of your record sheet but probably are the least important in the long run.

Other information to include in the beginning is the cost of a project, which is usually two different

amounts, your out-of-pocket expense and the actual cost of the project. If your piece has many stripes and you've used yarn that came premeasured (four-ounce skeins, two-ounce tubes, whatever), rather than in the exact quantity you need, you will likely have some left over. It may have cost you $40 to purchase all the yarn, but you may have $12 worth of yarn left with which to weave another project. Your out-of-pocket expense is therefore $40, but the project really cost only $28. Your next project may use some of this leftover yarn and so you may have an out-of-pocket expense of $3, with the project's real cost being $10. It's a good idea to keep track of both numbers because it is not at all unusual for someone to see something you've woven and ask you to make another just like it. You may agree to do so as a gift, but you may want to be paid for the cost of the materials and/or labor. In any case, it's much easier to make such arrangements if you have a record of how much money and time you spent.

When you are just learning, everything you do will take longer than it will once you've gained some experience. Sooner than you think, however, you'll be weaving in half the time you do now. If you expect you'll ever sell your weavings or weave for a deadline (such as a birthday present), you'll have a much better sense of what's feasible if you know how long a piece took to make, from conception on through to delivery. The best way to keep track of your weaving time is to buy a cheap alarm clock (not digital) and set it at 12:00 at the beginning of each new project. Every time you start to work on the project, plug the clock in; when you quit, unplug it. It will count your cumulative time and if you finish a particular project with

Record of a Project

Name of project:_____

Date woven: _____

Approximate time project took: _____

Yarns used: warp_____

             weft _____

Pattern:_____

Source: _____

Length of warp:_____   Dimensions on loom: _____

Width of warp: _____   Dimensions off loom: _____

Sett:_____   Dimensions after washing: _____

P.P.I.: _____   Cost of Project:_____

Total yarn used: _____

Out of pocket expense: _____

Goal of project: _____

Was goal met?: _____

Other discoveries: _____

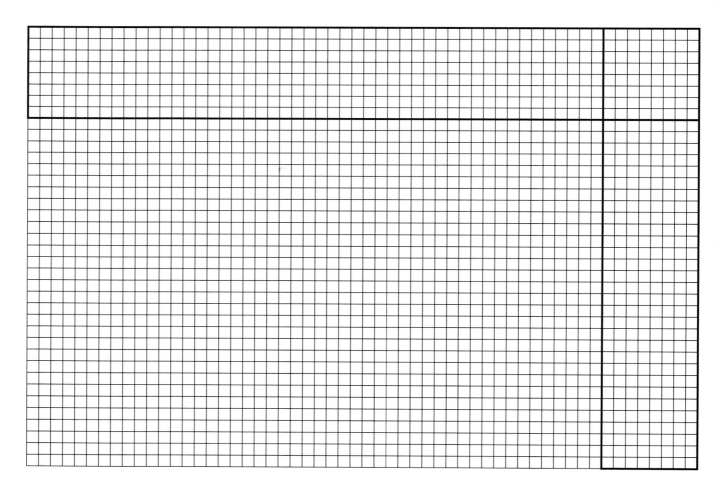

the clock reading 9:30, you'll know it took nine and a half hours to do that project. The only catch is remembering to plug and unplug the clock.

At this point, you may well think that each piece you weave has so much invested in it—time, planning, worry, love, decisions, frustrations, joy, and money—that you'll never forget it, and so keeping records isn't really necessary. That's what I thought for a long time. It's not so; you will forget. I've been to friends' homes in other parts of the country and seen things that looked oddly familiar, only to realize I had woven them years ago. One of the best reasons for keeping thorough, dated records is that a friend of a friend will see a pillow you wove and say, "Oh, I'd like one just like it only in blue!" Can you imagine trying to remember the threading for a pillow that you wove several years ago and haven't seen since?

What goes into a record sheet? Everything you might ever want to know. I've included a sample record sheet here. If you like this sheet, feel free to photocopy it for your own use. You may also want to include such other information as your name, special equipment needed, loom used, and finishing techniques.

If you plan to keep these notes only for yourself, then any paper will do. If you plan to share the sheets with other weavers or attach samples to them, stiffer paper such as card stock may be appropriate. Keeping sheets in a loose-leaf notebook makes them easy to remove for copying and sharing.

Discoveries

For me, the most important part of the record sheet is my notes on other discoveries. This is where I record surprises as well as disasters—all the true learning experiences: Sett too close for yarn—friction-caused breaking; Colors bled; Colors worked just right for couch; Selvedges terrible—floating selvedge needed; Beautiful yarn lost its character—finished piece not as pretty as I'd hoped; Softness and bumps perfect for slightly textured baby blanket; Pattern didn't show with this color choice; Forgot to compensate for stretchy yarn—piece ended up too short; Beat is just right—I'm getting better; Etc. There is no end to the discoveries you'll make, and it's a rare project that doesn't teach you something new. However, I've discovered that if I don't record what I've learned and then read over it once in a while, I have to learn the lesson all over again.

If this is your first experience with weaving, you may not know what everything on this record sheet refers to or what all the surprises listed above mean. Don't worry, you will in time. For now, just fill in what you do know; leave the rest for later.

Self-evaluation

Self-evaluation is a mystery, especially if you live in weaver-isolation. On the one hand, the real truth is if *you* like it, it's good; if you don't, it's not. As long as you are weaving for your own pleasure and satisfaction, the only thing that matters is that you are enjoying what you're doing or what you're getting, or both.

On the other hand, most weavers also want to know how their work rates alongside what other people are doing, what the standard is. If we never see what other weavers are doing, it's difficult to know what we could be striving for, either in quality or new ideas. To help you improve your weaving, consider the following guiding questions:

- Is your piece structurally stable, or is it likely to fall apart easily?
- Is the yarn appropriate to the project? Wool bikinis and linen rugs leave something to be desired.
- Does your piece look finished, or are there pieces of yarn hanging out? Look for evenness of beat, reasonably straight selvedges, good finishing of fabric and finishing techniques, no mistakes in the pattern.
- Is your fabric aesthetically pleasing—good color, design—to you?
- Does the piece fill the need for which it was intended?
- Is it better than your earlier work, either improving on old skills or experimenting with new ones?
- Are you proud enough of your piece to show it to your best friend, a total stranger, your parents, or your third-grade teacher? Or another weaver?

Weavers needn't feel totally isolated anymore, because of the existence of weaving magazines. (And electronic bulletin boards—see pages 223–224). As of this writing there are at least three magazines published just for weavers, several others for the fiber arts in general. A subscription to any one of them will connect you to thousands of other weavers. Weaving magazines show weavers' work, some by professionals and some by beginners, many in between. Each magazine has a different emphasis, and by reading them you can get a good idea of what's being done and how weavers feel about what they are seeing. Read the letters to the editor, find one you like, and ask that person to be your weaving pen pal, or write your own letter to the editor and offer yourself as one.

Meanwhile, if you're just starting out and you are alone, don't spend much energy wondering how your work ranks alongside others. Now is the time to learn, to let yourself explore all that's new and exciting and easily available. Look at each piece you finish, decide what *one* thing about it you want to improve on in your next piece, then work on that. Don't be hard on yourself. You are not going to be the world's greatest weaver this month; you are going to be the weaver you are. Enjoy it. Enjoy it. Enjoy it.

Planning A Project

The initial drawing

Warp calculations

Weft calculations

Now that you've woven a sample, you should have a pretty good feel for how your loom works and what weaving is all about. Although knowing how to warp your loom and throw a shuttle are essential, they are not all you need to know to become a self-sufficient weaver. To be able to truly weave on your own, you need to be able to make all the decisions for planning a project before you ever begin to measure your warp.

One of the most astonishing things I have ever witnessed was a student whose first step was to go to the warping board and begin measuring her warp. After a while, she asked me if she had measured enough.

"What are you making?" I asked.

"A shawl."

"Well, how many warp ends do you need and how many do you have?"

"I don't know."

"Where are your warp calculations?"

"I didn't do any."

"How did you know how long to measure your warp?"

"I thought this looked long enough."

It was one of the few times in my life that I was speechless. Only later did I learn that any number of people, for a variety of reasons, guess at their yarn needs, bluff their way through their projects, hoping they'll get something usable. Aside from the folly of omitting it, planning can be as much fun as any other part of the process.

For your first piece, I told you just what I wanted you to do. I wanted you to understand what I was asking you to do, and why, so that you would be able to do it on your own in your future projects. The skill to do what you want is my goal, and I hope it is one of yours, too.

The initial drawing

Planning a project is easiest for me when I start by drawing it out on paper. With that visual/graphic aid I'm less likely to forget details. For example, consider a set of four placemats. All four can be woven on one long warp.

A drawing of what the warp and mats would look like after being woven if they were all stretched out is on the next page. The loom waste in the front and back is the warp that never gets woven. In front, the yarn that is tied onto the front apron rod does not get woven. At the other end, you cannot weave the warp that goes behind the reed, through the shafts, and is tied to the back apron rod. We'll talk about how much yarn gets "wasted" when we discuss warp calculations.

Planning a project

front loom waste

Mat 1

fringe between mats

Mat 2

Mat 3

Mat 4

back loom waste

Draw a picture of what you want to weave.

Because I want to have fringe on these mats, I need to leave unwoven warp between them. If I were going to hem the mats, I could weave one long strip of cloth and simply cut and sew the ends. (But remember I'd have to weave enough extra in between each mat to make those hems, depending on the design.)

After you make an initial drawing of what you want to weave, the rest is simply a matter of filling in the details. To make your plan, you'll need to ask and answer these questions: How many mats? What dimensions? Fringed or hemmed?

How much length is needed for fringe or hems? You'll need to allow at least 3 inches between mats even if the fringe is to be only 1 inch long; it can be trimmed later. In planning hems, you'll need to decide how much to turn under.

What fiber do you want to use? Cotton, silk, rayon, wool, nylon, acrylic, linen, a blend?

What about shrinkage? You can get a rough idea of how much a yarn shrinks by washing a piece of yarn a yard long and then measuring it again, but the best way to determine shrinkage is to weave a sample and wash it as you would wash the finished project. Most yarns shrink 5 to 10 percent, though some can shrink as much as 25 percent, depending on how they're finished.

Thick or thin? Generally, thin yarn makes thin mats, thick yarn, thick mats. For in-between thicknesses, use one yarn for the warp, the other for the weft.

Design. There are many design questions you'll have to ask yourself, but right now I'd like to keep to the basics of planning. I'll talk about design gradually, throughout the lessons.

Warp calculations

Warp calculations are easy when you have answers to the questions above.

We already decided we'd make four mats. (Somehow saying "we decided" is like the teacher saying, "Now we are going to take a test," when you know full well the teacher is *not* taking a test. However, if you were in my classroom "we decided" would be accurate because I always have the students make the decisions; so I'm going to go ahead and say it here since I want you to feel that you are in a classroom.) However, placemats come in many sizes, from 9 by 11 inches to 17 by 22 inches. I like large mats myself, and I usually aim for a finished size of about 15 by 17 inches.

Fringe or hems? Let's go for fringe, hemstitched with a needle and yarn to match the warp. Hemstitching is an edge treatment that is done most easily on the loom while the warp is still under tension. It looks nice, and the piece requires no additional edge work when the piece is removed from the loom. (See page 97 for an illustration of hemstitching.)

Cotton is a good fiber for placemats. Mercerized cotton will barely shrink at all; unmercerized cotton may shrink a lot. (Mercerized cotton has been treated so that it won't shrink; you can recognize it because it is shiny. Unmercerized cotton has a duller finish.) For this exercise, let's assume that the cotton is preshrunk and allow only 5 percent for shrinkage.

As with choosing a fiber, choosing yarn is very arbitrary when we're making up an example. Let's have a thin warp and a slightly thicker weft.

Figuring your warp needs

Let's draw the picture again and add some dimensions. The four mats at 17 inches each will give a total woven length of 68 inches. Add the three 4-inch sections of fringe to get the total finished length:

finished woven length	
4 mats × 17" =	68"
fringe	3 × 4" = 12"
total finished length	= 80"

To be able to weave this total finished length, you have to add extra length to allow for shrinkage and take-up, the flexing and curving of the threads as they go over and under each other. That curving of the yarn shortens the length of the woven piece, and while it doesn't matter a lot on a placemat, it matters a great deal on anything that needs to be a particular size, be it clothing or curtains. (Before I believed in take-up, I made two sets of curtains too short for their windows. I could finally use them when I moved to a house with shorter windows.) Generally, 10 percent is a reasonable take-up allowance. For very fat yarns, allow more; for very thin yarns, you might be able to get away with less. If the weft is fatter than the warp, the warp will take up more, for it has to go over and under the fat weft. If the warp is fatter, the weft will have more take-up as it goes further under and over.

Between the 5 percent shrinkage and 10 percent take-up, a total of 15 percent of the weaving length is lost, and unless you allow for that 15 percent, you will run out of warp before you finish the last placemat. To be mathematically rigorous, you'd need to subtract the combined shrinkage

plus take-up from 100 percent and divide the total finished length by this number. If you're like me and prefer visual to abstract calculations, you can get a very good approximation by simply adding the shrinkage and take-up to the total finished length.

total finished length	80"
+ 5% shrinkage (0.5 × 80") =	4"
+ 10 % take-up (10 × 68") =	
6.8" round up to	7"
total project length	= 91"

(not total warp length yet)

Because only the woven part experiences take-up, the take-up in this calculation is figured for only the length that is woven; it excludes the 12 inches of fringe.

Next, you have to allow for *loom waste*, the amount of warp that never gets woven. Loom waste needs to be added on to get the total warp length. Loom waste varies with the loom, the weaver, and the warping method. An experienced, stingy weaver using a small loom may well get by with only 12 inches of waste, whereas a beginner using a large loom may have 30 inches or more. To determine your loom waste, pull your back apron rod (the rod attached to your warp beam) over the back beam and toward the castle. If it doesn't almost touch the last shaft, then either lengthen the cords holding it or, if you have a cloth apron,

As yarns are woven they curve and flex as they go over and under each other. This flexing and curving acts to shorten the distance a yarn is able to travel, and is called take-up.

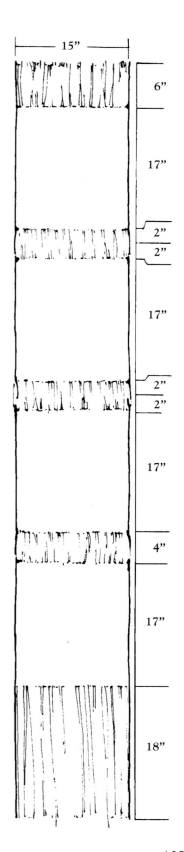

Planning a project

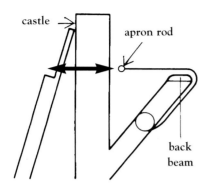

The distance from in front of the beater to behind the castle is the major part of your loom waste. To make the apron rod reach as close as possible to the castle, extend the apron cords or if you have cloth apron, lash a second rod onto the first.

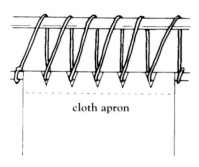

If you have a cloth apron, lash a second apron rod onto the first.

lash a second apron rod onto the first. Nearly any sturdy wood or metal rod will work as an apron rod. I prefer to use a round one because the warp knots roll and shift around it more easily. Hardware stores carry dowels and metal rods that will work fine. (Get one that is lightweight.)

Now tip the beater back against the castle. Measure the distance from the front of the beater to the back apron rod. That will be the largest part of your loom waste but not all of it. Tying the warp around the apron rods takes at least another 2 inches front and back (unless you warped from back to front, in which case there would be no knots in the back), and many people use 6 inches. Finally, it is rare that you will keep weaving until the apron rod reaches all the way to the castle, for reasons you'll understand the first time you approach the end of a piece. The closer you get to the castle, the smaller your shed will be, until finally you can't weave any further.

So, add together the distance between the rods, 4 to 12 inches for tying on, and 3 to 4 inches for shed room at the end. The best way to determine the loom waste for your own weaving is to measure it when you take a piece off the loom. Untie in-

stead of cutting at least two groups of warp, then measure all the unwoven warp. Do it for several warps, not just one. You can measure your take-up at the same time, though this will vary from piece to piece.

For this calculation, let's assume a loom waste of 24 inches. We then add this number to our 91 inches to get the total warp length.

91" + 24" = 115"
115" ÷ 36 = 3 yd 7 inches

The next step is to determine how many warp ends are needed. Although it can be avoided, most weavers experience some *draw-in* as they weave, causing the selvedges of the weaving to be pulled in a little from the original warp width. As you weave a variety of projects with a variety of yarns, you'll find that each draws in differently. Over time, you'll be able to predict how certain yarn and pattern combinations are likely to behave. Most weavers allow for an average of 1 to 2 inches of draw-in.

For these placemats, let's assume that you want a finished width of 15 inches, that there will be 5 percent shrinkage, and 1 inch of draw-in. The combined effects of shrinkage

Formula for figuring your warp needs

project length	finished width	
+ fringe	+ draw-in (1–2" average)	
+ take-up (10% average)	+ shrinkage (10% average)	total length in inches
+ shrinkage (10% average)	= on loom width	× warp ends needed
+ loom waste	× warp sett (e.p.i.)	= total warp needed in inches
= total length	= warp ends needed	÷ 36
		= total yards needed

Use this formula when figuring your warp needs. It's also printed on the last page of this book for quick reference.

and draw-in will be to make the placemat 5 percent plus one inch (which is about 7 percent of 15 inches) narrower. In other words, the 15 inches width you want to end up with is about 13 percent narrower than the width you'll want to start with. If you want to be mathematically rigorous, you'll need to figure out how wide to make your warp by subtracting the combined shrinkage and draw-in percentages from 100 percent and then dividing the desired finished width by this number. But, as with the warp length calculation, you can get a good approximation by simply adding the shrinkage and draw-in to the desired finished width.

desired finished width	15"
+ shrinkage (5%)	0.75"
+ draw-in	1"
weaving width	16.75"

which we'll round up to 17"

So we know that we want to put a 17-inch-wide warp on the loom. The warp yarn I'm thinking of will be good set at 12 warp ends per inch (e.p.i.) in the reed.

12 e.p.i. × 17" wide = 204 warp ends

If you have plenty of yarn on hand, then you now have enough information to measure your warp. You know you need 204 pieces, each 115 inches long. However, if you are going to go purchase the yarn, you need to find out how many yards you'll need in total so you'll know how much to buy. (Or spin!)

115" × 204 ends = 23,460"
23,460" ÷ 36 = 652 yards

Weft calculations

The formula for determining weft needs is as simple and straightforward as the one for warp. The difference is that unless you've woven a sample you can only make an educated guess at how many weft shots you'll pack in per inch. Warp ends per inch are determined by you and the reed, and stay constant. Weft shots per inch, or picks per inch (p.p.i.), are determined by the tension of the warp and how hard you beat, and they can vary with every inch. For that reason, weft calculations are rarely as precise as those for the warp, but they can certainly be close enough to be valuable in figuring how much weft you'll need.

Before you start filling in numbers, consider take-up again. As the weft goes over and under the warp threads, it is no longer in a straight line, therefore it needs to be longer than just the width of the warp.

Ten percent take-up in both warp and weft is a typical amount to

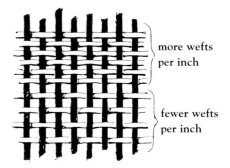
more wefts per inch

fewer wefts per inch

warp
weft
Open shed with weft going through.

Closed shed with weft going over and under warps.

Formula for figuring your weft needs

length of one weft shot in inches
× shots per inch
= inches needed to weave one inch of fabric
× inches to be woven (project length + shrinkage)
= inches of weft needed to weave all of project
÷ 36
= yards of weft needed

allow for a balanced fabric, one with about the same number of ends per inch as picks per inch. Therefore, if the warp is 17 inches wide in the reed, then one weft shot will be about 17" + 1.7" (10%) = 18.7", or almost 19" long. When calculating yarn needs, round fractional figures up, as it's always better to have a little more yarn than you need than a little less. If you have a long warp, wait to round up until the last steps.

For these placemats, let's assume that the weft is slightly thicker than the warp, with 10 weft picks per inch (p.p.i.).

Now let's fill in the blanks in the formula.

length of one weft shot	19"
× p.p.i.	10"
= total weft per inch	190"
× inches to be woven	72"
= total inches needed	13,680"
÷ 36	÷ 36
= total yards needed	380

When you get to the inches-to-be-woven line, omit the inches that will be fringe and not woven. You won't need weft for these areas. For our example, the entire mats account for 80 inches of warp length, but only 68 inches of this amount is woven. You'll also have to account for the 5 percent shrinkage, so in this case, add 4 inches to 68 to get 72 inches. The rest is fringe.

If you haven't woven a sample to find out how many weft shots per inch you'll have, you can estimate this number in a couple of different ways. The easiest way to do this, if you've decided that your piece is going to be a balanced fabric (equal e.p.i. and p.p.i.) and your weft and warp are the same yarn, is to say that

the p.p.i. will equal the e.p.i. Then when you're weaving, be careful to beat so that it is. If you are planning a balanced weave, your weft and warp needs will be approximately the same, though you won't need quite as much weft because you won't weave the loom waste. The longer the total warp (and therefore the lower percentage of waste), the closer the warp and weft quantities will be. If your warp is only 1 yard long, then half or more could be waste, so you won't need nearly as much weft. If your warp is 10 yards long, then the waste is only about 5 percent, making your weft and warp needs nearly equal. If your weave is unbalanced (more weft per inch than warp, or vice versa), use the formula given here to determine how much weft you'll need.

Another method to determine your p.p.i. is to wrap your weft yarn around a ruler at the density you think you'll pack it in, then count how many wraps there are in 1 inch.

That's really all there is to it. After you've woven a few pieces and practiced using the formulas a few times, you'll find that you'll begin to remember them much of the time.

Planning a shawl

Let's go through another project planning exercise, this time without so many words.

Shawl: 24 by 72 inches, in wool, loosely woven, smooth warp in two colors, fuzzy or bumpy weft in one color. Let's allow for 5 percent shrinkage and 10 percent take-up. First figure the total warp needed.

Because there are two colors in the warp, the total needs to be broken down into two numbers, one for each color. Say you have two blue

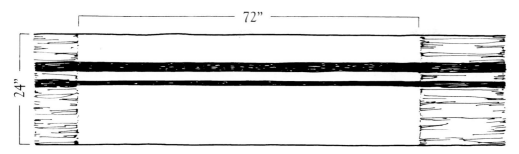

A shawl, 24" × 72", in wool, two colors in warp and one color in weft.

Warp

project length	72"	finished width	24"	total length in inches		110"
+ take-up	7"	+ draw-in	1"	× warp ends needed		216
+ shrinkage	3.5"	+ shrinkage	2"	= total warp needed in inches		23,760"
+ fringe	3" *	= on loom width	27"	÷ 36		÷ 36
+ loom waste	24"	× warp sett ×	8 e.p.i.	= total yards needed		660 yards
= total length	109.5" or 110"	= warp ends needed 216 = 23,760				
		÷ 36 = 660 yards				

* The rest is coming from loom waste.

Weft

length of one weft shot (27" + 10%)	30"
× p.p.i. (estimate)	× 8
= inches of weft needed per inch woven	240
× inches to be woven (project length + shrinkage)	× 76
= total inches needed	18,240"
÷36 = 507 yards	

---

stripes on a white background. Let's say that one stripe is 2 inches wide and the other is 1 inch wide for a total of 3 inches of blue.

$$8 \text{ e.p.i.} \times 3" = 24 \text{ blue warps}$$
$$\underline{\begin{array}{r} 216 \text{ total} \\ -24 \text{ blue} \end{array}}$$
$$= 192 \text{ white}$$

To figure the total yardage needed for each color, use the warp calculation formula above, inserting 24

and 192, respectively, for the warp ends needed.

There are many routes to determining how much of each color you'll need. If you need equal amounts of four colors, simply divide the total by four. Sometimes you won't figure the total first; instead you'll figure each color on its own. Whichever way seems easiest at the time is the one to use.

Six dishtowels with fringe.

Check designs.

Another planning exercise

Here's one for you to figure out. Six gingham dish towels, red-and-white checks, cottolin (a great cotton/ linen-blend yarn), 18 by 24 inches, short fringe, stitched across the ends with a zigzag stitch. Checks are made by striping both warp and weft, in equal-size stripes for gingham, other proportions for other designs. For equal-sized stripes, you would need half red yarn and half white.

Warp and weft are the same yarn this time, so you can add the two totals to obtain the total yarn needed. Then decide how much will be red, how much white (unless you determined that stripe by stripe already).

Because calculating warp and weft is in many ways subjective and because take-up, draw-in, and shrinkage depend on many factors—the yarn, the sett, your beat, how you wash the project, etc.—this exercise has no exact right answers. To find out if your totals are somewhere in the ballpark (assuming 10 percent shrinkage and take-up), look on page 232.

By now you should be getting the idea; getting comfortable with calculating yarn needs is a matter of practice more than anything else. The first time it takes just short of forever, but later it takes only a few minutes. If you want it to become easy, figure out one project every day. It doesn't need to be real; that's not the point. Repetition will make it automatic, and in time you'll be able to figure yarn needs for the most complex project in fifteen minutes, or for an easy one in two or three. You'll find that a calculator speeds up the process considerably.

Warp

project length	finished width
+ fringe	+ draw-in
+ take-up (10%)	+ shrinkage
+ shrinkage (10%)	= on loom width
+ loom waste	× warp sett (15 e.p.i. for this)
total length ×	warp ends needed
	÷ 36 = yards of warp needed

Add the column on the left, add and multiply the column on the right, multiply the two totals, and divide by 36 to get a more reasonable number to work with. That's all you need to do to determine your warp needs.

Weft

length of one weft shot (warp width + 10%)
× p.p.i. (15 p.p.i. for this)
= inches of weft needed per inch of weaving
× inches to be woven (project + shrinkage)
= inches of weft needed
÷ 36 = yards of weft needed

PART II:
Now That You Know the Basics

Reading Drafts

The four parts of a draft:

Threading

Tie-up

Treadling

Drawdown

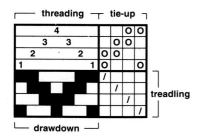

The four parts of a draft.

> *The threading tells you on what shafts and in what order to thread the heddles.*

Drafts are the weaver's blueprints. They tell you in what order to thread the heddles and when to raise which shafts. Just as musical scores tell musicians what notes to play, drafts are the weaver's notation for creating weaving patterns.

True weaving literacy comes with the understanding of drafts and drafting. As with reading, it's not difficult when you understand the basic principles. And, as familiarity with reading eventually enables you to write, so familiarity with reading drafts gradually enables you to make up your own designs. Just as some people write as little as possible while others write constantly for the sheer joy of it, so some weavers use their drafting skills only to use or adapt existing patterns while others invent their own patterns for everything they weave. I want to give you enough information about drafting here so that you will be comfortable with the basics of reading and designing. When you want to learn more, I suggest you read Carol S. Kurtz's *Designing for Weaving*, (Interweave Press, 201 East Fourth Street Loveland, Colorado 80537), an excellent book that contains a very thorough section on drafting, or Madelyn Van der Hoogt's *The Complete Book of Drafting for Hand-*

weavers, (ShuttleCraft Books, PO Box 550, Coupeville, Washington 98239), a comprehensive exploration of the subject.

The four parts of drafts

There are four parts to a draft: threading, tie-up, treadling, and drawdown. The threading tells you in what order to thread the heddles. The tie-up tells you which combinations of shafts to raise together. (On some looms the shafts are lowered, not raised; I'll address this later. Because most weavers in the United States use rising-shed looms, for the sake of simplicity I will always refer to raising shafts. For most of the discussion, it doesn't matter which type of loom you have, but when it does, I'll say so.) The treadling tells you the order in which to raise the shafts. The drawdown is a graphic picture of the pattern.

Threading

Although many different symbols are used in writing drafts, the important factor is *where* the symbols are located.

Each of the notations below says the same thing. The bottom row represents the first shaft, the second row up the second shaft, the third the third, and the fourth the fourth. Each notation says to thread 1, 2, 3, 4. That means that the farthest left thread will be threaded through a heddle on shaft 1. The second thread will go through a heddle on shaft 2, and likewise with 3 and 4. This most basic of all threading pat-

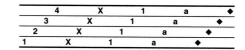

terns is called a straight draw because warp ends are threaded on one shaft after the other (one thread per shaft) in a straight line from shaft 1 to shaft 4.

The sample threadings below are not straight draws and yield different patterns. The threading on the far left of the example below, a point twill, says that after you've threaded the first four threads onto each shaft respectively, thread five goes onto shaft 3, thread six onto shaft 2, and thread seven onto shaft 1.

For the middle pattern the threading reads 1, 2, 1, 4, 3, 4. The threading on the right of the example says 1, 2, 1, 2, 3, 2, 3, 4, 3, 4, 1, 4. Threading variations are unlimited, and each change results in a different pattern. What makes it all manageable is that there are families of weave structures or patterns related by common characteristics that make it possible to predict how a particular threading (in combination with specific treadlings) will look and behave. Later on in this course, we'll cover some of the families.

Each of the threadings discussed above shows one repeat of the pattern. One time through a threading (or treadling) pattern is called a "repeat", even though you don't repeat it until you thread that sequence a second time. Most drafts will show you only one repeat of a threading sequence to save space and because there is no need to rewrite the same thing again and again. It is up to you to start over, to repeat the repeat. You may thread it as many times as needed to achieve the width you want.

Some drafts read from right to left; others read left to right. Either way is correct. What is important is always to work in the same direction. Most books and magazines will tell you in which direction to read their drafts, especially when a threading is so long that it is continued on two or three lines.

Tie-up

The tie-up tells you in what combinations the shafts need to work. Each horizontal row of the tie-up represents the corresponding shaft in the threading. Thus, the bottom row is shaft 1, the next one up shaft 2, etc. The circles or markings in the boxes indicate shafts to be raised during weaving. The marks in each column tell which shafts to raise together. In the tie-up here, you'll first raise shafts 1 and 2 together, next shafts 2 and 3, next 3 and 4, and finally 4 and 1. The combinations depend on the pattern to be woven. There are fourteen combinations possible with four shafts (eliminating raising all or none at once since that would create no shed). A tie-up will include only those combinations necessary to its particular pattern, so you'll probably never see all fourteen combinations at once. Four or six are most common, and sometimes two are enough (for tabby, for instance).

The reason that this part of the draft is called the tie-up has to do with floor looms. On floor looms, the treadles are "tied up" to the shafts. Four-shaft looms usually have six treadles (not 14). Therefore, it is

> *The tie-up tells you which combinations of shafts to raise (or lower) together.*

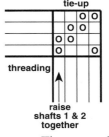

Sample tie-up. The tie-up tells you in what combinations the shafts need to work.

There are fourteen possible combinations with four shafts. A tie-up will include only those combinations necessary for a particular pattern.

Sample threadings. Different threadings yield different patterns.

necessary to be able to tie different combinations of shafts to the treadles so that you can get the sheds that you want. A tie-up for a given draft may not require all six treadles; it may need only two or four. Simply use however many you need. (The only exception to this rule that I know of is for some countermarch looms, which require the weight of the treadles for the counteraction, and so all treadles must be tied up even if not being used.)

When translating the information in the tie-up to your loom, think of each column as a treadle and tie the shafts indicated to that treadle. On the tie-up shown on page 113, you'd tie shafts 1 and 2 to your farthest left treadle, shafts 2 and 3 to the second treadle, etc. Whenever you need to raise that combination of shafts simply step on the treadle that is tied to them.

Other looms, including table looms, have what is called a direct tie-up in which the four shafts and four treadles (levers on table looms) are tied directly to each other. Treadle 1 is tied to shaft 1, treadle 2 to shaft 2, 3 to 3, and 4 to 4, and none can be changed. With a direct-tie-up loom, you'll need to raise each combination of shafts individually, using

two or three fingers or both feet simultaneously as needed. Because most drafts use essentially the same tie-up and treadling format, you need to know how to read it no matter which type of loom you use.

Now that you understand the tie-up, in theory anyway, I must tell you that the treadles on jack-style looms are not actually tied to the shafts. Instead, they are tied to the lamms, horizontal pieces that act as intermediaries between the treadles and the shafts. When the treadles are pushed down, the lamms push up or pull up the shafts. They are part of the jacking system of the loom and provide the lifting action.

Treadling

The treadling tells you in what order to raise the shafts. It is read vertically. The sample treadling on page 115 reads from the top down; sometimes, drafts are written the other way, starting at the bottom and working upward to correspond to the direction the cloth is woven. If you have a loom with multiple-tie-up treadles, in which several shafts may be tied to one treadle, and have tied them up according to the tie-up, then all you need to do is follow the

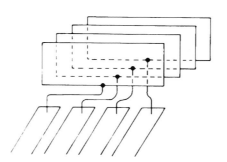

On looms with direct tie-up systems, each treadle is tied directly and permanently to one shaft.

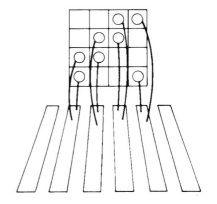

When translating information from the tie-up to your floor loom, think of each column as a treadle and tie the shafts indicated to that treadle.

pattern. In this example you would step first on the left treadle, second on the second treadle, third on the third, fourth on the right treadle, fifth back on the third treadle, sixth on the second from the left, and seventh on the left treadle again.

If you are working with a direct-tie-up loom, you'll need to translate the information to exactly which shafts are being lifted (even if your loom has multiple-tie-up capabilities, you certainly need to know what it is you're really doing). The illustration below shows you how to translate the information.

To read the treadling, look directly above the treadling symbol to the tie-up at the top of the column; whichever shafts are indicated are the ones you need to raise. Where this symbol is in vertical sequence tells you when to raise those shafts. As in the threading, different symbols are used in different books. If two or more symbols are used in the same draft, it indicates a change in weft threads, by color, thickness, texture, or the like. When numbers appear in the columns, however, instead of different wefts, they denote how many weft shots should be woven in a given shed before moving onto the next number (usually this involves other factors which I'll explain later in the lessons on summer & winter and overshot).

Look now at the differences between these treadlings: the one at the bottom of the page tells you to use one weft; the upper one in the sample treadling at right tells you to alternate between weft A and weft B; the lower treadling at right tells you how many weft shots to throw in each shed.

When working on a table loom or a direct-tie-up floor loom, you may find it easier to rewrite the treadling in numerical form. That way, you won't need to keep looking up and down the columns to see what's next. If you write the numbers in a staggered sequence so that the angles of the pattern show, in time you'll learn to recognize the pattern of the weave even before you do the drawdown or actual weaving.

12
  23
    34
1   4

One last very important consideration is that some tie-ups and treadlings are written for rising-shed looms, others for sinking-shed looms. On a rising-shed loom, the shafts go up to make the shed; on a sinking-shed loom, they go down. On a rising-shed loom, for example, if shafts 1 and 2 are raised, 3 and 4 are left down. To open the same shed on a sinking-shed loom, you would tie up

> *The treadling tells you in which order to raise the shafts.*

Sample treadlings. When different symbols appear in the treadling, it means that different wefts should be used. Numbers in the treadling indicate how many weft shots should be put into the same shed.

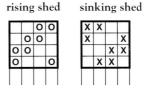

rising shed   sinking shed

Most often, Os in the tie-up signify rising-shed looms and Xs signify sinking-shed looms. Both of these say, from left to right:

1&2 up/3&4 down
2&3 up/1&4 down
3&4 up/1&2 down
4&1 up/2&3 down

← says that for the 1st weft shot you should raise shafts 1 & 2
← says that for the 2nd weft shot you should raise shafts 2 & 3
← says that for the 3rd weft shot you should raise shafts 3 & 4
← says that for the 4th weft shot you should raise shafts 1 & 4
← says that for the 5th weft shot you should raise shafts 3 & 4
← says that for the 6th weft shot you should raise shafts 2 & 3
← says that for the 7th weft shot you should raise shafts 1 & 2

shafts 3 and 4; they will be lowered, and shafts 1 and 2 will remain up.

At one time, it was reasonably safe to say that Os in the tie-up indicated a rising shed, Xs indicated a sinking shed. While this is still true most of the time, it is not always the case. You'll find many other symbols used as well. Older books were usually written with a sinking shed in mind. Newer books, those written since the surge of jack-action hand-looms in the United States in the 1950s, have been written for rising-shed looms. Some books include tie-ups for both, most notably, Mary Black's *Key to Weaving* (Macmillan, 55 Railroad Avenue, Greenwich, Conneticut 06830)

If you weave on a rising-shed loom but use a sinking-shed tie-up, you'll be treadling the exact opposite of what's intended. The result is that you'll get the intended fabric but you'll be weaving it upside down. Instead of the pattern facing you, it will be facing down and you'll be looking at the back side. (Often you won't be able to tell the difference.) Just turn the fabric over when you

take it off the loom. If you want to weave a sinking-shed tie-up on your rising-shed loom right side up, simply tie up the empty boxes instead of the filled-in ones.

Drawdown

With the information you have so far, you can read a draft and weave the fabric. An equally important skill is being able to create a drawdown. The drawdown will show you what the fabric will look like (in most cases) and where to begin and end the threading and treadling to have a centered or balanced pattern. In some books, a full pattern threading may start in the middle of the design instead of on the edge. If you've done a drawdown of the pattern, you can easily determine where to begin and end it. More on that later in the lesson on altering drafts.

Filling in a draft's drawdown is like doing a puzzle. First, think of each column on a piece of graph paper as a warp thread, as if you were facing your warp on your loom. Think of each row as a weft thread

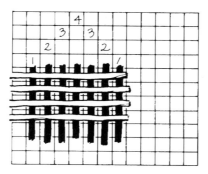

Think of each column of the draw-down as a warp thread, as if you were facing your loom; think of each row as a weft crossing the warp.

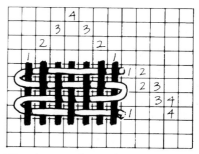

This drawing shows the actual interlace-ment of threads as called for in the draft. When the treadling calls for shafts 1 and 2 to be raised, the warp threads go over the weft.

crossing the warp. If you were to lay yarn in the spaces between the vertical lines on the illustration at the bottom left of page 116, each warp thread would be threaded on the shaft indicated at the top in the threading. Now take the yarn away and remember that the column of boxes represents the yarn. In the same way, each horizontal row represents a weft thread. In the lower left illustration on page 116 the yarns are shown laid on the paper, not woven together at all. The lower right illustration shows the actual interlacements of the threads as called for in the draft. As you can see, when the treadling calls for shafts 1 and 2 to be raised, those warp threads lie over the weft threads. The same weft shot goes over the warps on shafts 3 and 4 because they were not raised. The second weft shot goes over the warp threads on shafts one and four because they were left down when shafts 2 and 3 were raised. For the third shot, shafts 3 and 4 were raised, so those warp threads lie on top of the weft, or on the surface of the weave. The fourth row shows that

shafts 1 and 4 were raised, for those are the warps passing over the weft. Thus the warp threads that are raised have been lifted up out of the way and will lie on top; those that remain unlifted may then be crossed by weft and are on the bottom.

The illustration at right shows explicitly the pattern of intersecting threads a draft will give, but drawing every pattern like this would be ridiculous—you could weave it faster. Instead, a shorthand version of the same idea is used. The boxes representing the warp lying on top of the weft are filled in; those representing the weft on top are left blank.

Doing your own drawdown from a draft is simple. When the treadling says to raise shafts 1 and 2, go across that row filling in all the boxes under the 1s and 2s in the threading, as shown. When it says to raise shafts 2 and 3, fill in the boxes under the 2s and 3s, etc.

Trace along the weft shots that are drawn in until you see how it all works. Then take a pencil and fill in the rest of the drawdown. (The completed drawdown is on page 232.)

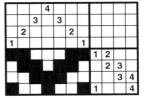

To do a drawdrawn from a draft, fill in the boxes that correspond to the shafts the treadling says to raise. For example, if the treadling says to raise shafts 1 and 2, fill in the boxes across that row under the 1s and 2s in the threading.

The drawdown is a graphic picture of what the pattern will look like.

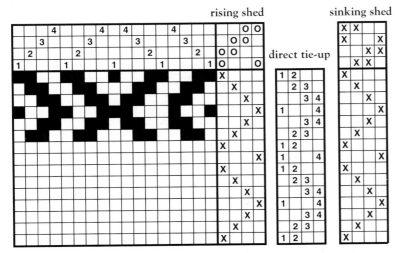

Fill in the rest of this drawdown. Tie-ups and threadlings are given for rising shed, direct tie-up, and sinking shed looms. (The completed drawdown is given on page 232.)

Your assignment

The following exercises will give you practice at doing drawdowns and start your library of drafts. I recommend that you use a pencil so that you can erase if (when) necessary. Completely filling in the squares makes a beautiful draft which is easy to see. Faster alternatives for filling in the squares include Xs or dots or Os or vertical and horizontal lines (to look like warp and weft). You can put anything you want in the squares as long as the ones you fill in are the warps on the surface of the weave. It will be evident almost immediately that the denser or bigger the mark, the more clearly the pattern will show; use whatever is fast enough and dark enough to please you. And have fun. (Completed drawdowns are shown on page 232.)

Plainweave.

Plainweave.

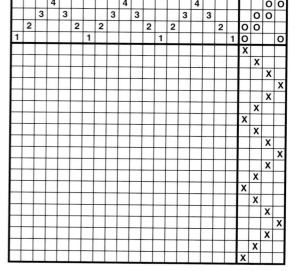

Point twill.

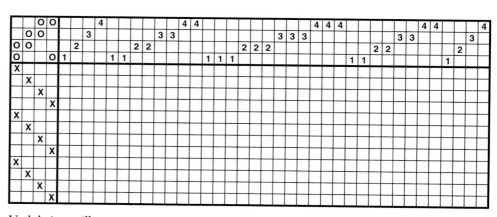

Undulating twill.

Plain-Weave Variations

Structure variations

Color variations

Texture variations

Plain weave and its variations, though simple in structure, can be tremendously complex. One way to achieve fabrics with dramatically different qualities is by altering how much warp or weft shows. Here, working clockwise from the far left, we see a balanced plain-weave fabric where equal amounts of warp and weft show. This fabric will drape well and is suitable for a shawl or non-tailored garment. The next two fabrics have the warps set very close together; the first is referred to as a warp-predominant fabric because only a little of the weft shows; the second is called a warp-faced fabric since no weft shows at all. The first of these two would be ideal for table runners or placemats; the second fabric would make a sturdy belt. The fourth fabric, bottom right, is a weft-faced rug sample where the weft completely covers the warp. For a weft-faced fabric the warp needs to be set wide enough so that the weft will cover it easily. While warp sett is important, notice here, too, how yarns—whether they are thick or thin, smooth or coarse—play a part in determining a fabric's character. *Fabrics by Bethany Thomas, Jane Patrick, Yvonne Stahl, Linda Ligon.*

119

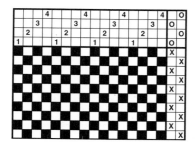

Plain weave or tabby.

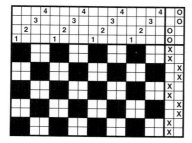

Basket weave.

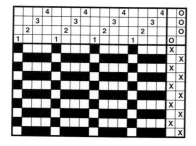

Rib weave.

All of these are threaded on a straight draw.

Before moving on to more complex weave structures, I'd like to dwell a while longer on some variations of plain weave. Although an entire book could be written on these, here I'll just give you a representative offering.

The first variations have to do with weave structure, all of which could be done on two shafts, though each would require different threadings. All can be done on the same threading on four shafts with only a need to change the treadling, just as you did when you wove plain weave and twill on your first sample. These weaves are the most basic of weave structures and have much to offer. They'll expand your understanding of drafting and put it to work. They also permit sampling a few of the infinite design possibilities which exist when color and texture are introduced. I'll discuss a few of these variations and hope that they inspire you to explore many more.

Structure Variations

Now that you have been through the drafting lesson, I hope you can look at the drafts at left and see that first you need to thread your loom just as you did the first time— 1, 2, 3, 4, etc.

Plain weave or Tabby

"Tabby" is another name for the plainest plain weave—a simple over-under sequence of warp and weft threads. To weave tabby, you need to raise shafts 1 and 3 alternately with shafts 2 and 4. Since you've already done that, it should be old hat by now.

Basket Weave

Basket weave is kind of a doubled tabby; it has the same over/under pattern but all threads are doubled. As you will quickly discover, if you try to weave two shots successively in the same shed, your second pass of the shuttle may well pull out your first weft shot. Wrapping your yarn around a selvedge thread (or two) will secure it.

If I am going to weave a lot of basket weave, then I usually wrap two wefts together on one shuttle, eliminating the need for doubling back in the same shed. Sometimes that's not good because the two yarns won't always lie exactly parallel but will tend to cross over each other. If you are using two colors or a very fat weft there will be a marked difference between using a double versus a single weft. With one color and finer yarn, the significance of the difference is debatable. Try it both ways for any given project, and decide what's acceptable to you.

Despite their similarity, I'm always surprised at how different a basket weave and a plain weave appear. Always one or the other is more appropriate for what I have in mind; I've never found them to be aesthetically interchangeable.

Structurally, too, they differ significantly. In any fabric, the more intersections (crossings) of warp and weft there are, the stiffer the fabric will be; the fewer the intersections, the softer, more pliable it will be. Therefore, since a basket weave has only half as many intersections as plain weave, basket weave will be much more pliable and drape better than its plain-weave counterpart. The same is true with twills and many other weaves; pay attention to the frequency of intersections.

The difference in numbers of intersections has another effect. In plain weave, which has the maximum number of crossovers, the threads will be pushed as far apart from each other as possible. When threads can draw in together, share space, they will. Since basket weave has fewer intersections than plain weave, more threads will group together, resulting in a piece that is somewhat narrower and thicker. If you weave 4 inches of basket weave, then 1 inch of tabby, then another 4 inches of basket, the tabby area, being forced apart by many intersections, will be wider, and your piece will look like a snake after a large meal. It's fine to combine equally pliable weaves, but inserting a stiffer tabby will cause a change in fabric quality that you may or may not like. Basket weave, rib weave, and twill all draw in to a similar degree.

Rib Weave

A rib weave creates another interesting texture. Using one color and a balanced weave you'll get a nice texture, nothing very "ribby". But if you pack the weft a little harder, a pronounced vertical rib will begin to appear, wide and narrow stripes alternating. To make it show the most, use two weft colors, one the same as the warp. Use this color when you lift shafts 2-3-4 together; use the contrasting color when you lift shaft 1. As the second color crosses over three warps, it visually begins to build a wide vertical line while the weft that crosses over only

one warp will join with the warp in serving as background. The back side of the rib weave will be the exact opposite, having a narrow rib in contrasting color. How would you reverse the pattern—bring the narrow contrasting rib to the side facing you?

When you use two colors, you will need two shuttles, which introduces another concern: preventing skipped warps at the selvedges. When the shuttles are on the same side, wrap them around each other, twisting the wefts together to prevent them from missing the selvedge warp as shown in the illustration. Try it. It's easier to do than to explain.

Aside from these variations in structure, all three of these weaves can have a wide variety of appearances depending on how close or far apart the warp is set and how hard the weft is packed in. A balanced weave, you may recall, has equal warp ends per inch (e.p.i.) and weft picks per inch (p.p.i.). If your warp is widely spaced, your weft will pack in more, resulting in a weft-predominant or even weft-faced fabric, one in which the warp doesn't show at all. If the warp threads are very close together, then the weft won't be able to pack in as much because of their resistance. Depending on how close the warp is set, the fabric can have a predominance of warp or even be totally warp-faced, the weft showing only where it turns the corner at the selvedge. Navajo rugs are weft-faced; inkle bands are warp-faced. Whether we're discussing tabby, basket, rib weave, or another weave altogether, altering your warp sett will affect to a great degree the proportions and appearance of your fabric.

Basket weave, rib weave, and twill, when used together with tabby, will draw in more because they have fewer intersections than tabby. When threads share space they have a tendency to draw in more which results in a somewhat narrower, thicker fabric.

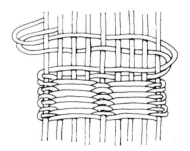

When you use two colors, two shuttles are required. To prevent skips at the selvedge, wrap the shuttles around each other when they are on the same side.

Color variations

Working with color opens up another world of possibilities. You probably had an inkling of this when you wove your first piece and noticed how the colors blended together to make a third one when they crossed each other. If not, take note of this when you weave your next piece. To get a better idea of how color and weave interact, take out your sample and look at it up close. You can see the individual colors quite well. Now tape it to the wall and stand on the other side of the room. Notice how your eye blends the two colors together where they cross each other to make a different, solid-looking color?

Using color in a woven piece can be as simple as crossing a solid color in the warp with a different single weft color, or it can be as complicated as a Scottish tartan with many colors used in warp and weft.

Stripes

In your first piece, you put stripes in your warp, so you understand how to do that. Any time that you have more than one color in either warp or weft, and cross it with a single color, you have stripes. They can be very wide and colorful like awning stripes, or very subtle monochromatic ones.

Plaids

Plaids are really only stripes going in both the warp and weft directions. They may be balanced or not, many colors or few, wide or fine, bright or subtle, complex or simple. If you are interested in traditional Scottish tartans, there are books that include color formulas for them. If not, go look in your closet, choose

Three fabrics with warp stripes. Stripes may be in a regularly repeating sequence as in the larger fabric at left, or in random order as in the fabric at right. *Fabrics by Lisa Budwig, Debbie Redding, Awyn Combs.*

several plaids and study them, decide what you like and why, then make up your own. Use crayons or short pieces of yarn, rearranging colors until you get a sequence you like.

Weave structure is a factor to consider in planning either stripes or plaids. A rib weave, in which you weave three warps up against one down, would look a lot different than a plain weave plaid with the same color sequences. Generally, it is best to avoid mixing too much color and structural texture in one piece because they compete and create chaos instead of harmony. A plaid rib weave could be very nice, or it could be awful. Try a little at the beginning of a plaid warp and see how it looks.

Color and Weave

Color-and-weave effect is a phenomenon which happens when weave structure interacts with color changes in the warp and/or weft to create pattern. Such a pattern can look very complicated even when the weave structure is simple.

Log cabin is one example which is simple to do and fascinating to look at. The usual structure is plain weave, though what happens to log

Plaids can be thought of as stripes going both ways. Consider scale of project and yarn size when planning plaids. As always, weaving a sample first is a good idea. *Fabrics by Ardis Dobrovolny, The Weaving Shop*

Plain-Weave Variations

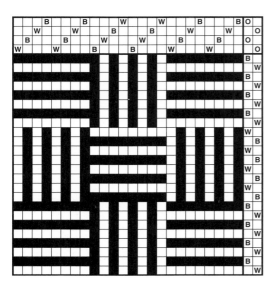

This color draft shows three sequences of a two-block log cabin. The symbols in the threading and treadling indicate which color to thread on what shaft and in what sequence the two colors should be woven.

W = White
B = Blue

Log cabin, complex in appearance, is simple in structure. This log cabin piece features borders of solid-colored warp stripes. When crossed with two alternating weft colors, dots appear.
Fabric by Selena Billington.

cabin when woven in twill is lots of fun, too. Log cabin requires two colors. If they are highly contrasting, such as black and white, the effect is extra dramatic. If the colors used are similar in hue, the effect is more subtle. Complimentary colors such as blue and orange create an electric effect that will make your eyes dance.

The basic requirement of log cabin is that the two colors alternate consistently, then shift. For example, a log cabin color sequence may be blue, white, blue, white, then shift to white, blue, white, blue, then shift to blue, white, blue, white, and so on. The weft sequence would be the same: blue, white, blue, white; white, blue, white, blue; etc. The

weave must be fairly balanced to work. If you pack your weft so tightly that it covers the warp, you'll probably get something interesting but it won't be log cabin.

Looking at the log cabin fabric shown below, the intrigue is in the blocks of design, the changes from horizontal stripes to vertical. To get the blocks to switch, you simply switch from BWBW to WBWB in threading and treadling. You can reverse as often as you want the blocks to reverse.

The draft here shows three sequences of a two-block log cabin. Remember, the location of a symbol tells you what shaft to thread. The symbol itself, B (blue) or W (white), tells you which color to thread on that shaft. The drawdown shows the color pattern, not the weave structure that we discussed in the lesson

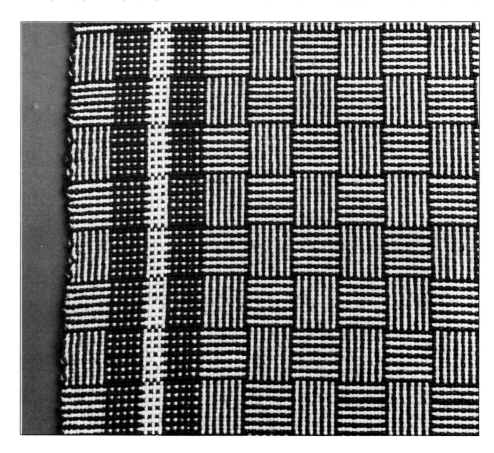

on drafting. Color drafting is different from structure drafting, but you don't need to concern yourself with it now. If you want to know more about color drafting, see Carol S. Kurtz's *Designing for Weaving* (Interweave Press, 201 East Fourth St., Loveland, Colorado 80537).

Texture variations

Everything has texture. Whether it is smooth or rough, cotton or wool, all yarn has texture.

When you think about texture in weaving, you need to consider both the visual and tactile aspects. What do you want your piece to feel like, and texturally how should it look?

Choosing appropriate yarn comes from asking yourself what the piece will be used for. If it's a fabric to be worn against the skin, then a scratchy yarn would be undesirable. If it's to be a table mat, then you won't want very fuzzy yarn that could reach up into your food and be harder to clean.

Textural considerations can be purely visual. You can alternate very thick yarns with very thin ones for a striped effect. Crossing these stripes will give you textured checks.

Using different kinds of yarn even when they are all the same color can produce interesting results. As you've noticed, some yarns are shiny and others dull. For example, a mercerized cotton is very shiny and will reflect more light because of its smoothness than a fuzzy wool yarn will. By mixing bumpy and looped yarns with fuzzy and smooth ones, you can produce a fascinating fabric with just simple plain weave.

Yarn choice is probably the most important factor in determining the overall tactile result of a fabric. Soft, loopy yarns, loosely set, create an inviting, cuddly looking fabric in the sample at top left. Similar effects are achieved when a large, bumpy, wooly yarn and a plied wool yarn are set openly to create a squishy blanket-like fabric. Contrasted to these two highly textured fabrics are the two smooth swatches at right. All four swatches are plain weave; notice what a difference yarn choice and sett makes! *Fabrics by The Weaving Shop, Sharon Alderman, Bethany Thomas*

In conclusion

In this lesson, I've introduced just a few of the possibilities of plain weave. You can expect that any given weave structure will have many options.

The three structural variations, plain, rib, and basket weave, can all be done on any straight-draw (1, 2, 3, 4) warp you set up. Color variations in the warp require separate warps for the separate colors, of course. But you can weave many different colors of weft into one warp just to see what you get.

Next are several ideas for homework. You can use any one or more of these or make up your own. From here on, I'll make suggestions and let you make up your own assignment. If a lesson really turns you on, weave several variations before going on to the next. If it's boring, weave one so you'll learn about it. You'll probably discover some merit in it after all.

I've pondered the idea of taking a single weave structure and weaving it with every yarn I could find, and trying different warp setts within each yarn. I'm sure a project like that would be very enlightening.

basket weave

rib weave

1/3 twill

2/2 twill

plain weave

Weave sampler; balanced weave, light color in warp, dark color in weft.

I'm also sure I'd be very sick of that weave before I was done. But once you've had some experience with yarns and how they are transformed, just thinking about it can give you an idea of the potential that is always present. Just think, after you've used every smooth yarn you can find—in a variety of colors, of course—you can get into novelty yarns, substituting bumps and loops for blues and greens. With so many yarns available to us, that kind of exploring can go on forever.

Your assignments

1. Thread a single-color warp, set for a good balanced weave, and weave plain weave, basket weave, rib weave, and twill, each with a single color that contrasts with that of the warp; then do it again, this time alternating two colors. Then pull your warp forward, cut the first sample off, resley to a closer sett, and repeat the whole sequence. Then cut that sample off, resley the warp looser and weave it all again. To resley in the same reed: if you had one thread per dent, starting in the middle and working your way out to the sides, change to two threads in every even dent and one in every odd dent. That will give you a sley sequence of 1/2/1/2/1/ etc. If your warp sett was 12 e.p.i., it will now be 18 e.p.i. To resley looser, try one thread every other dent (6 e.p.i. in a 12-dent reed) or skip every third dent, giving 1/1/0/1/1/0/1/1/0/, etc. (9 e.p.i.).

2. Plan a plaid, weave it in plain weave, basket, and rib (and perhaps a 2/2 twill as you did in your first piece). For a symmetrical plaid, be sure that your beat is balanced and look for squares of solid color along a diagonal line from the lower right corner up to the upper left corner (or vice versa).

3. Set up a log cabin, perhaps trying different color combinations side by side. You could have 3 inches of your warp width in highly contrasting colors, 3 inches in mildly contrasting colors, and 3 inches in subtle colors—for instance black and white, black and light gray, black and dark gray. Then weave each of those combinations using the same color sequence. Log cabin is a plain weave, but try other weaves as well just to see what happens.

4. Rib weave variations. Use one color for half of the warp and add a second color on one shaft only to the other half (see draft on page 128). Weave using a single weft color, two weft colors, two wefts of different thicknesses, and two wefts of which one is a novelty yarn. In all cases, try medium beating and hard beating. Then try changing the treadling to raise a different shaft by itself, so instead of 1, 234 try 2, 134, then 3, 124, then 4, 123; you can make checks by weaving 1/2 to 1 inch (or at least four treadle repeats) with one pair, then changing to a different pair for a short distance (see draft on page 128).

5. Use different weights and textures of yarn in the warp, and then weave with each one to see how the character of the texture changes. Weave a few inches with each warp yarn used singly; then try alternating two differ-

ent yarns. You could do the same with a many-colored striped warp to see how the colors of the stripes change when crossed by different colors. Because you are experimenting with textural yarns, stick to plain weave for a while to get used to how the yarn handles. Later try basket or rib to see the differences.

What could you do with all these variations? Think about a set of placemats or towels, all on the same warp, each having one variation. Or two afghans or scarves that for the sake of efficiency you want to weave on one warp but for variety you want to look very different. What changes could you make to achieve that variety?

Rib weave variations.

Weave (treadle) each repeat at least four times before going on to the next one.

Basic Twills

Ratios

The patterns, the drafts

Miscellaneous information to know about twills

Setts for twills

Weaving balanced twills

Using a floating selvedge

Twills, their diagonal lines pointing in one direction or the other, are full of possibilities waiting to be discovered. Even the very simplest straight and point twills have much to offer: set them close for belts; use them for luxurious mohair scarves; try them with lots of color contrast between warp and weft; combine diamonds and straight twill, or 1/3 and 2/2 twill treadlings. Mix and match; experiment! *Fabrics by Mary Peterson, Ardis Dobrovolny, Jane Patrick.*

On your first sample you wove some twill, a weave that is identified by its diagonal lines. I just touched lightly on the problems of uncaught warp at the selvedge and gave you the treadling for a 2/2 twill. Now I'll tell you more about twills so that you can begin to understand why it may be the weave most often used by both handweavers and the textile industry.

Ratios

As you know already, when weaving with four shafts you can raise either one, two, or three shafts at a time to make a shed. A 1/3 twill is woven by raising one shaft at a time so that the weft goes under one warp and over three. You can also think of these numbers as the visible ratio of warp to weft; for example, in a 1/3 twill you'll see one part warp for every three parts weft. Because what you see is mostly weft, it is called a weft-predominant twill.

A 2/2 twill has two warps up for every two down, thus is balanced. You see as much warp as weft.

A 3/1 twill has three shafts raised for each weft shot, putting more warp on the surface than weft. This is called a warp-predominant twill.

If you turn a 3/1 twill fabric over, you'll find a 1/3 twill on the opposite side. One side (the 3/1) will show mostly warp, the other (the 1/3) mostly weft. If your warp is blue and your weft is green, one side will be mostly blue, the other mostly green. Likewise, if your warp is striped and your weft is a single color, the 3/1 side will have a very strong stripe, the 1/3 side very subtle stripes. A 2/2 twill will look the same on both sides.

The patterns, the drafts

In weaving a twill, each weft float appears slightly to the right or left of the weft float in the row before it. As they "climb", the diagonal appears. There are many, many

Each weft float in a twill climbs to the left or right to make a diagonal pattern.

In a 1/3 twill the weft goes under one warp and then over three.

1/3 Twill.

In a 2/2 twill the weft goes under two warps and then over two.

2/2 Twill.

In a 3/1 twill the weft goes under three warps and then over one.

3/1 Twill.

possibilities for varying your threading and treadling to make twill patterns. Discovering these can be a lot of fun.

The four drafts below show the most basic of twills. If you reverse the direction of your threading, as in B, then the direction of the twill will reverse horizontally. If you reverse the direction of your treadling, as in C, the twill will change directions vertically. A twill that reverses horizontally is usually called herringbone, or point twill; one that reverses vertically is called a reverse twill, or sometimes a vertical herringbone. If you change directions in both the threading and treadling, you'll get diamonds, and that's where the real fun begins. The next twill lesson is mostly on making diamonds of different sizes, so for now we won't do any more with them.

There are many names for the various twill variations, and often it is difficult to distinguish which is which. Therefore, I prefer to avoid using names at all. I use point twill to mean a twill in which the threading and/or treadling reverses direction and otherwise refer to specific threadings or treadlings.

When you are threading for a twill, it is not crucial that you end on shaft 4 or 1. If you come to your last thread and you've only made it to shaft 3 in the sequence, don't worry about it. If it's a straight twill, it will be impossible to tell because the twill line is the same in all places. If it's a point twill, then not finishing a threading sequence will give you an unbalanced pattern, which you may not want. (If you want a balanced pattern, you'll want to be sure you've planned for enough threads before you begin measuring your warp.) Structurally, however, the fabric will be fine.

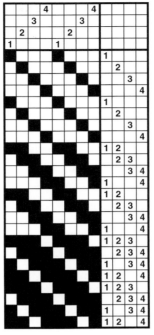

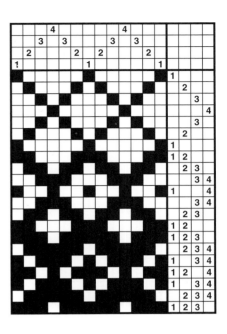

Examples of 1/3, 2/2, and 3/1 twills on straight (left) and point twill (right) threadings.

Basic twill drafts

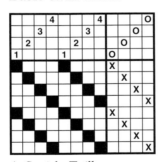

A. Straight Twill.

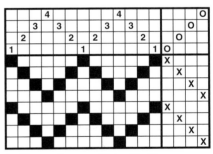

B. Herringbone or Point Twill.

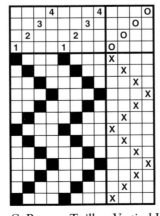

C. Reverse Twill or Vertical Herringbone.

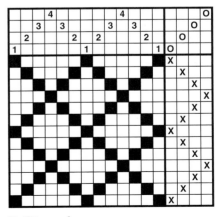

D. Diamonds.

131

Plain weave.

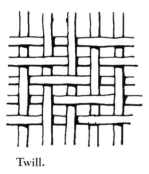

Twill.

The threads pack in more in twill than in plain weave because adjacent threads share some space and tend to group together.

The same is true of the treadling. If there is a changing pattern, then you'll probably want to complete a sequence, but if it's a straight treadling, you can stop at any point.

This is enough information for you to embark on basic twills. So far you've threaded the loom in a straight draw (1, 2, 3, 4) every time. Now it's time to open your mind to new threading patterns. After all, there are two reasons that the heddles slide back and forth to wherever you want them. One is to accommodate varying thicknesses of yarn and warp setts; the other is so that you can use them in whatever order you want.

These drafts are so basic that you may feel bored and want something more challenging. That's understandable, and you have at least two options. One is skip ahead to the next lesson, which is an expansion of this one. A second option is to play around with different yarns, some in the warp, even more in the weft. The assignments at the end of the chapter will give you some ideas to explore.

Miscellaneous information to know about twills

In the section on basket weave, I said that the more intersections there are, the stiffer the fabric (plain weave), and the fewer, the more pliable (basket, twill). That rule, and the resulting characteristics of twill fabrics, make twills very desirable for clothing; they flex to respond to body movement. Although almost no woven fabric is as stretchy or flexible as a knitted fabric, twills are among the most flexible of woven

fabrics. Jeans are woven in a 1/2 twill on three shafts. Jeans may seem very stiff, but notice how they bend at the knees, thousands of times, even when they're too tight. Look at your clothing and notice which garments are twill, which are plain weave, which are knitted. Can you tell what difference structure makes in how each feels when worn? How tight or loose can any structure be and still be comfortable?

As you may have noticed already, when you wove twill your weft tended to pack in a little more than when you wove plain weave. That's part of the grouping effect, in which the wefts share some space and so slide on top of each other somewhat. (The warps do it, too.) The result is that if the twill fabric is as solid as your plain weave was, then it's not a balanced weave; it leans toward weft-predominant because more weft is packed in. For many projects, that doesn't matter at all, but sometimes it will. If you have more weft, the fabric is likely to be stiffer (less pliable) across than it is up and down. Carried to an extreme, if you wove a scarf that was too weft-predominant, it would have the characteristics of a collar more than a scarf. It would be too stiff to wear comfortably.

Setts for twills

To compensate for the tendency of the weft to pack in, set your warp slightly closer. The resulting resistance will prevent too much weft from packing in. If you like the balanced tabby you got with a particular yarn set at 10 e.p.i., try twill at 12 e.p.i.; if you liked the tabby at 12 e.p.i., try the twill at 15 e.p.i. This is not an exact science.

Weaving balanced twills

As you weave, you can tell immediately whether your twill is balanced or not by the angle of the twill diagonal. A balanced twill has a 45° angle, a weft-predominant one a smaller angle, a warp-predominant one a larger angle. Watching that angle is a good way to check your beat, a gauge for its evenness. If the angle changes, your beat has changed. Visually that's distracting, and it also means that your fabric will be softer or weaker in some areas, stiffer or tougher in others.

The twill line is a useful tool for checking the consistency of your work, but its primary function is to provide interesting design. If that is your goal, then think about colors. If your warp and weft are the same color, the twill will be there but it will be hard to see. The more contrast between the two, the easier it will be to see the pattern. Or try a fatter weft, maybe a lot fatter, and see what happens.

When weaving a 1/3 or 3/1 twill, most of your weft is on one side, warp on the other. If the weft is a stretchy yarn or if you've laid it

into the shed stretched taut and allowed for very little take-up, it will relax back into its unstretched state, pulling the warp with it. The result is that the selvedges of the piece will curl toward the weft-predominant side. This doesn't always happen, but if it does, try leaving more for take-up.

Using a floating selvedge

When you weave twills, you will with regularity have to decide what to do about the edge warps not being caught by the weft. We've already discussed some of the alternatives (see pages 84–85 for others), and the floating selvedge is just one more. Some people like floating selvedges so much that they use them all the time, even when technically they are unnecessary. Other weavers find them very distracting and use them as little as possible. It is a matter of preference, so give them a try and see where your preference falls.

As the name implies, we're talking about a selvedge thread, the rightmost and/or leftmost edge thread. "Floating" refers to its position relative to the rest of the warp.

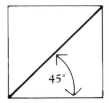

Balanced twill 45°.

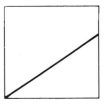

Weft predominant.

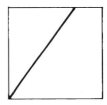

Warp predominant.

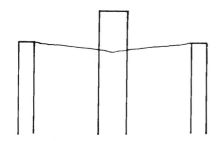

On a jack loom, with no shafts raised, the warp dips an inch or so as it travels from front to back.

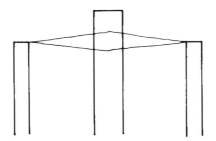

When the shed is opened, the warps on top and bottom are equidistant from an imaginary line traveling from front to back beam.

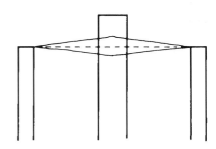

The floating selvedge rests in the middle of the shed.

Choose a sequence for going over and under your floating selvedge and use it all the time. Here are a few possibilities.

Measured, sleyed, and beamed with the rest of the warp, the floating selvedge is not threaded through a heddle. If you look at your jack loom from the side, with no shafts raised, the warp should dip an inch or more as it travels from the front to the back beam. The shafts on a jack loom are set so that if you draw a straight line from front to back beam, the heddle eyes are below that line. Thus, when you raise one set of warps, they will be lifted above the midline the same amount as the rest of the warps are below it. This maintains the same amount of tension on both sets of warps. Counterbalance and countermarch looms pull warps both up and down. At rest, with no shed, the warp will go straight from beam to beam. Since the floating selvedge does not go through a heddle eye, it always sits in the middle of the shed, along the imaginary straight line from beam to beam. As you weave, you'll take your shuttle around the floating selvedge, just as you may have done with your other selvedge threads before.

Wrapping your shuttle around a floating selvedge has several advantages over going over a threaded selvedge thread. First of all, it's easier to use and easier on the yarn. Because the floater is always right there in the middle of the shed, it is easy to pass the shuttle over and under it. It speeds weaving because less manipulation is needed. A floating selvedge is less likely to be stretched or frayed from the constant rubbing of the shuttle, and so it will be both more stable and better looking. When it's woven you'll never be aware of it; it will look like all the other warps.

For efficiency, speed, comfort, rhythm, or simplicity, choose a sequence for going over and under the floaters and use it all the time. You can enter the shed under one floater and exit the shed over the other one, or go over upon entering and under as you exit, or go under both going one direction and over going the other way. Do whichever one feels most comfortable to you.

A very soft yarn, one that is loosely twisted, may be weak and not very resistant to abrasion. While that can be fine as warp, the extra rubbing that the floating selvedge gets may be more than it can stand. Consider using two together to provide the extra strength needed. If you don't want the extra bulk that will give you, choose another strong, smooth, fine thread, such as sewing thread, nylon fishing line, or another yarn, and run that with your floating selvedge(s). After you've finished the piece, slide the guest yarn out by pulling from one end; that's why it needs to be smooth and fine.

Conclusion

The information on twills given in this chapter has only scratched the surface of what there is to know about them. The next lesson on altering drafts will begin to expand on the information already mentioned in this chapter, as will the rest of the lessons in Part II. I'd been weaving several years before it hit me how incredibly versatile twills are and how it would be possible to spend years just exploring their many possibilities, but like so many things, I couldn't recognize or appreciate that until after I'd been out exploring other areas.

So start here, move on quickly, and have fun with starting to make up your own patterns.

Your Assignments

1. Plan and set up a single-color warp that has a point twill-threading (i.e., 1, 2, 3, 4, 3, 2, 1, etc.) for a few inches on each side and a straight-twill threading (1, 2, 3, 4, etc.) in the center. Use a different color for the weft and weave a 2/2 twill. Treadle a point-twill border (treadle 1-2, 2-3, 3-4, 4-1, 3-4, 2-3, 1-2, etc.), a straight twill center (1-2, 2-3, 3-4, 4-1, etc.), and another point-twill border. (See draft below.)

Repeat the entire weaving sequence with a thinner weft, then a thicker one, then a novelty yarn (lots of bumps, slubs, loops, or other textures), then a colored variegated yarn. Record how well each one shows off the pattern. Do the drawdown for the draft below, *before* you weave the fabric.

2. Plan and set up a striped warp, part straight twill, part point twill, as shown in the draft on page 136. Weave 1/3, 2/2, and 3/1 twills with one color of weft, then the three again striping the

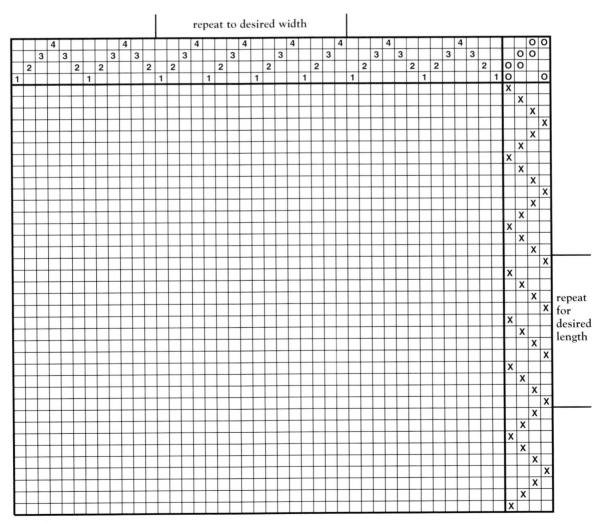

repeat to desired width

repeat for desired length

Draft for Assignment 1.

weft. When does it look plaid, when striped, when solid? The colors may coincide with the threading pattern of the point twill, or not. Try it both ways.

3. Plan your own sampler, trying all of the following in one piece: straight and point twill threadings; straight and point twill treadlings; 1/3, 2/2, 3/1 twill ratios; same and contrasting weft colors. Have it all balance so that it looks unified instead of like a conglomeration. You could put a black thread between each section, warp and weft, to designate change, or use two colors alternating in blocks. Below are two threading possibilities.

Draft for Assignment 2

Threading possibilities for Assignment 3

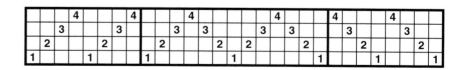

Altering Drafts

Doing drawdowns to make pattern decisions

More twills, a little less basic

Drafting from cloth diagrams to threading and treadling

Doing drawdowns to make pattern decisions

You know how to read drafts, how to do drawdowns, and how to tell which parts of the drawdown represent which threads in the threading and treadling drafts (look straight up, or straight across). Some of the drafts you've seen repeated the same sequence over and over, for

example, 1, 2, 3, 4, 1, 2, 3, 4, etc., while others gave you only one repeat of the pattern, leaving it to you to repeat it at the loom. For many projects or patterns, repeating the given draft for the width of the warp works fine. For others, an intermediate step is essential. This step may be the most compelling reason for doing drawdowns.

The draft here is shown just as it is given in *A Handweaver's Pattern Book* (Marguerite Davison, Box 263, Swarthmore, PA 19081). It is not centered, probably because the threading sequence is easier to keep track of this way than if it were to start where the design looks best. If you were using this pattern to weave a bedspread, whether the diamond on the edge ended at its point would probably not be as crucial as it would be on placemats or a table runner. On a bedspread, you will see dozens of diamonds all over, but few people will lean over the side of the bed to look at the selvedge. On placemats or a table runner, the selvedges are obvious, and thus it's far more likely that you'll want the diamond to end on the edge.

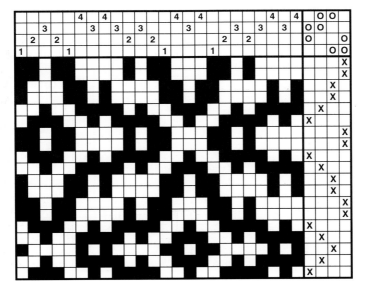

This draft is called "Periwinkle" and comes from page 131 of *A Handweaver's Pattern Book* by Marguerite Davison.

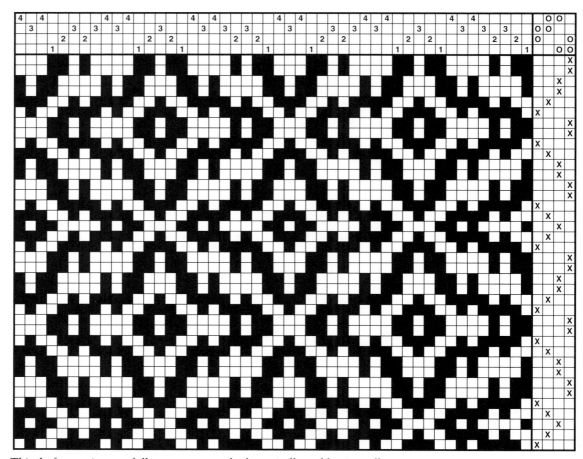

This draft contains two full pattern repeats both vertically and horizontally.

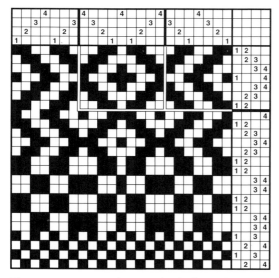

If you want to use only part of a draft, mark off the section you like and then do a two-repeat drawdown.

Two-repeat drawdown of the section marked off in the draft at left. To close the top and bottom of the diamonds, one more shot in the twill progression was added before reversing direction, as seen in the lower half of the drawdown. This not only changes the outside of the large diamonds, but the inside of the center pattern is altered as well.

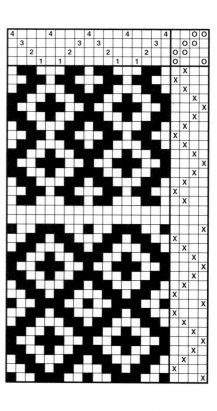

To decide where you want the pattern to start and stop you need to do a drawdown of two repeats of the pattern, repeating both threading and treadling.

The draft on page 138 contains two full repeats. In the first draft (page 137), if you didn't know enough to look for diamonds, you might not have seen one, as the two shown are each dissected into three pieces. The draft on page 138 contains two full re-peats and you can see three whole diamonds, and several others that are convincing even if not quite complete. To get the diamond point on your selvedge, draw lines through the drawdown and draft where you think the edges should be, as in the draft at lower left, and then start your threading and treadling from there.

One repeat of the pattern might be enough when weaving something tiny: a bookmark, tree ornament, gift-wrapping decoration, pieces to make a mobile. One single diamond could be very pretty for any of these. In that case, you'd start and stop on the edges of one diamond. Look carefully at the diamonds in this draft. They are not identical. The diamond whose center is threaded 1, 2, 3, 2, 1 is both taller and wider than the one with the center threaded 4, 3, 4. Look at the centers to see the difference. (Just in case you're considering it, don't weave this pattern until after you've done Lesson 15: Overshot. It might work well for you, but it's more likely not to.)

Now let's say you come across a draft that you like only part of. Treat it the same way as the draft we just worked on. Block off the part you like and use it. This is another occasion for doing a two-repeat draw-down, for the way a pattern looks where it joins when repeated is sometimes a surprise.

In the example at the bottom of page 138, notice that the treadling is changed on the second half of the new draft. In the top half, I didn't like the opening left between the bottom and top of the diamonds. To close the diamonds at top and bottom I added one more shot in the twill progression before reversing direction. Notice that while the added weft shot changed the outside of the large diamonds, it also changed the design in the center of the pattern. The motif changed from a white (weft) cross to a small diamond with a black (warp) dot in the center. Becoming aware of those small changes and how to create them will help you to begin designing your own patterns and make slight alterations in existing drafts to help them suit your taste a little better.

More twills, a little less basic

I spent an hour or two (with a computer drafting program it could be done in a couple of minutes— see page 223 for more on that) drawing out the random assortment of twills on the next two pages, and I hope you have as much fun looking at them as I did making them up. By changing the threading only slightly, I came up with surprisingly varied effects.

Each treadling follows essentially the same pattern as its threading. The only change is that I started with treadle 4 instead of 1 and went in reverse. Had I started with 1 in the treadling, the drawdowns would be varied Xs instead of varied diamonds; try a few yourself and see.

While all of these except D are drawn as 1/3 twills, they would probably be more practical woven as 2/2 twills. To change from a 1/3 to 2/2

Altering Drafts

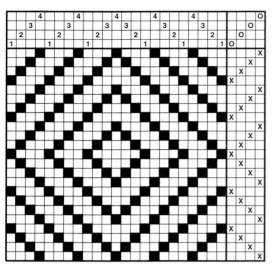

Draft A.

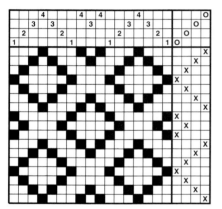

Draft B.

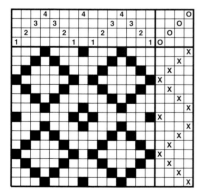

Draft C.

twill, simply treadle 1-2 for every 1, change 2 to 2-3, 3 to 3-4, and 4 to 4-1. My concern for practicality comes from looking at some of the long rows of white space, which mean long weft floats (wefts not intersecting warps) on the face of the fabric, warp floats on the back. Too many long floats make a fabric unstable and likely to snag. The actual length of a float depends on the warp sett. If a weft is floating over seven warps at 6 e.p.i., that's more than an inch, but at 24 e.p.i., it's only about 1/3 of an inch and not very dangerous.

Let's discuss the following five drafts for a moment. Draft A shows you how to get diamonds inside of diamonds, or bigger ones than you did in the last lesson. (I'll speak of 1, 2, 3, 4 as forward, 4, 3, 2, 1 as backward.) To get larger diamonds, go forward (1, 2, 3, 4, 1, 2, 3, 4, etc.) in your threading several times before reversing. Where you reverse direction will be the point of your twill, and each repeat out from that center point will be one more concentric diamond. The same is true in the treadling. With your hand, cover the lower half of the draft. If you never reversed the direction of your treadling, you would have a very large herringbone.

Draft B has lots of small diamonds that are not connected to each other as they were on the preceding page. The diamonds in Draft C also aren't connected; notice that in this draft one diamond is smaller than the others. In an expanded draft of more repeats, you'd see that there are as many smaller diamonds in C as there are larger diamonds. It

doesn't look that way now because of where the draft starts and stops—a good case for a larger drawdown.

Draft D combines small and large diamonds, another very simple way to design a pattern with a lot of variety. Draft E has a wonderful assortment of diamonds with differing notches and differing centers.

Again, any of these can be woven in a 1/3, 2/2, or 3/1 twill. Depending on your yarn and color choices they can look markedly different from one another.

There is no great secret to making up these designs. All I did was write out a threading that seemed interesting and a treadling that followed the same sequence, and draw the drawdown to find out what I'd concocted. Were I to weave one now, I'd probably pull a section out of E, and then do a two-repeat drawdown of that section. If I still liked what I got, I'd try it in a sample.

Notice, too, that the pattern of the treadling marks is the mirror image of the pattern created in the drawdown. As you work more with drafts, you'll begin to recognize predictable combinations of threading and treadling, knowing in advance what causes what.

In designing twills, the size and number of diamonds you get will be determined by how often you reverse direction in your threading and treadling. I'd like you to play around with these, make up your own, combine the various threading or pattern units (1, 2, 3, 4—1, 2, 3, 4, 3, 2, 1— 1, 2, 3, 4, 1, 4, 3, 2, 1—1, 2, 3, 4, 3, 4, 3, 2, 1, etc.) and do drawdowns to see what you'll get. Then weave some. Use a variety of yarns, try different warp setts, experiment with colors if you want. In Marguerite Davison's A Handweaver's Pattern Book, (Marguerite Davison, Box

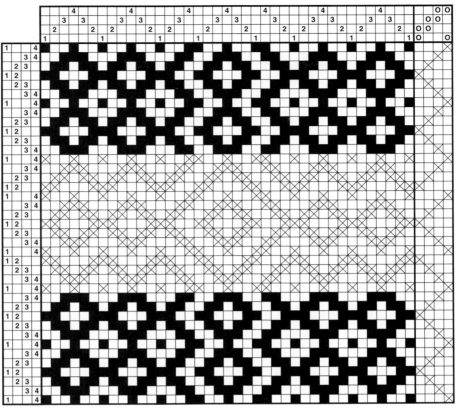

Draft D.

Direct tie-up treadling
in easy-to-read form.

Multiple tie-up
and treadling.

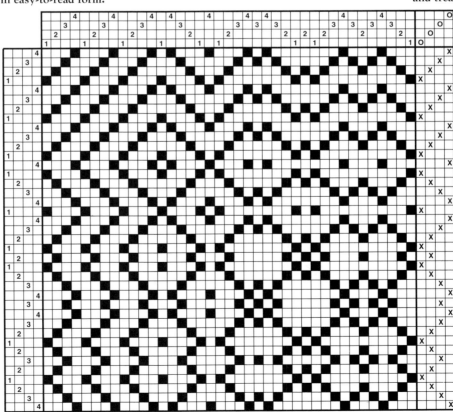

Draft E.

Direct tie-up treadling
in easy-to-read form.

Multiple tie-up
and treadling.

263, Swarthmore, PA 19081) the first 54 pages are devoted to straight and point twills. Take a look at them if you like, but please don't decide to just copy hers and forget about making up your own. Twills are easy to understand and execute, and this is the beginning of some of the fun you can have adding your own personal touch to all you weave.

Your assignments

1. Choose one of the drafts from this lesson and weave it as is, then again as a 2/2 twill (or 1/3 if you choose D). Remember that the weave needs to be fairly balanced for the pattern to show up well. If you pack your weft in too tight, you'll lose the visual relationship of the warp and weft.
2. Pull a section out of one of the drafts from this lesson and do a two-repeat drawdown. Weave it as a 1/3 twill and also as a 2/2 twill.
3. Choose the threading from one twill draft and the treadling from a different one and make up a new drawdown. If you like it, weave it using two different colors or textures of weft.
4. Make up your own twill, planning for a particular project. It could be skirt fabric, a border on kitchen or camper curtains, a pillow, a baby blanket. Plan it so that the pattern is symmetrical across the warp. You don't have to do a drawdown of the entire warp to know this, just one repeat or a repeat of each section will do.

A quick design shortcut is to use diagonal lines in place of numbers as shown below. Use numbers for the first repeat, lines to get an idea of what the whole piece will look like. Weave it if you like the design.

Drafting shorthand: use numbers for first repeat, and then diagonal lines to give an idea of what the whole piece will look like.

Drafting from cloth diagrams to threading and treadling

Now, let's approach the draft from the other direction. So far, we've started with threading and treadling and then figured out what it would give us, but often you'll have a picture in your mind of how you want a pattern to look. You need to know how to thread and treadle to get that particular pattern. To make up threadings and treadlings and then do drawdowns to see if you got what you wanted would be ridiculously time-consuming—you could spend days hoping for your pattern to show up. Instead, you can draw a draw-down, now called a cloth diagram, of what you want to weave and determine the threading and treadling from it. Then you only have to do one draft, the one you want.

Actually, you may need to do more than one. The only problem with starting with an original cloth diagram is that until you've done enough of them to understand how they work, you are fairly likely to draw a design that takes more shafts than you have. When that happens, you need to simplify the pattern, maintaining its character while curtailing its flair. If you enjoy doing your own designing and keep practicing and exploring, you'll get to the point where you can count shafts in your head as you draw and you'll know when you've reached your loom's limit.

The other reason for knowing how to derive threading and tread-ling from cloth diagrams is that you will begin to notice fabrics that you want to duplicate. Commercial clothing, upholstery, bedspreads, and table linens often have fabric struc-

tures that can be duplicated with four or eight shafts. You will also come across other handwoven things you'd like to try your own version of, and being able to figure out how they were done makes this possible.

At right is a cloth diagram, which is a picture of a fabric structure. As before, the black squares represent the warp threads going over the weft threads. From the general design, you can see that it is a point twill (squint your eyes to see it better), but you need to know more than that to weave it. Each column represents one warp thread, so if our example here were a whole fabric swatch, it would be nine threads wide. *All columns that are identical in pattern represent warp threads on the same shaft.* Thus, the first, fifth, and ninth columns/threads are all on the same shaft, which we'll label 1 because it's a convenient place to start. Any column/thread that is different in pattern from those is on a different shaft, so the second column/thread, being different from the first, will be on shaft 2. Identical patterns to column 2, all the way up and down the row, are in the fourth, sixth, and eighth columns. These threads are all threaded on shaft 2. Finally, the two remaining columns/threads are identical, so they can both be labeled 3.

From the completed threading you can see that it takes only three shafts to weave this pattern.

To determine the treadling order is even easier. You know that to weave a shot you need to raise some shafts, and that the black squares represent warp on top, or threads/shafts raised. Each row across represents one weft shot, and the squares that are filled in show which shafts are up when that weft shot is thrown. Look above the filled-in

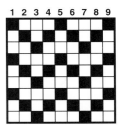

Cloth diagram.

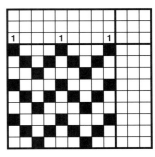

Begin filling in the threading by writing in all the ones.

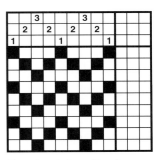

Completed threading for cloth diagram.

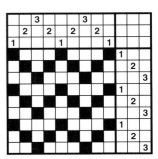

Completed threading and treadling.

Altering Drafts

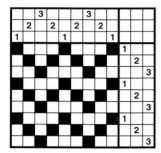

Completed threading and treadling.

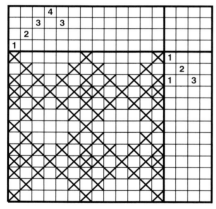

Complete the threading and treadling for this cloth diagram. Check yourself on page 149.

squares to see what number is at the top of the columns they are in, and write those numbers down at the end of the row. Those are the shafts you need to raise for that weft shot.

In this draft, for the first weft shot the squares under the 1s are filled in, which means that the threads on shaft 1 are raised. For the second weft shot the number 2 boxes are filled in, so you will want to raise shaft 2 to weave it. The boxes below the number 3s are filled in in the third row, so shaft 3 is to be raised for the third shot. And so forth.

That's really all there is to it. The system is easy, but some drafts are more complex than others. It takes practice and a watchful eye to do this easily.

Let's do a few more, only this time you do more of the work. And remember, just because you have only four shafts does not mean that the draft will.

Start with the cloth diagram shown at left. If you begin assigning shafts with shaft 1 and count up, you can go as high as you need to. You could begin with any number, but starting midway of an unknown quantity can get confusing. Thus, we'll say that the first thread is on shaft 1.

The thread next to it is raised at different times (you know this because the squares are filled in in a different pattern), so it must be on a different shaft. We'll assign it to shaft 2.

How about the next thread? It's different again and should be threaded on shaft 3. And the fourth thread? The fifth thread is the same as the third, so it's on shaft 3. You do the rest.

With the threading done, you can easily figure out the treadling. When the first shot was woven, the warps that are filled in in the first row were raised, so look above the filled-in boxes to see which shafts were raised. For the first shot only shaft 1 was raised. For the second weft shot, the boxes under the 2s are filled in, so shaft 2 was raised. The third shot requires two shafts to be raised, 1 and 3. While for most of the weaving you've done so far you have lifted the same number of shafts for every shot, that is not a rule at all. The rib weave alternated one shaft against three, remember? The draft we're working on right now is for a waffle weave, called that because the fabric looks like a waffle, and it will use varying numbers of shafts for each shot. To weave the fourth shot, you need to raise shafts 1, 2, and 4. Now you finish.

All of the cloth diagrams on page 145 are equally simple, and your biggest problem will be trying to make them too hard. If it's difficult to follow the rows, which it often is, use a ruler or some other straightedge. The solutions to all of these begin on page 151, at the end of the next lesson.

I told you that analyzing cloth diagrams is useful if you want to copy an existing fabric. The way to do that is to mark off a section of the fabric with pins and then trace the warp or weft in the swatch. Record on graph paper when the warp covers the weft: follow one thread, whichever direction is easier, and fill in the squares when the warp is on top. Leave them blank when the weft is on top. You are creating a cloth diagram from which you can determine the threading and treadling just as you've done above.

How soon you'll actually do this I can't say. But whether you choose to create your own draft or not, knowing how to alter drafts and work from cloth diagrams will help you to catch errors: your own, a book's, or a loom's. You will have a broader base of understanding to work from, which will make all your weaving easier. In fact, most of the techniques and specific information I've learned in weaving have turned out to be most valuable at times that would have seemed unrelated to their subject matter. A bit of information from category A solves some problem in category C. Now I'm glad to learn new things not so much for themselves as for what they will add to my general store of knowledge. It's fun to mix and match, and what you learn about drafting definitely falls under this heading. You'll rarely use one phase of it without incorporating others.

From here on, I'll be using drafts to explore other weaves, and I will assume a degree of drafting knowledge on your part. Using drafts will make you more comfortable with them. Later, we'll talk about block theory and block drafting, another segment of drafting. What I've given you here are the basics.

Your assignment

Make up your own cloth diagram and fill in the threading and treadling. Add direct tie-up treadling to the left of the diagram. To draw a multiple tie-up, take the shaft numbers of each shot and write them vertically in the tie-up box—first shot = first column, etc. Refer to drafts on pages 115 and 117.

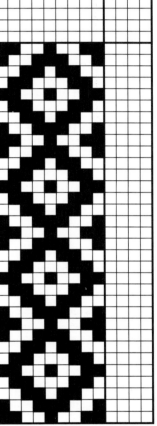

Multiple tie-up and treadling.

Fill in the threading and treadling for these cloth diagrams.

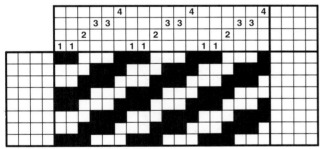

Direct tie-up treadling.

Multiple tie-up and treadling.

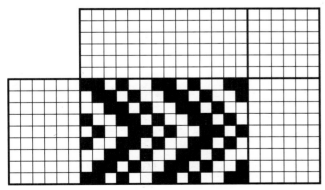

Direct tie-up treadling.

Multiple tie-up and treadling.

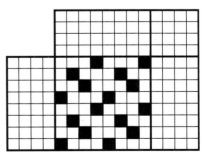

Direct tie-up treadling.

Multiple tie-up and treadling.

145

An Introduction to Other Kinds of Twills

Offset and broken twills

Waffle weave

Combination twills

Weaving on opposites

Treadling variations and combination threadings expand the realm of twills. Here, at lower left, is a soft, waffle weave fabric. The threading is an ordinary point twill, and the secret to the waffles, or floats, is in the way the treadling is varied. Compare this waffle weave with the fabric at top right, also a waffle weave, to get an idea of the possibilities and different results which can be achieved when color is an added element. The fine fabric at center combines stripes of point twill and basket weave. It would be suitable for a dress or jacket. At bottom right is another example of this same combination threading, only done in heavier yarns. Again, this is only a taste of what's possible. As always, note that fiber choice, sett, and color usage are important factors to keep in mind when planning projects. *Fabrics by Debbie Redding, Sharon Alderman, Yvonne Stahl, The Weaving Shop.*

The twills you've done so far have been straight and point twills. That's only the beginning. In addition to variations of these, there are many other categories of twills, each with its own variations. Steep, low, undulating, satin, mock satin, extended, double-faced, offset, broken, waffle, and combination twills are some of the variations. The vocabulary overlaps, and many of these share characteristics even beyond their common twill identity. Some can be done only with more than four shafts, most have four-shaft versions as well as others. The drafts that you worked on in the last lesson come from this list, and they as well as some others are shown with their threadings, treadlings, and names at the end of this lesson. They are there for your reference, to try whenever you feel so inclined. In this lesson I want to talk about only three: offset and broken, waffle, and combination, and a treadling option, weaving on opposites.

More twills! At left is an undulating twill; the white warp and the black weft provide lots of contrast for this threading where the optical effects can be played up for electrifying results. Another threading which lends itself well to "op art" interpretation is the extended twill fabric shown at bottom right. Again, highly contrasting colors increase the effect of this threading. Mock satin weave is used for the fabric at top right. On one side the warp predominates; on the other side only specks of warp show. Experiment with one color in the warp and one color in the weft, or cross warp stripes with one color of weft. All three of these threadings invite lots of color play, whether your color choices are conservative or bold and bright. *Fabrics by Judy Steinkoenig.*

Offset and broken twills

In offset and broken twills, the twill line is broken. "Offset" is the word applied to straight twills; "broken" refers to point twills, but the principle is the same for both.

If you look at the threading of this offset twill, you'll see that the offset of the pattern occurs where one shaft was left out of the threading sequence. It can be any shaft; it can happen at any interval. I recommend that you plan your breaks often enough that they look intentional instead of like threading errors.

In a broken twill, the shaft deletion occurs on one side or the other of the point; thus, instead of threading 1, 2, 3, 4, 3, 2, 1, you'd thread 1, 2, 3, 4, 2, 1 or 1, 2, 4, 3, 2, 1. Creating this break is a slight variation that adds new character to a point twill, one you might like.

Both of these twills can be created with interruptions in treadling as well as threading. Just leave one shot out of your treadling sequence and you'll have the same kind of interruption. Whether you have a point or straight threading will, of course, affect the design dramatically.*

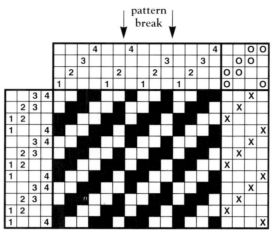

Offset twill.

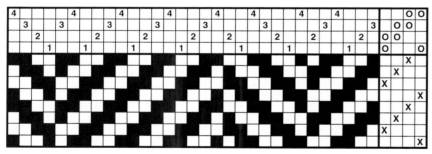

Broken twill.

*One of the ways to experiment with alterations in drafts or ways of accomplishing patterns is to take a cloth diagram or drawdown and turn it 90°, refigure the threading and treadling, and see what happens. On simple drafts, such as plain weave or 2/2 twills, there may be no difference. On others, there is a tremendous difference in how you would arrive at the same fabric, which often won't be exatly the same.

Waffle weave

I've included waffle weave because it's one of the most fun of all weaves. It has great possibilities for color arranging and intrigues nearly everyone. Waffle weave has a point-twill threading. The treadling, which creates an arrangement of warp and weft floats with few intersections, is the key to creating the waffles of waffle weave. This has two significant results to be aware of.

First, the fabric does not look like the drawdown. In the drawdown you see diamonds; in the fabric you'll see squares. Look at the draft again. Notice where there are warp threads staying up for a relatively long distance without intersecting any wefts. Also notice weft floats, rows in which no warps appear for a distance. Those warp and weft floats will outline the depression of the waffle. The insides of the square actually are at a lower level, just as in a real waffle. The stabilizing intersections occur in the centers of the waffles.

Because there are so few intersections, it is all too easy to pack the weft in too much. The warp is putting up almost no resistance to the weft, and so first-time waffle-weavers often end up with a weft-faced fabric and no waffles. For the waffles to show, you must have a balanced fabric

(e.p.i. = p.p.i.) or nearly so, so beat lightly, or set your warp half again as close as you normally would, for example, 18 e.p.i. instead of 12 e.p.i.

While the warp is on the loom under tension, the waffles will be flattened; only when the tension is relaxed will the depth appear. As this happens, the fabric will draw up a lot in length and width. Depending on your yarn and your beat, the external dimensions of your fabric could shrink as much as 30 percent, and this is only structural shrinkage; it does not take into account yarn shrinkage from washing. I once wove a four-shaft waffle weave out of linnay, a very nice linen/rayon yarn that shrinks a fair amount. Between the structure and the yarn shrinkage, the piece shrank 47 percent and was about three times as thick as when on the loom. Do a sample. I didn't on that one and never did figure out what to do with it in its changed state.

Rather than try to explain all the color possibilities that exist for waffles, I'm going to give you some color-coded threading drafts. Use the same color sequence in your treadling, and make up more of your own.

The threads that outline the waffles on the face of the fabric will be the bottom of the waffle on the other side and vice versa. When you start weaving, look on the other side just to see what's happening.

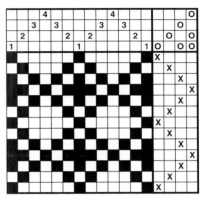

Waffle weave drawdown.

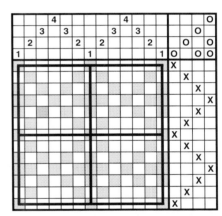

Illustration of woven fabric. Note that the fabric does not look like the drawdown. Squares appear in the fabric although there are diamonds in the drawdown.

A		B		C				D		E		F		G	
	a		b		b		a		d		c		b		b
	a	a		a	a		b a	a b		c c		b b		b b	b b
a		a	b		b	a		a b	b	b	b	b	b	a		a	b		b
a		a	a		a	a	b		a	a		a	a		a	a		a	a	a

Seven possible color threading sequences for waffle weave.

Combination twills

When your warp is threaded to a straight draw, you can treadle to achieve a variety of weaves: plain weave, twill, basket, rib, etc. You can also combine weaves in the threading so that different patterns occur side by side across the warp. With an unlimited number of shafts, you could combine anything, using an entirely new group for each pattern. Because most of us have a limited number of shafts, however, it is necessary to play around to discover feasible combinations.

You've already mixed straight and point twills. Here we're talking about combining less related weaves. I'll save you some time by telling you that you cannot combine twill and tabby on four shafts. You can, however, combine twill and basket weave, as in the drafts below. It must be a 2/2 twill, but it can be straight, point, broken—try anything you can think of, and remember that by changing colors or textures as you change pattern you can amplify the effects.

This is a perfect opportunity to try out your inventing and designing skills, making drawings of what you want to try and then determining the threading and treadling to see if you can weave them on your loom. At this point, you may not do much inventing, but as you get more comfortable with the designing process, you may begin to, and may really enjoy it.

Weaving on opposites

Weaving on opposites is a technique that I'll mention briefly here because twills lend themselves so well to it. It's a method of treadling rather than a specific weave structure, and can apply to other weave structures, too. Instead of sleying for a balanced weave, to weave twills on opposites you'll need to space your warp farther apart so that a weft-faced fabric can be woven.

Weaving on opposites means just that. After you throw a pick in one shed, the one that follows it will be woven in the previous pick's opposite shed. Two shuttles are needed, a leader (color A) and a follower or opposite (color B). So, if you weave shed 1-2 with color A (the leader), you'll follow it with 3-4 and color B; shed 2-3 (leader, color A) will be followed by 1-4 (color B); shed 3-4 (color A) will be followed by 1-2

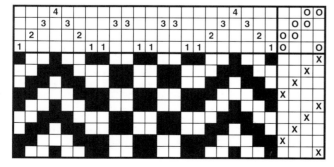

Combination twills.

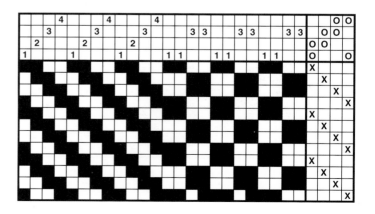

Twill variations

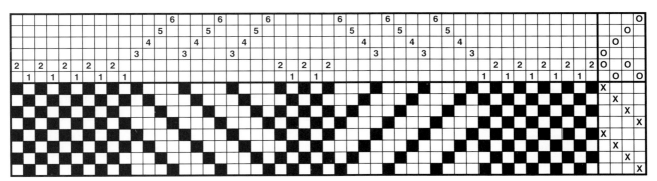

Combination of twill and plain weave.

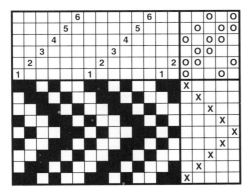

Point twill-herringbone.

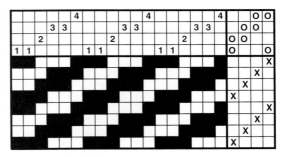

Undulating twill.

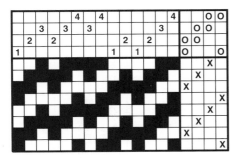

Extended twill.

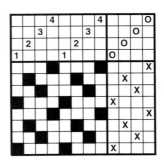

Mock satin.

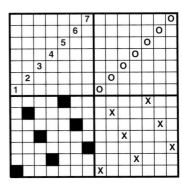

Satin.

More twill variations

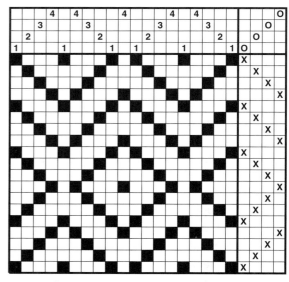

Point twill.

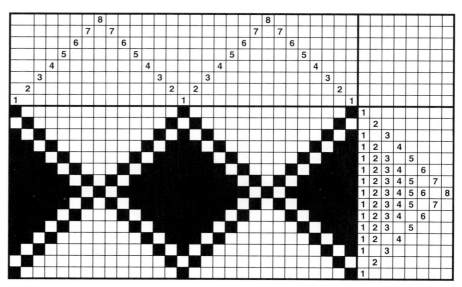

Double-faced twill. The cloth looks different than the drawdown.

Waffle weave.

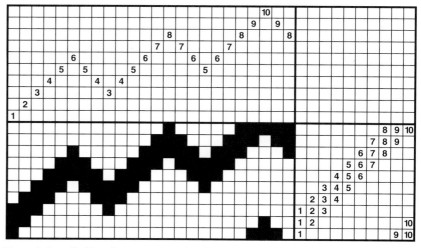

Point twill.

Extended twill. (Just because it can be drawn doesn't mean that it should be woven.)

(color B), and so on. In other words, for your follower raise whatever shafts weren't raised the last time. The leader can go into any shed you want; because the next shot is its opposite, the fabric is structurally sound no matter where the leader leads. Pack your weft in well so that the warp is completely hidden, and use two colors at a time or your pattern won't show. This technique is ideal for rugs, purses, bags, and footstool cushions. It may also be used for table mats, runners, belts, or even vests and jackets, if lighter-weight materials are used. For inspiration, take a look at the pillow on page 82.

In conclusion

As always, these are the basics. Try what you like, know that there's more if you want it later. In general, twills are softer and thicker, may need a closer sett, may benefit from a floating selvedge, may look different on the two sides, are versatile, and are easy to weave. You can use any yarn, but a very complex yarn will obscure a small or complex pattern. Any thickness of yarn can work, provided the e.p.i. and p.p.i. are appropriate, and you can go wild with color if you want to.

Your assignments

1. Design and weave an offset twill with the breaks coming at regular intervals, and another one in which the intervals are not all the same size; for example, 1/2-to-1-inch repeat, and repeats of 1, 2, 1, and 3 inches.

2. Design and weave a broken-twill fabric suitable for a winter coat or man's sport jacket. Think of using one color in the warp and another in the weft, with perhaps a single warp end of a third color at the break in the twill.

3. Design and weave a waffle weave using a color sequence that will emphasize the depth of the waffle cells; for example, light on the top, dark on the bottom.

4. Design and weave a waffle weave with one color in the warp and a slightly different color in the weft for more character than a single color would produce.

5. Design and weave a waffle-weave sample with three color combinations side by side in the warp, each 3 to 4 inches wide. Repeat this sequence in the weft. What happens when color sequence B crosses C?

6. Design and weave a combination twill/basket weave with three colors in the warp, perhaps one as accent only.

7. Design and weave a combination twill other than the one(s) given; combine some twills in new ways.

8. Choose a point-twill draft and weave it on opposites. You might want to label your shuttles "A" and "B" to help you keep track of which is which; B always follows A.

PART III:

For Those of You Who Know What You're Doing

Double Weave

Setting up

Threading

Warp sett considerations

Sleying the reed

Methods of weaving

An alternative threading

Yarns

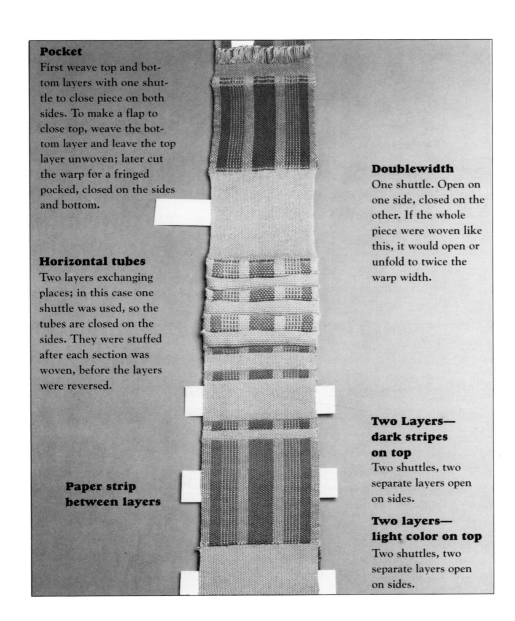

Pocket
First weave top and bottom layers with one shuttle to close piece on both sides. To make a flap to close top, weave the bottom layer and leave the top layer unwoven; later cut the warp for a fringed pocked, closed on the sides and bottom.

Horizontal tubes
Two layers exchanging places; in this case one shuttle was used, so the tubes are closed on the sides. They were stuffed after each section was woven, before the layers were reversed.

Paper strip between layers

Doublewidth
One shuttle. Open on one side, closed on the other. If the whole piece were woven like this, it would open or unfold to twice the warp width.

Two Layers—dark stripes on top
Two shuttles, two separate layers open on sides.

Two layers—light color on top
Two shuttles, two separate layers open on sides.

Double weave draft.

157

Double Weave

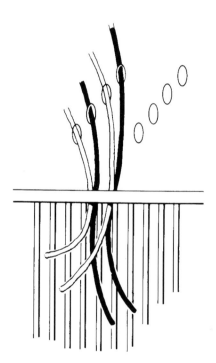

Threading for double weave. One layer (A) is threaded on shafts 1 and 3, the other layer (B) on shafts 2 and 4.

Double weave threaded on straight draw. The threads on shafts 1 and 3 form one layer; those on 2 and 4 form another. Here, threads on shafts 1 and 2 are threaded through the same dent in the reed; threads on shafts 3 and 4 are threaded through the next dent.

Double weave is a way to weave two layers of fabric at one time. Its versatility lies in how these two layers can be connected. Double weave can be used to create sculptural and three-dimensional effects that are great for everything from toys to contemporary art. In practical ways, double weave allows you to create fabrics twice as wide as your loom, clothing without seams, and tubes that can be stuffed (such as pillows), to name just a few of the many possibilities. This chapter will get you started with this fun type of weaving.

Setting up

Double weave is surprisingly simple. You already know that you can weave one layer of fabric, plain weave or variations of it, on two shafts. From this you can deduce that you can weave two layers of fabric on your four-shaft loom, two shafts for each layer. Because each layer is limited to two-shaft weaves, no twills or other weaves that take more than two shafts are possible. (However, if you have eight shafts on your loom, each layer can use four shafts. Or you can have four layers, each using only two shafts.) But because there are many variations of plain weave, including color arrangements and the use of textured yarns, the limitations to double weave on four-shaft looms are not terribly restrictive. Although the structure of double weave is very simple, what can be done with it can be tremendously complex if you choose to make it so. But let's start at the beginning.

Threading

Double weave can be threaded on a straight draw: 1, 2, 3, 4. (I'll tell you an alternative later on.) The threads for the two layers are interspersed. Those on shafts 1 and 3 form one layer; those on 2 and 4 form the other. The first time you weave double weave, consider alternating two colors in your warp so that one layer is color A, the other, color B; if you do that, you cannot possibly raise the wrong shaft (wrong layer) without knowing it immediately. (Note that capital A and B represent colors; lowercase a and b will represent the two tabby shots.)

Warp sett considerations

One of the most important aspects of double weave is the warp sett. If you use a yarn that you want set at 12 e.p.i. per layer, you need to have 24 e.p.i. altogether. If your warp is set at 12 e.p.i. total, each layer will have 6 e.p.i. You can weave a double weave with a much looser sett (for example, 6 e.p.i.), but with the warp so far apart it is likely that your weft will pack down a lot and you'll end up with a weft-faced fabric on each layer. That's okay if it's what you want, but frustrating if it isn't (and slow to weave).

Sleying the reed

The number of threads you sley in each dent of the reed depends on the yarn and the reed you choose. A yarn you want to set at 10 e.p.i. per layer, threaded in a 10-dent reed, will need to be double-sleyed to give 20 e.p.i. (Double-sleyed means two threads per dent; you will still thread one thread per heddle.) On the other hand, if you use the same yarn and warp sett and sley it in a 5-dent reed, you'll need to have four threads per dent to make 20 e.p.i. If you want a warp sett of 4 e.p.i. per layer and you have an 8-dent reed, you could have one thread per dent.

Sometimes it is better to have four threads per dent in large dents than two threads per dent in smaller ones. If the yarn is at all bumpy or fuzzy it will be less crowded in a reed with large dents. Remember that as you weave, the warp threads need to pass by each other in the reed, especially if you are changing layers a lot. Rubbing against another yarn, which flexes, is easier on a yarn than rubbing against a steel bar, which has no give.

Methods of weaving

Let's say you've threaded a straight draw, using a different color for each layer, and set your warp at twice the normal sett for the yarn you've chosen. Now that you're warped up, what can you do with it? Descriptions of the most basic double-weave possibilities follow. Weave several inches of each one before going on to the next*.

Two shuttles, two separate layers

First, try weaving two layers completely separately. You'll need two shuttles, one for each layer. I've given you the treadling in the draft, but think about the theory of what you are doing also. Each layer is tabby, and tabby has two shots, tabby a and tabby b. (When you first started weaving, tabby a was raising 1 + 3, tabby b was 2 + 4; that's not what

*No matter what kind of loom you have, weaving double weave will be much easier if you start with a direct tie-up. Because the treadling and layers change so often, you could spend as much time changing tie-ups as weaving. For a sample designed to try many double-weave options, tie one shaft per treadle and then move your feet a lot. Doing this also helps you really understand what's happening, which then makes it easier to plan your own double-weave adventures.

you'll treadle now, but I want to be sure you understand what I mean by tabby a and b because we'll use them a lot in this lesson and from now on.)

To weave the top layer, you'll alternate tabbies a and b by raising shafts 1 and 3 alternately. To weave the bottom layer, you need to raise all of the top layer to keep it up out of the way, then alternate the a and b tabby shots of the bottom layer, shafts 2 and 4. Thus, to weave the bottom layer, you will raise three shafts, the two top-layer shafts and one for the bottom layer. (1 + 3 + 2, then 1 + 3 + 4). Use the first shuttle for the top layer, the second shuttle for the bottom layer. Be careful not to twist the shuttles around each other on the side or your layers won't be completely separate.

You can weave two shots on one layer, then two on the other, then back to the first again, etc. The less often you change shuttles, the faster and more easily your weaving will go. If you weave more than two shots per layer, the beater will not be able to pack in the weft on the other layer because the shots from the first layer will be in the way.

Next, try weaving two separate layers again, this time with the 2-4 layer on top. The principles are the same, only this time shafts 2 and 4 will make the top layer, and shafts 1 and 3, the bottom. To weave the top layer, you will raise shaft 2 for tabby a, then shaft 4 for tabby b. To weave the bottom layer, you'll need to hold up the top layer (shafts 2 and 4) and then raise tabby a of the bottom layer (shaft 1), then tabby b (shaft 3).

Weaving two layers completely separately is a good exercise for understanding how double weave works. Practically speaking, however, weaving an entire warp off as two separate pieces has some real drawbacks.

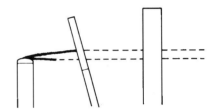

Two shuttles, two separate layers.

If you weave more than two shots per layer, after weaving one layer the beater will not be able to pack in the weft on the other layer because the shots from the first layer will be in the way.

I remember thinking how clever it would be to weave two sets of placemats at one time, one set on each layer. And while it would seem as though I was weaving one, when it came off I'd really have two sets. I thought about that for a little while, and I began to realize potential problems. First, errors are more likely in the bottom layer because you can't see it. Therefore, my bottom placemats might need a lot of repair work. Then there's the matter of speed. While weaving two sets off at once might seem efficient, the constant shuttle exchange consumes more time than you might possibly save. Using one shuttle and weaving off a warp twice as long would be faster. And finally, a warp twice as long would have one set of loom waste, whereas a double-weave warp, with twice as many warp ends, would have twice the loom waste. About that point in my pondering, I abandoned the idea of weaving off a double-weave warp as two entirely separate layers, for placemats or anything else.

There are, however, good uses for two layers woven separately. By weaving an inch or so, then reversing the layers and weaving another inch or so, and continuing to reverse the layers, you can weave a very sturdy fabric. Depending on the yarns used, this can be a great way to weave a rug or saddle blanket. Woven of lighter-weight yarns, it can be a beautiful reversible jacket fabric. One fun option is to weave a kid's nap mat or grown-up's yoga mat by stuffing the sections with some kind of batting just before you reverse the layers; you'll end up with a custom-designed padded mat. If the fabric and padding aren't too heavy, you can make your own version of a down vest.

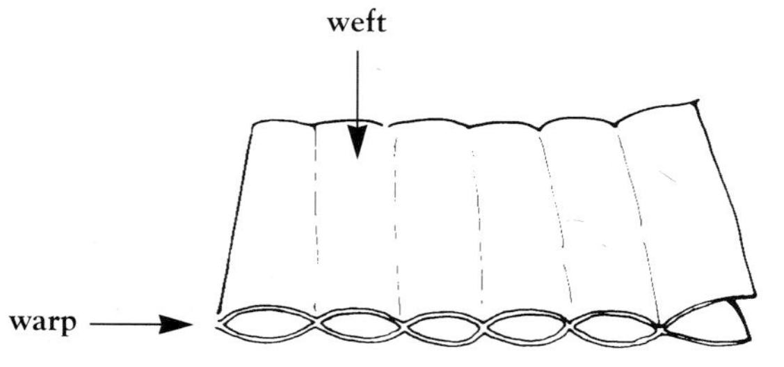

Two layers, woven separately, exchange places to form horizontal tubes.

Reversing layers can also be woven with a single shuttle in any of the methods below. The advantages are quicker weaving and the ability to seal the selvedges (to keep the stuffing in). A disadvantage is the loss of exclusively solid-colored stripes if your layers are separate colors. Working with a single shuttle means you'll have only one color of weft; it can match one of the warp colors, or be completely different. For a rainbow effect, you can weave with a different color weft every time you change layers. (Any plain-weave variation is possible, remember, and color variations may be the easiest to plan and execute.)

One shuttle

When using one shuttle, you cannot keep the layers entirely separate. Stated another way, the various methods of joining the layers are accomplished using only one shuttle. As the weft proceeds from one layer to the other, it connects them. The path of the weft determines whether the resulting piece is double width, vertically tubular, or some other shape.

Doublewidth

The ability to weave blankets, tablecloths, and other projects wider than the loom is possibly one of the most popular advantages of double weave. Some special problems come up, but they are relatively easy to remedy.

To create a piece that will unfold

to twice its width, simply connect the two layers on one side. That selvedge then becomes the center of the larger piece.

To join the layers on one side, weave tabby a of the top layer, tabby a of the bottom layer, tabby b of the bottom, and then back to the top and its tabby b. The side that is closed will be the side opposite from where you started your shuttle. Which side is closed makes no difference unless you have a particular color plan or your selvedge control is much better on one side than the other. (Make the better selvedge the folded/connected side.)

If your tension on the closed side is consistent and neither too tight nor too loose, then the piece will come off looking like one large piece woven the normal way. However, if you get much draw-in, the warp on the center line will be closer together and make a visual line. You would get the same kind of stripe in any weaving if you sleyed some of your warp closer together. If the closed side is woven very loosely and has weft loops extending out, then you'll

have a loose center, as if some warps had been pulled out. Either of these problems can be fixed by pulling some warps out or stitching some additional ones in. The biggest aggravation comes when your folded side is inconsistent—sometimes fine, sometimes loose, sometimes tight. To fix that, you need to pull some warp out, stitch some in, and try to make it look like it's all the same. And while you're adding and subtracting all these warps (or pieces of warps), you need to maintain the weave structure. For plain weave, this means always adding or subtracting two threads, not one.

Repairing the problem is possible; preventing it is much better. If you have pretty good selvedges, you shouldn't have a big problem. Different yarns and setts have different needs, so feel your way accordingly. I'll give you two fairly simple preventive measures, and add that there are others as well. Read, talk to other weavers, or make up something and then share it.

If you are going to have stripes in your warp, especially bold stripes,

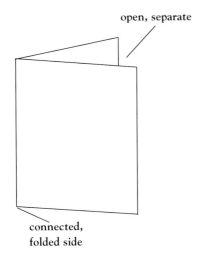

open, separate

connected,
folded side

The fabric is folded while being woven.

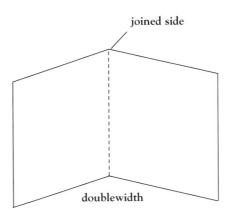

joined side

doublewidth

The fabric unfolds when removed from the loom.

plan a color change at the selvedge on the closed side. When the piece is opened out, what will be most obvious is the color change. A slight variation in the sett will be totally camouflaged, a drastic one obscured.

Another option, especially good for large pieces that you'll be weaving for a fairly long time, is a separately weighted floating selvedge. Use the strongest yarn or cord you can find. When the loom is all warped and ready to go, tie it to the front apron rod, run it through the reed in the same dent as your selvedge thread(s), through no heddle, and then hang it over the back beam. Tie to your floater as much weight as it will support (a gallon jug with as much water as the yarn or cord can hold is good), making it much tighter than the rest of your warp. As you weave, keep the yarn/cord

floating inside the fold of the cloth. Go over it when you come from the top layer, under it when you come from the bottom. Because it is so tight, you can pull your weft up against it without the selvedge drawing in. Because it will not be woven into the fabric but simply riding between the layers, you can use anything. Fishing line is good if you can get the knot to stay tied; seine twine will work if it's fine enough. Or use any very strong yarn. I keep mine so tight that sometimes it breaks. If I repair it immediately, I'm fine; if I wait a few shots out of laziness, I'm sorry.

Weaving doublewidth is really very easy, and even if you rarely do it, it's nice to know you have the option. A 15-inch-wide loom can suddenly go beyond samples, placemats, scarves, and neckties.

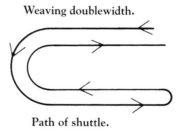

Weaving doublewidth.

Path of shuttle.

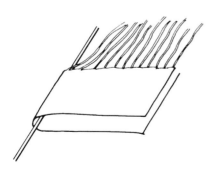

Use a floating selvedge on your closed side to help prevent draw-in on this edge. Use a strong yarn and weight it separately with a lot of weight off the back of the loom.

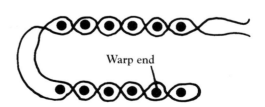

Warp end

Weaving tubes

Closing both sides of your weaving will create a vertical tube. People laugh, but one of the biggest kicks in weaving is sticking your fingers down inside a pocket or sack you are weaving to feel the fabric above and below your hand. To weave a tube, weave tabby a across the top, go back with the bottom layer tabby a, back across the top with tabby b, and finally, across the bottom with its tabby b. By weaving top-bottom-top-bottom, your weft will close both sides.

Tubes, in various shapes and sizes, have many uses. The padded mats mentioned earlier can have closed sides to keep the stuffing in. Although the tube is then only an inch or two tall and many inches wide, and so looks more like a horizontal tube, it is the same thing.

A narrow warp woven into a long, skinny tube can be stuffed and made into a snake. If it's a fairly short tube, you can add ears, legs and a tail to make a bunny or some other animal. You can weave a wall hanging with pockets, closing a section of the tube at one end and leaving it open at the other.

By combining tubes and double width you can make a "shawl" with sleeves. Sometimes this is called a granny shrug, but you don't have to be a granny to wear it. When worn, the center section will open up and cover your shoulders; the tubes on the ends become the sleeves. They are comfortable, light, quick, something like a fitted afghan.

There are so many other uses for double weave that rather than try to tell you more I suggest you look for other books and magazine articles on the subject. There are at least three books dealing with double weave, and many others that have good sections on it.

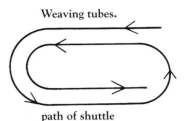

Weaving tubes.

path of shuttle

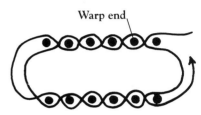

Warp end

Closing both sides of your weaving will create a tube.

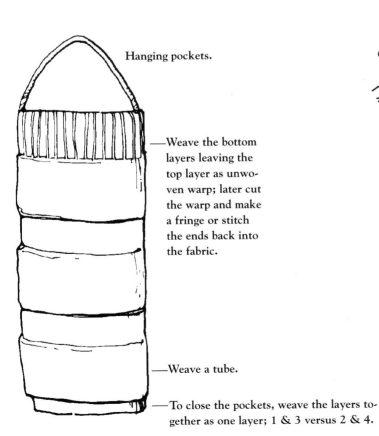

Hanging pockets.

—Weave the bottom layers leaving the top layer as unwoven warp; later cut the warp and make a fringe or stitch the ends back into the fabric.

—Weave a tube.

—To close the pockets, weave the layers together as one layer; 1 & 3 versus 2 & 4.

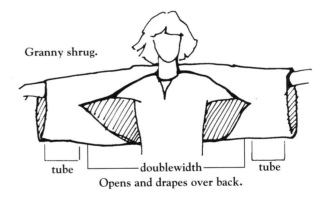

Granny shrug.

tube doublewidth tube

Opens and drapes over back.

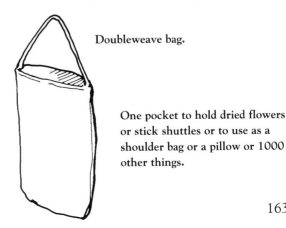

Doubleweave bag.

One pocket to hold dried flowers or stick shuttles or to use as a shoulder bag or a pillow or 1000 other things.

An alternative threading

Here's the alternative threading I mentioned earlier. I've put it at the end so that you can consider it when you want to, and not get it confused with the threading I mentioned first.

A straight draw, which is easiest to thread, puts one layer on shafts 1 and 3, the other on 2 and 4. The alternative threading shown here is very slightly more awkward to thread but easier to treadle (for me, anyway) as it puts the layers on adjacent shafts. One layer is on shafts 1 and 2, the other on 3 and 4.

On a multiple-tie-up floor loom, it doesn't really matter much because after you've tied up the treadles, you concentrate on the treadling sequence without having to think about what the individual shafts are doing. But with table or direct tie-up looms, you have to be constantly aware of the individual shafts. When I think of a layer on shafts 1 and 3 and another on 2 and 4, I feel as though my mind is being split up. Thinking of layers on adjacent shafts is so much more cohesive to me that I almost always use this threading.

I avoid trying to keep lots of numbers in my head, probably because I'm not very good at it. For this reason, I plan my double-weave projects by drawing very simple pictures or by building models out of paper. I do have a good mechanical sense and can think of planes and surfaces, three-dimensional shapes, and how puzzles go together. For me, the fun of double weave is planning shapes, layers, and connections. Having my layers on adjoining shafts seems to make planning more unified and neater.

Use whichever threading meth-

od makes the most sense to you. Try both and see which you prefer.

Yarns

As always, your weft can be anything; it can change as often as you want a color stripe. What to use for warp depends not only on what you're making, but on which form of double weave you'll be doing. If you are going to weave a whole piece as double width or a tube in which the layers will never switch places, then you don't need to be concerned with how easily they will pass by each other in the reed. The top layer of warp will always be above the bottom, and the space the layers share will be vertical which allows plenty of room.

If you plan to change layers, however, then the warp needs to be able to be crowded and yet be able to free itself again. For this, a smooth warp is far more cooperative than a sticky one. Hairy yarns grab onto each other and don't want to let go. A sticky double-weave warp requires constant manual opening of the shed, using your hands to pull the yarn apart. It's a hassle, destroys any rhythm you might develop, and often makes your beat uneven. I'm not advising you not to use wool, but a brushed wool or mohair might spell disaster. If you want a fuzzy piece, use fuzzy weft instead of a fuzzy warp.

As for color, you may want to use just a single color if your piece is to open out, as a blanket or shawl. Just be careful not to raise the wrong shaft and weave your layers together; stick your hand in between the layers frequently to check. On your first sample, consider using two colors, one for each layer, just to see clearly how it works.

An alternative threading for double weave.

Your assignments

1. Put on a narrow warp and try all of the double-weave options, then weave the rest of your warp off as a tube for a stuffed toy, such as a snake or baseball bat.

2. Figure out how to weave a striped or plaid baby blanket double width. Draw what you want to weave, then fold the paper in half.

3. Design a double-layer saddle blanket or hanging pockets for shuttles or wooden spoons.

4. What are some options for a shoulder bag? Tubular with no seams? Tubular with pockets woven in, seams necessary? Reversing layers for stripes, then folding and sewing it into a bag? Others?

5. Weave a tubular pillow. Tie the two layers of warp together at the ends as a finish.

Honeycomb

Size and shape of blocks

Color considerations

Uses for honeycomb

Honeycomb, with its undulating weft, is the epitome of the theory that threads don't want to be woven, that when they can, they will try to escape. For the two-block honeycomb shown here, while one block weaves plain weave, the other block simply floats, so that you have warp floats crossing weft floats. To visually isolate the blocks, and to provide stability, a heavy or outline weft is woven between the blocks. Because the threads need to relax in order for them to shift, most often you won't see the cells until you've removed the fabric from the loom. You can have a lot of fun playing around with color and thick and thin threads. Try different colored warp stripes each time the blocks switch, different colors of wefts for each line of cells, or experiment with very heavy or very thin outline wefts. Try using shiny yarns for the cells and a dull yarn for the outline weft, or vice versa. Keep in mind that understated, solid colored fabrics, in fine threads, can be very effective, too.
Fabrics by Debbie Redding, Jane Patrick, Betsy Holdsworth.

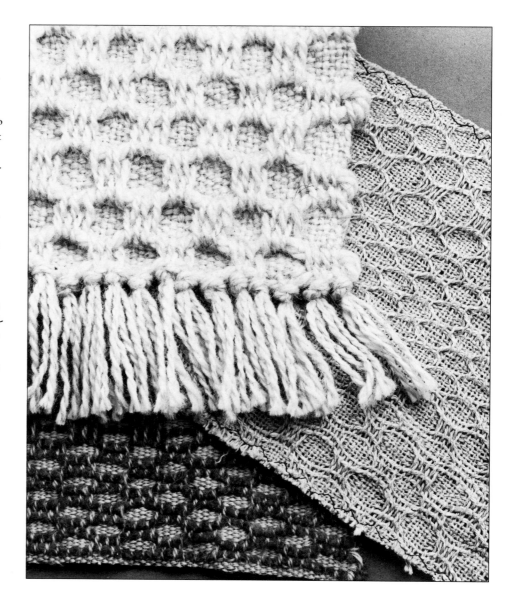

Honeycomb derives its name from its cellular structure, which resembles a bee's honeycomb. There are many variations, the differences being in size and the patterning of cells. We're going to look at the most basic, a two-block honeycomb.

In the draft shown here, it is easy to see that one section of warp will be on the first two shafts, another section will be on the other two shafts. These sections are called blocks. Block A is on shafts 1 and 2, block B on 3 and 4. (Notice the capital letters. Blocks A and B are noted with uppercase letters; lowercase letters a and b denote tabby shots.)

In two-block honeycomb, blocks A and B are alternately woven in plain weave. An outline or heavier weft separates the two blocks. If you compare the treadling to that for double weave, you'll see some similarities. When block A is being woven, shafts 1 and 2 alternate (weaving tabby) and block B (shafts 3 and 4) is held up out of the way. When block B is being woven (alternating shafts 3 and 4), block A is held up. Although the principle of lifting threads up out of the way is similar to double weave, the results are completely different. In honeycomb, the blocks are threaded side by side instead of in separate layers as in double weave. (I want you to be aware of how some practices and principles apply to different weaves. The more you understand in generalities, the easier it will be to learn new weaves and to adapt what you know to what you want to weave. There are probably no weaving rules that apply in only one case; all of the information gets used in many forms in a kind of mix-and-match that creates new results by rearranging old principles.)

There are two weft shots labeled H in the treadling. The H stands for heavy weft yarn, or honeycomb outline. In the photo of honeycomb, opposite, you can see cells in the fabric outlined by heavier, curving, or flexing weft. Those are H shots. While most of the weft is woven into block A or B, H is woven as a tabby that goes through both blocks. The curving which you see results from the woven cells' pushing that weft into the unwoven areas above and below them. Block A pushes H up, and block B pushes it down. For this reason, the family of which honeycomb is a member is called deflected-weft weaves.

Many weaves have an added dimension that comes from the threads not being straight all the time, and while the threads in most do not flex as much as in honeycomb, the principle is the same. (I learned it as one of the first principles of weaving: threads don't want to be woven, and when they can escape they will.) Deflected wefts (or warps) are straight when woven, but curve when the tension is released and they can respond to the pushing and pulling of threads around them.

Size and shape of blocks

Blocks of honeycomb can be threaded as wide or narrow as you want and woven as tall or short as you want. Remember to throw outline shot(s) between each block to hold the fabric together and to provide stability. The yarn in the outline shots doesn't have to be heavier, but it shows up better if it is. Using a different color would also help define the blocks. These three

Honeycomb draft.
The "H" represents the outline or heavier weft.

elements, block A, block B, and honeycomb outline wefts, work together to make the cellular shapes of honeycomb.

While blocks can be of any size, there are some practical factors you need to consider. First, notice in the draft that only one block is woven at a time. While one block is being woven in tabby, the other block isn't being woven at all; it consists simply of warp floats floating over weft floats. The woven block is stable because it's being woven; the block not being woven is very unstable because it's all floats. If your blocks are large, the floats will be long, and the longer they are, the weaker your fabric will be.

Your honeycomb outline weft needs to be flexible. A heavy, very stiff weft won't be able to curve, especially if the cells are very small. How small is too small depends on the yarns you are using and your warp sett. Big yarns need big cells, and small need small. Experiment with different-sized cells and different yarns and see what works and pleases you. As a starting point, I suggest keeping your blocks less than an inch wide and weaving them less than an inch tall.

Color considerations

How you use color with your honeycomb can be the most intriguing part of the design. You can thread block A in one color, block B in another, weave each block with its own color, and use a third color for your heavy outline weft. Or have all your warp one color and weave each new row of blocks with a different color. In this case, you could have your honeycomb outline weft match the warp and be more subtle. You could have it change as the blocks do or use it as an accent color

and outline the color changes. You could make each section of warp a different color as well as each block of weft, creating a color gamp with a black heavy weft to outline each color combination. On the understated side, some of the most beautiful honeycombs I've seen have been all one color, texture being the focus of those.

Uses for honeycomb

A tightly woven honeycomb can be quite sturdy and can have a wide variety of uses. Pillows, bags, clothing, and blankets are all good uses for honeycomb. Avoid heavy fabrics with heavy outline wefts for placemats or tablecloths which require relatively smooth surfaces. Honeycomb, with its ridges of outline weft, generally makes a poor choice for upholstery because the raised yarns will wear out before the rest of the fabric. Honeycomb can be used to produce a tough or gentle fabric, depending on how tightly you weave it. In fact, how tightly it's woven is usually more crucial than what yarns you use. Your warp and weft can be the same yarns or different ones, the cells balanced or not, oblong or more nearly circular. Because honeycomb is so versatile, you can use any yarn or fiber; choose according to the project you have in mind.

These are the basics of honeycomb. Variations you'll find will be honeycombs with more blocks which have overlapping cells. Those can be quite elegant as the cells can create a diamond or other pattern. You will still need to keep in mind the proportions of tabby areas to float areas appropriate to the degree of stability you want. As you explore honeycomb you'll learn the differences and find out what will work.

Your assignments

1. Make a single-color warp and use a variety of wefts to weave the cells or blocks. Use several heavy wefts of differing textures to see which curve best. The flexing probably won't be evident until you release the tension, but you can preview the results while the warp is still on the loom just by releasing your brake and scrunching up the cloth a bit.

2. Try a multicolored warp. Alternate colors within blocks or make stripes that correspond to blocks.

3. Put on a sample warp that has blocks in ever-increasing sizes. For instance, start with 4 threads per block, then 6, 8, and so on up to 20. Weave the sample with the same gradation in the weft, and when it's done, study it to see what works and what doesn't and why. Take measurements on the loom, off the loom, and after washing. That flexing outline weft may draw the piece in a lot.

Loom-Controlled Lace Weaves

The lace unit

Blocks

Threading

Tabby

Weaving it

Yarn choices

Sett

Color

Heddles

Lace weaves have a lot to offer. You can use them for a variety of different projects, such as curtains, blankets, placemats, blouse fabrics, or shawls; they are equally suited to heavy- and light-weight fabrics. Lace is effective used all over as in the two bottom fabrics shown here, or in blocks as in the top fabric. Explore texture, color, yarns; experiment with lace stripes, borders, and checks. *Fabrics by Lisa Budwig, Bethany Thomas, The Weaving Shop.*

A lace weave is one in which there are open spaces in the fabric. There are many ways to achieve such an effect, including finger manipulation of the warp, leaving empty dents in the reed, and weaving a pattern that causes some threads to group together leaving gaps where they were before they grouped. The last of these is what this lesson is about.

Swedish lace, Atwater-Bronson lace, mock leno, huck-a-buck, barleycorn, and canvas weave are names of weaves in the lace-weave family. Some of these are identical, some have only slight differences, some can be distinguished very easily. One pattern may have different names in different books, and the same name may have a different pattern in different books. For more information on lace, look in books under all these names.

The weave we're going to learn is variously known as Atwater-Bronson lace, Swedish lace, and 5/1/5 mock leno. In the more traditional books, it is called Atwater-Bronson lace because of the threading we're going to use, but the structure of all three is virtually the same.

The lace unit

Atwater-Bronson lace is a two-block weave (on four shafts) that is structured so that some threads group together, leaving spaces or windows in the fabric. The combination of threads grouping and spaces being left is what creates the lace and is another example of the escape principle that we found in honeycomb: when a thread is allowed to escape, it will.

One unit of lace consists of six threads and takes three shafts. On paper it looks like a tic-tac-toe game plus one thread on the side. In the draft and drawdown at right, there is yet one more thread drawn in just to balance the draft. If you have only a single isolated unit, you won't get the lacy effect characteristic of this weave; you'll get a "spot". Because it is the space *between* the spots that creates lace, to get the airy, lacy effect, you must have several units together, separated by only one thread, a dividing or tie-down thread.

Blocks

The draft at right has two units of block A (one unit of block A = 1, 3, 1, 3, 1, 2). You could thread this same block over and over across your entire warp width, and weave it for your entire warp length. The resulting fabric would have lace all over. On the other hand, if you wanted to have blocks of lace, you could thread a second block, block B. The threading for block B is the same as block A, except that where you used shaft 3 in block A, you use shaft 4 in block B. So a unit of block B = 1, 4, 1, 4, 1, 2. Block B will look exactly like block A; the only difference is that it will weave lace in a different place.

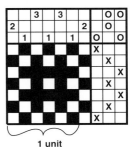

1 unit

A single unit of lace structure takes three shafts.

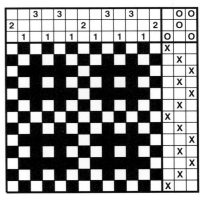

Lace is formed when there are several units together.

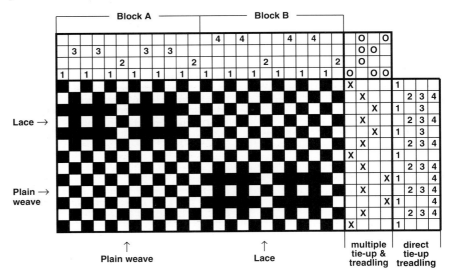

By using two blocks you can get lace in some areas, plain weave in others.

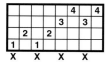

Tabby is woven by raising every other thread (x). Up to this point that has meant raising shafts 1 and 3 followed by shafts 2 and 4. With lace it's different.

Threading

What makes this lace so simple to comprehend and design is that no matter where you want the lace to appear, shafts 1 and 2 always do the same thing. Shaft 1 is called the ground shaft, shaft 2 the tie-down shaft.

Every other thread across the entire warp is on shaft 1; it provides the ground or stabilizing force for all else going on. The threads between each unit of lace are always on shaft 2. Look at the lace drafts on page 171 again and notice that the horizontal lines of the tic-tac-toe pattern represent five adjacent warps raised at once. That tells you that there is a weft float on the other side floating across (or under) those five warps. The dividing thread, the thread on shaft 2, serves to tie those floats down. It is the only place where those wefts quit floating. Thus shaft 2 is called the tie-down shaft, and every sixth thread needs to be on it.

Shafts 3 and 4 (and any more you have) are your pattern shafts. Each unit is composed of six threads; the five threads between those on shaft 2 plus one thread on shaft 2. You can put your lace blocks in any

pattern you want as long as each *unit* is complete—1, 3, 1, 3, 1, 2 or 1, 4, 1, 4, 1, 2. So first write in the constant 1s and 2s, then just fill in the rest of the draft with 3s and 4s. How many units you use before changing is determined by how wide you want your blocks to be.

Tabby

Up to now, you've usually woven tabby by raising shafts 1 and 3, then 2 and 4. That was because regardless of the actual sequence you were threading, you went from an odd-numbered shaft to an even-numbered shaft. Raising all the odds (1 and 3) gave you every other thread, the evens (2 and 4), the remaining threads. Look at the threading sequences at the left to see that.

This time, however, you are not threading odd-even-odd-even. Since every other thread is on shaft 1, tabby a will come by raising shaft 1 alone, tabby b by raising all of the other shafts together. Look at the large draft on page 173 and verify that the odd threads (1st, 3rd, 5th, 7th, etc.) are all on shaft 1; therefore the even threads (2nd, 4th, 6th, etc.) are on all the other shafts.

Lace threading

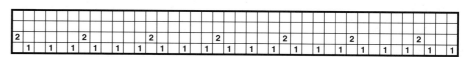

Every other thread is on shaft 1. The threads between each unit of lace are always on shaft 2.

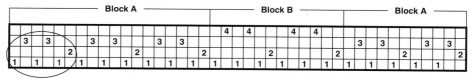

Pattern threads are on shafts 3 and 4. A single unit of block A is circled.

Weaving it

Now notice that the draft shows both blocks and the two faces of the lace. As always, where there are warp floats on one side, there are weft floats on the other side. Although it is the spaces or openings between the lace units that give the lace effect, the presence of warp or weft floats is very much a part of the overall appearance of this weave. On most pieces, you'll like one side or the other better, and if your warp is 1 color, your weft a second color, the two sides will have different colors predominating. You can weave with either the warp or the weft floats toward you, or some of each; just change your treadling according to which you'd like to see.

Some lace designs

Lace threading:
Block A: 1,3,1,3,1,2
Block B: 1,4,1,4,1,2

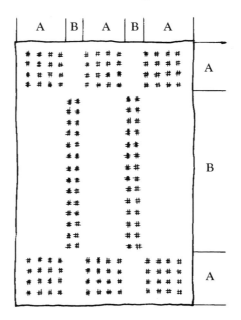

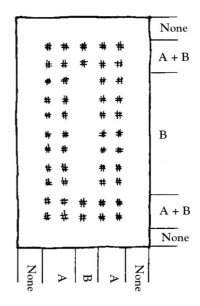

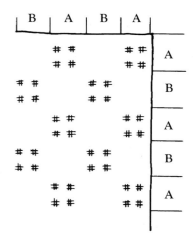

Looking at the treadling on the draft on page 173, you'll notice that to a great extent it's as regular as the threading. Shafts 1 and 2 are being raised alternately throughout, regardless of what the pattern shafts are doing. When you want a lace block woven with warp floats, keep its pattern shaft up for five shots, the length of the lace unit. When you want a lace block woven with weft floats, keep the appropriate pattern shaft down for five shots. The pattern shaft(s) not being used for lace is always raised with shaft 2, and because of that, all areas that are not lace are tabby, a good, solid, inconspicuous background.

You can weave block A alone, block B alone, both blocks at once, or neither block. If you want a vertical stripe on this draft to be entirely tabby, with no lace at all in it, you can thread this block alternating ends on shafts 1 and 2; no pattern shafts required. Because your treadling always alternates shafts 1 and 2, it can't help but produce tabby all of the time. (This works on this draft, *not* necessarily on other lace drafts; you cannot combine two different threadings and expect only one result. When in doubt, do a drawdown.)

Yarn choices

Because you are trying to create openings, and the openings occur when the yarns slide together, the harder, crisper, and smoother your yarn, the more the lace will open up. If you're weaving a scarf or shawl, you won't want a hard yarn, so choose a smooth soft yarn. (One of the prettiest lace pieces I've seen was woven with alpaca, about as far from crisp as you can get.) The texture of the weave is pretty, and the openness

of the lace here is secondary. Curtains are a nice way to use lace, for they let in lots of light but still afford privacy. In this case, you will want to be sure that the openings will remain open. About the only yarns that will really defeat lace are very hairy or very bumpy yarns, for example, brushed wool or mohair, or heavily textured novelties.

Sett

Your warp sett is at least as important as your yarn choice. Often a major portion of a lace weave is tabby, and that is what to gauge your sett by. A balanced tabby will give a balanced lace as well, which is definitely desirable—weft-faced lace weaves won't be lacy. However, you can weave a balanced tabby very tightly or very loosely or somewhere in between. If you want your lace to be fairly open, aim for a looser tabby. If you have only one reed, which gives you a nice, medium-balanced tabby with the yarn you've chosen, but you want a little more openness in your lace, leave an empty dent between threading units, that is, to the right or left of each tie-down thread (on shaft 2). That will give a little more space where you want it.

Color

Lace weaves have a wide range of color options even without getting complicated. When the warp and the weft are the same color, the lace structure itself is what is most visible, for nothing about the color pulls your attention away. Using a slightly different shade for one will add some depth without being distracting. Likewise, a heathery yarn will have depth whereas solid-colored yarns will look flat.

If you want to use more than one color, you can thread each warp block with a different color, then weave with all one color and get warp stripes or weave with two and get a more checkered effect.

You can have the threads on shaft 2, those separating the lace units, be a contrasting color from all of the others. The result will be a kind of overall check with the lace units bordered by the contrasting thread. As you weave, use your base color for most of your weft, your contrasting thread for the weft shot that divides the units vertically (shaft 1 by itself between warp float units, shafts 2, 3, 4 between weft float units).

The way you plan your colors will be determined in part by the way you plan your blocks and overall design. Draw a simple sketch of where you want lace to appear on your piece, then plan your colors accordingly. The drawings on page 174 suggest possible designs. If your colors change in the middle of your lace units, they will compete with the lace and the lace will be obscured. In a "visibility" contest between color and structure, color always wins.

Heddles

One other consideration: half of your warp is threaded on shaft 1. That means you'll need a lot of heddles on that shaft. Usually heddles are divided evenly, with each shaft having the same number, and usually you have more than you need. You may have enough heddles on shaft 1 for whatever you plan, especially if you have a wide loom and a narrow project. But count the heddles before you start threading; it's much easier to move heddles before you've begun threading. If you must move some heddles, and it seems like a major hassle, turn to page 213 for some ideas on making it easier.

Your assignments

1. Plan and weave a lace sample with three colors, each for approximately one-third of the width. Weave it using the same three colors, the idea being to see which color combinations you like best and why. Have warp floats on top, then weft floats on top. If you have both types on the same side of the sample, you don't have to flip it back and forth to see the differences, which is nice if you mount it on a record sheet or bulletin board.

2. Plan a set of placemats all using lace weave but each with a different arrangement of blocks. Make the changes in the treadling only so that all can be woven on the same threading.

3. I once wove a set of lace curtains for a living room that had just been carpeted. I planned carefully, wove samples, matched the colors with the new carpet, and when they were done they looked magnificent on the carpet. Unfortunately they were made to hang next to the wall, not the carpet, and against the wall they almost disappeared because the colors of the curtains and wall were so close. See if you can plan a set of curtains better than I did. The lace, by the way, worked very well for letting the light in, as did the light blond yarn I chose.

4. Design a summer top with lace sleeves or lace across the bodice. Draw pictures of pattern pieces as you'll weave them to plan where your lace areas need to fall.

5. Do you like sets of things? A set of things for the kitchen, all in lace weaves, could include curtains, dish towels, dishrags, placemats, table runners, tablecloths, napkins, aprons, a wall hanging, and a bread basket cover. For the living room, you could weave an afghan, pillows, curtains, cabinet scarves, and a wall hanging. Some projects would require different yarns than others, but a feeling of unity can easily be maintained if the colors and patterns are similar. Plan two warps that will give you related products, both in lace weaves, of course.

LESSON 13

Block Theory

Block patterns
Profile drafts

Blocks apply to many weave structures. Here are a few examples of some of the possibilities. From the top, working clockwise, are samples of lace weave, double weave, double binding, and overshot. One exercise which you might find instructive, as well as intriguing, is to make up a block pattern and try to weave it in a couple of different weave structures. Up to this point you've woven one block weave which lends itself to this kind of interpretation; summer & winter in Lesson 14 introduces another one. *Fabrics by Audrey Kick, Jane Patrick, Judy Steinkoenig, Yvonne Stahl.*

Block patterns

In the last two lessons, you planned your threading partly according to how wide you wanted blocks A and B to be. In honeycomb, the threading unit for block A is 1, 2, repeated as many times as desired. For block B, the threading unit is 3, 4, repeated. In Atwater-Bronson lace, the threading unit for block A is 1, 3, 1, 3, 1, 2; for block B, it's 1, 4, 1, 4, 1, 2. Every weave has its own threading unit, and units may be repeated as often or as wide as you want a block to be. Threads combine to form units, units combine to form blocks, blocks combine to form overall patterns.

The table below lists threading units; I'll talk more about them later.

Not all, but many weave structures use blocks. Each has its own threading unit (see examples in the table below). For this chapter, we'll be talking about the big picture, the overall pattern of a piece.

In some weave structures, some shafts are shared by blocks; Atwater-Bronson lace, summer & winter, and overshot. In others, each block gets its own shafts. However, when you are designing block patterns, you are not yet concerned with how many shafts are needed or whether or not you can weave something. For the time being, forget about shafts, threading, treadling, and weaving.

Think about the overall pattern you'd see in a fabric if you were standing far enough away that you couldn't see the weave structure. The illustrations below can be thought of as block patterns. Some are balanced or squared in that they look the same no matter which way you turn them.

From these illustrations or block patterns, it is a simple matter to determine how many blocks a given pattern has. In the same way that

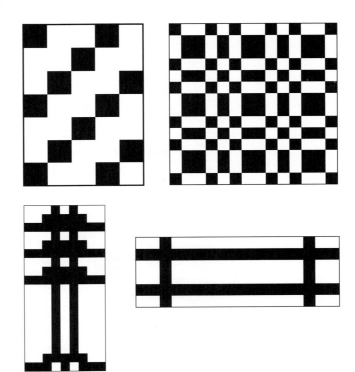

THREADING UNITS

Weave Structure	Block A	Block B	Block C	Block D
2-block honeycomb	1,2	3,4		
4-block honeycomb	1,2	2,3	3,4	4,1
Atwater-Bronson lace	1,3,1,3,1,2	1,4,1,4,1,2	1,5,1,5,1,2	1,6,1,6,1,2
Summer & Winter	1,3,2,3	1,4,2,4	1,5,2,5	1,6,2,6
Overshot	1,2	2,3	3,4	4,1
Twill blocks	1,2,3,4	5,6,7,8	9,10,11,12	13,14,15,16
Double-weave blocks	1,2,3,4	5,6,7,8	9,10,11,12	13,14,15,16
Ripsmatta	1,2	3,4	5,6	7,8

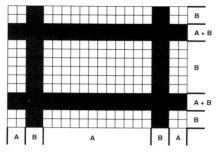

Combine blocks to build a pattern.

you determined how many shafts a cloth diagram used, you can now determine the number of blocks used. Each vertical column is a block, and each one that has pattern areas filled in in the same places is the same block. Each one that is different is another block. The pattern of the column is of no significance at this point, only its similarity to other columns. Look at the illustrations on this page and trace the columns to remind yourself how this works.

To find out which blocks to combine to build a pattern, you'll do the same as you did to find out how to treadle a particular cloth diagram. Consider the black areas as the pattern being created on a white background. To create the pattern at left, you'll need to first weave block B alone, then A and B together, then B alone again, then A and B, then finish up with B alone. Remember that we are not yet concerned with whether it is possible to weave this, rather how to create the design.

Profile drafts

A profile draft can be called the threading draft of a block diagram. The moose on page 181, which is different from the moose below, requires eight blocks, seven for the moose and one more for the borders on the sides. The profile draft below the moose shows the block sequence, including block changes and block widths. To thread from a profile draft, you insert the chosen threading unit for the block shown, repeating it as many times as necessary for the block's width. Let's translate part of the moose's profile draft on page 181 into a couple of threadings just to see how it works.

Block A is four squares wide, so whatever weave structure's threading unit you choose, it needs to be repeated four times. For simplicity let's use Atwater-Bronson lace because you know how it works and summer & winter because it's the subject of the next lesson.

Block patterns

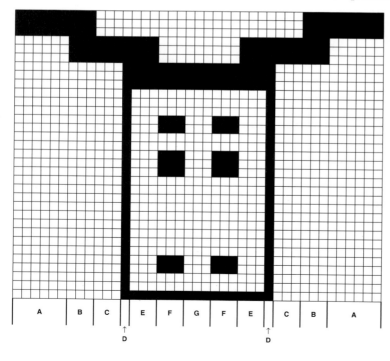

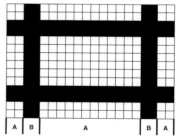

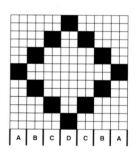

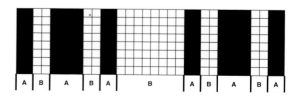

As you know, to thread block A in Atwater-Bronson lace you thread 1, 3, 1, 3, 1, 2. In summer & winter, you thread 1, 3, 2, 3. Block A is four squares wide, so the threading unit needs to be repeated four times. Block B is two squares wide, so its threading sequence—1, 4, 1, 4, 1, 2 for lace, 1, 4, 2, 4 for summer & winter—is repeated twice. Look at the threadings below.

You can insert any threading unit into any block pattern that easily. These two happen to be very similar and require the same number of shafts; others may require more or fewer. Also, not all weaves work well with all patterns.

The honeycomb you wove relies on alternating A and B blocks to reveal the honeycomb pattern. You can't weave two threading units of the same block side by side in a two-block honeycomb and still get honeycomb; you'd have plain weave instead. With lace, however, that's no problem; you can weave as many or as few threading units of the same block side by side as you want.

This is a very basic discussion of block theory. You'll understand it more as you learn more weaves and see how blocks apply. I will mention block theory more in the following lessons, as it applies.

For your reference, now and later, a two-block design is shown on pages 182 and 183 in profile draft, block pattern, and full thread-by-thread drafts and drawdowns for both Atwater-Bronson lace and summer & winter.

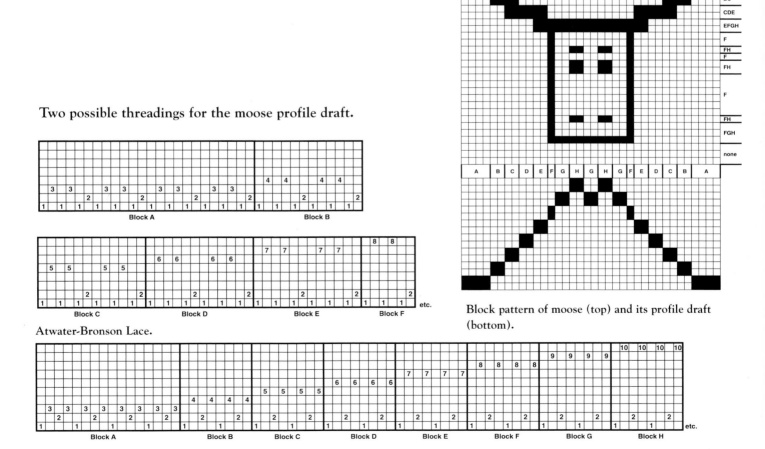

Two possible threadings for the moose profile draft.

Atwater-Bronson Lace.

Block pattern of moose (top) and its profile draft (bottom).

Summer & Winter.

Your assignments

1. Using graph paper, draw some block designs that you find interesting and then make a profile draft from your block pattern. Referring to the chart at the beginning of the section, determine which weaves you could do in the design you've drawn with the number of shafts you have. (For now, don't be concerned with which ones would actually work.)

2. Design a block pattern and weave it in Atwater-Bronson lace.

Profile Draft

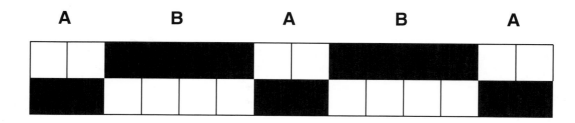

Block Diagram

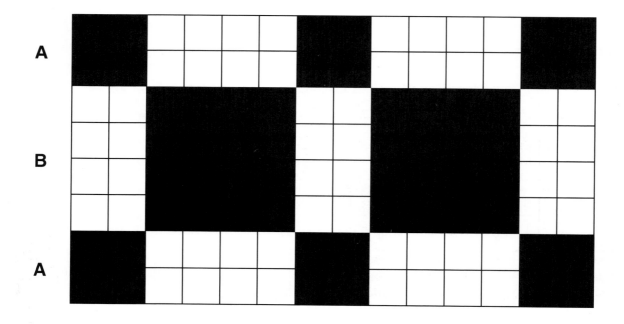

Atwater-Bronson Lace

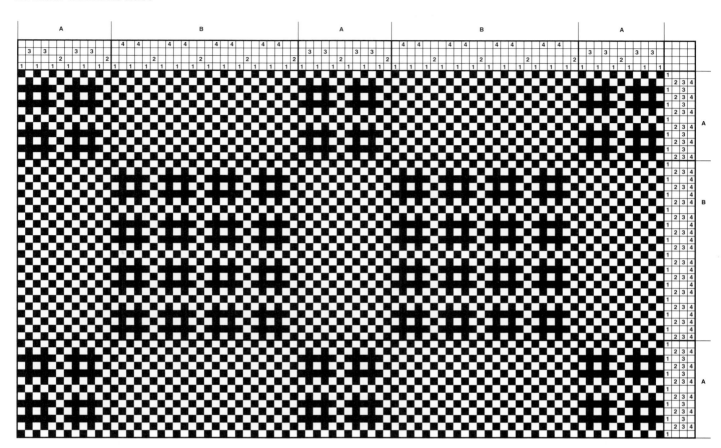

Summer & Winter

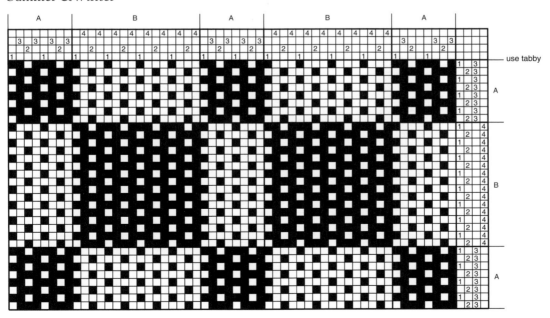

LESSON 14

Summer & Winter

The basics of summer & winter

Using two wefts

Yarn and color choices

Treadling summer & winter

Summary

Variations

Uses

Summer & winter is a versatile block weave. As in Atwater-Bronson lace, the blocks can be as wide and long as you wish to make them. Two wefts (requiring two shuttles), a pattern weft and a tabby or background weft, are needed to weave summer & winter. Notice in the samples shown here that both the background weft and pattern weft are integral parts of the pattern. That is, the pattern weft predominates in some blocks, the background weft in others. This allows much for the imagination! *Fabrics by Lisa Budwig, Bethany Thomas, The Weaving Shop.*

The basics of summer & winter

Summer & winter is one of my favorite weaves because it's easy to design and the fabric has great versatility. It is both stable and durable. After you've woven one summer & winter piece, you'll find it's easy to understand, and it has so many variations it's unlikely that you'll ever exhaust the possibilities.

Like Atwater-Bronson lace, summer & winter has two shafts whose threading remains constant from block to block and two shafts that create the pattern blocks. In summer & winter, every other thread is alternately threaded on shafts 1 and 2, consequently they are called ground shafts, each acting as a tie-down shaft. As in Atwater-Bronson lace, you can start a draft by drawing in the 1s and 2s because they are always the same, and after that add the 3s and 4s where you want your pattern blocks to be.

A threading unit for summer & winter is 1, 3, 2, 3 or 1, 4, 2, 4. Your blocks can be any width from one unit on up. Again, you can weave any two-block pattern, including any of the assortment on the next page.

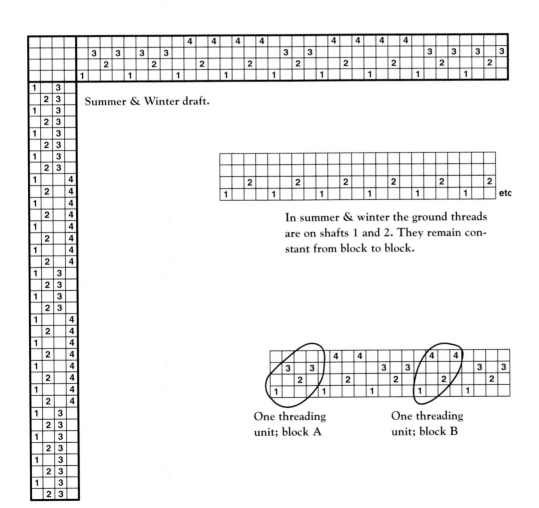

Summer & Winter draft.

In summer & winter the ground threads are on shafts 1 and 2. They remain constant from block to block.

One threading unit; block A

One threading unit; block B

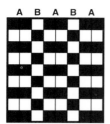

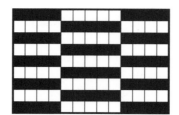

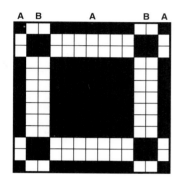

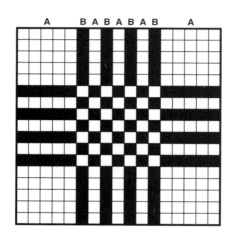

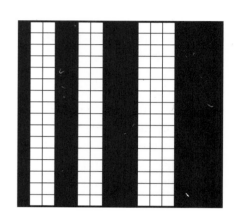

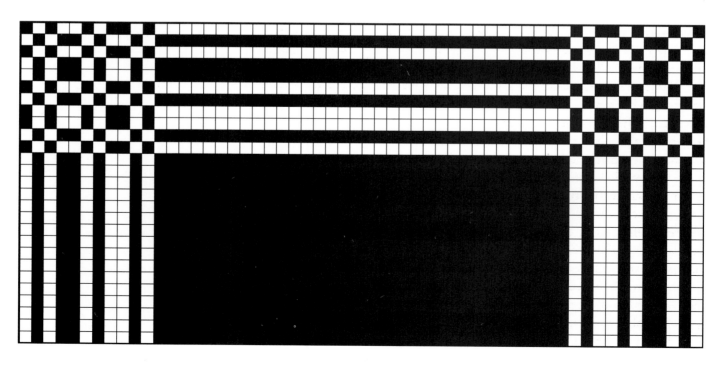

Using two wefts

The treadling for summer & winter is where we begin to get into new material.

Summer & winter uses two wefts, a pattern weft and a tabby weft. The two are used alternately throughout the piece: tabby, pattern, tabby, pattern, etc. The pattern treadling will vary according to which blocks you are weaving. The tabby weft *always* weaves tabby, regardless of what the pattern is doing. In most books, the draft gives only the treadling for the pattern weft because that is the only part that changes. It may say, "Use tabby", or it may not even say that, expecting you to know that you are supposed to use it.

As you know, tabby is woven by alternately raising the odd threads and then the even threads. Look at the threading draft on page 185. Every other thread is on shaft 1 or 2, and the remaining threads are on 3 or 4. Therefore, you can raise shafts 1 and 2 for tabby a, and shafts 3 and 4 for tabby b. Put in your mind that your tabby a weft will always go through shed 1-2, then a pattern weft, then tabby b (3-4), pattern, tabby a, pattern, tabby b, pattern, etc.

With two shuttles going and a constantly changing pattern weft, it is practically impossible to remember which tabby shot you threw last, so determine which shed is open when the shuttle is going from right to left and know that the other needs to be open when the shuttle goes from left to right. From then on, the direction in which the shuttle is going will tell you which shed to open. If you have treadles, turn to page 194 and read the section on tying up tabby treadles.

The purpose of weaving tabby is to provide a ground under the pattern that makes the fabric stable. By using a tabby ground, consecutive pattern shots can change sheds or repeat in the same sheds, depending on the pattern desired. If tabby is not used, weaving a lot of shots into the same shed again and again can make a weak fabric structure.

Yarn and color choices

In summer & winter, the tabby weft is an integral part of the design just as the pattern weft is. When you raise the shafts to make block A an area in which the pattern weft predominates, block B will be an area in which the tabby background is the strong design element. For this reason, color is very important. Summer & winter has three yarn elements: warp, tabby weft, and pattern weft. For the pattern to show off to its maximum, the warp and tabby weft should be the same color (even the same yarn); the pattern weft should be another color and a somewhat fatter yarn. How much fatter depends on the quality or style of the yarn you choose. If the yarn is soft and fluffy, it can be as much as three or four times fatter; if it's a hard-twist yarn, twice as fat is probably better. Try several wefts on your first sample so that you can see and feel the differences.

For a softer visual effect, use a tabby weft of a color that falls between the other two. If you use three very contrasting colors, you are likely to lose a lot of your pattern. The tabby is meant to be background, and several strong color choices will compete and obscure all the work you're doing. Weave some samples to help you decide whether this is the effect you want.

If you pulled all of the pattern wefts out of a finished summer & winter piece, you would (ideally)

Weaving Summer & Winter

Weft shot	Shafts raised	Shuttle direction
pattern	1 3	pattern weft ←
tabby a	1 2	tabby weft ←
pattern	2 3	pattern weft →
tabby b	3 4	tabby weft →

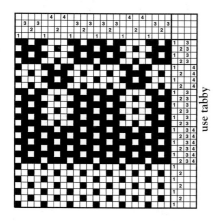

A full treadling unit is:
shaft 1 plus pattern(s),
tabby a
shaft 2 plus pattern(s)
tabby b
Tabby a = shafts 1 & 2
Tabby b = shafts 3 & 4

have a balanced tabby fabric left. To do this, you would need to weave your fabric so that you are putting in twice as many wefts per inch as you have warps per inch. For instance, if you set up a warp at 12 e.p.i., you'll weave in 12 pattern wefts and 12 tabby wefts per inch, 24 shots altogether. It may seem hard to believe that you can get that many shots in there, but the pattern weft takes up less space than you would expect because it slides on top of the tabby weft that is next to it across most of the fabric. So choose a warp sett that is appropriate for a balanced tabby or maybe slightly looser.

Treadling summer & winter

In terms of durability, one of the big advantages of summer & winter is that no weft ever passes over more than three warps before it is tied down again. (This is perhaps the greatest difference between summer & winter and overshot, which are often confused because both are traditional coverlet weaves. In overshot, however, weft floats can be very long and can snag easily. More on this in the next lesson.) In summer & winter, the even distribution of the warps threaded on shafts 1 and 2, which act as tie-down threads, limits the length of the pattern floats. To weave a pattern shot, one of the ground shafts is raised along with whichever pattern shafts are desired. Shafts 1 and 2 are raised alternately, and a full treadling unit (comparable to a threading unit) consists of shaft 1 plus pattern(s), tabby a, shaft 2 plus pattern(s), tabby b. For a block to show up at all, the pattern shaft(s) raised throughout the treadling unit

need to be the same. With this information, you can now make up any treadling you want to try.

Look at the draft on the left. Only the pattern shot treadlings are noted. Drawn like this, the draft looks more like what the fabric will actually look like than if the tabby shots had been drawn in also. Because the tabby shots are relatively obscure in the actual fabric, drawing them in will throw the proportions of the drawdown way off.

Because the drawdown shows warps as *filled-in boxes,* the blackest areas are those in which the warp is mostly raised. The pattern weft will predominate in the blocks in which the drawdown looks whiter. In other words, the fabric looks backwards from what we expect when looking at the draft.

Shafts 1 and 2 alternate with every pattern shot; 3 and 4 are raised as needed for pattern blocks.

Summer & winter is so named because the two sides look opposite from each other. What appears black on one side is white on the other side and vice versa. If your pattern is evenly divided between blocks A and B, then the two sides will be fairly balanced. Block A predominates on one side, block B on the other. One of the customs that goes with summer & winter weave is that the dark side of a summer & winter bedspread faces out in the winter, the light side in the summer. For the two sides to look significantly different, the blocks need to be unbalanced. Look at the assortment of two-block patterns at the beginning of the chapter again, and think about which would look approximately the same on both sides. Which ones would have two sides that appeared as different colors?

Summary

To summarize the basics of summer & winter, choose a warp yarn that will make a good visual background (smooth and solid-colored). Set it for a balanced tabby, perhaps slightly looser than normal. Thread your warp according to one of the drafts shown here or one you make up from your own block pattern. You'll have two wefts, one the same as the warp (or close to it) to use as tabby weft, the other fatter and of another color or texture to use as your pattern weft. You can use a treadling from a draft or make up your own. You need to always intersperse tabby shots with the pattern shots, alternating 1 and 2 versus 3 and 4. You can remember which one to throw by looking at the direction in which the shuttle is going.

Variations

The lesson up to this point has been for what is called "weaving singly". You can also weave summer & winter "in pairs", a phrase that refers to the pattern shots. You will still alternate tabby, pattern, tabby, pattern, but this time, instead of al-ternating the ground shafts with each pattern shot, you'll repeat them once. For example, instead of weav-ing 1-4, 2-4, 1-4, 2-4, you'd weave 1-4, 1-4, 2-4, 2-4, 1-4, 1-4, 2-4, 2-4, al-ternating tabbies a and b between each pattern pick. The effect is a blockier pattern and stronger color. It also changes the background de-sign. Look at the draft below to see how it works, then try it on your sample. Also look at the summer & winter fabrics on the first page of this chapter. The one on the right is woven in pairs on both ends, singly in the middle.

You can start and stop your trea-dling units at any point. The treadlings you choose will affect what the pattern looks like at the corners where the blocks connect. The differences can be quite surpris-ing, so try them all. Some examples are at right. Look at the treadling changes and block corners. For even more variations, these examples can be woven in pairs.

Uses

Woven in a lightweight fabric, summer & winter could be used for an entire piece of clothing; more

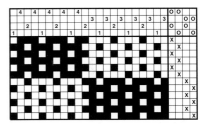
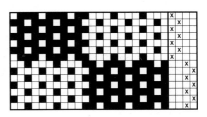
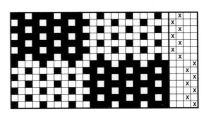

The point at which you change blocks in your treadling will alter the appear-ance of you pattern as illustrated in these three variations.

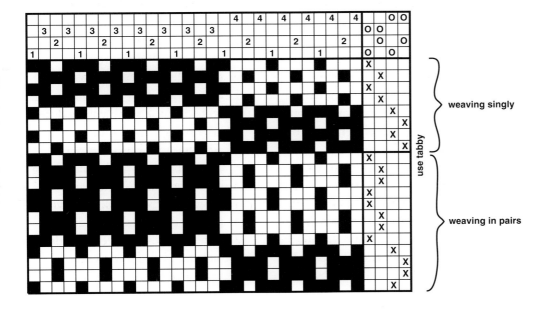

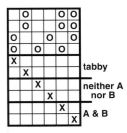

More treadling options.

often it is used as a border design with most of the garment being tabby. As a border, summer & winter can be a beautiful accent on elegant towels, table linens, cheery curtains, scarves, shawls, blankets, etc. As a border or the whole fabric, it is sturdy enough for pillows, shoulder bags, backpacks, upholstery, and great for placemats. It made a durable coverlet fabric during colonial days and still does.

I must admit that part of why I like summer & winter so much is that my loom has eight shafts, and as with lace, with two shafts for ground shafts I then have six for pattern blocks. With six pattern blocks, I can make many, many designs: stars, animals, letters, flowers, and many others. I try hard not to make people think they *need* eight shafts, for there are thousands of designs possible with four; but it is also true that if you like drafting and making up patterns, you are likely to enjoy having eight shafts. Lace and summer & winter are perfect weaves to show how easy it is to use an additional four shafts.

Your assignments

1. Put on a sample with blocks of varying widths. Treadle to get block A alone, block B alone, blocks A and B together, and no blocks on the surface. Go through this sequence with at least two different pattern wefts, woven singly and in pairs. Then, alternate from block A to B and back again, trying each of the corner variations shown on page 189.

2. Set up a warp with blocks in the center one threading unit wide, and repeat these for several inches. Surround these by wider blocks. Then, treadle a variety of patterns, including a sequence to match the threading sequence. In older books, you'll find only the profile draft given for summer & winter, nothing else. It may be called a "short draft". The intent is for you to treadle according to the threading pattern. This is called "tromp as writ" or "weave as drawn in". To do this, weave as many pattern shots as there are warp threads in the block, throwing 1-3, 2-3, etc., for the pattern block on shaft 3, 1-4, 2-4 for the block threaded on shaft 4.

3. Try using pattern wefts of varying thicknesses. If you use a very fat pattern weft, try using a skinnier tabby weft to balance it. See how it affects the appearance of the pattern, then try a slightly fatter tabby weft, and see what that does.

4. Plan a bedspread. Weave a sample or two (or more) to find out whether the fabric you are thinking of would be a good weight for a bedspread you'd like. Will your bedspread be primarily for decoration, or is it intended to keep you warm? (Do you live in Bangor or Atlanta?) Does it need to be machine washable, dog- or kid-proof? Do you want a design with seams down the middle or down the sides where they are likely to be less conspicuous? How big does your sample need to be to get an accurate idea of weight and drape? Do you want something subtle or flashy?

5. Design a set of summer & winter pillows that are all woven on the same warp but which have different treadlings so that each pillow has a different design.

LESSON 15

Overshot

The pattern blocks and threading
Tying up the treadles for tabby
Yarns and related information
Miscellaneous notes

Overshot, with its overlapping blocks, brings curves and circles to your weaving repertoire. Try it for borders on skirts, placemats, or dishtowels; use it all over for pillows, seat cushions, or table runners. This is a good one for exploring pattern and color. *Fabrics by Lynda Short, Eric Redding.*

Overshot

As a new weaver, my initial reaction to overshot patterns was that it was a good thing that someone had written down all those patterns because no one could figure them out again. It took awhile before I learned enough to make sense out of overshot and really believed that someone—even I—could create an overshot pattern. If you've understood everything up to here, you'll have an easier time with overshot than I did. Just weave some for a while, and sooner than you think it will make sense to you and you'll be able to alter or design your own.

This last lesson is a compilation of many of the things you've learned already together with a few new things. The patterns of overshot look complicated, but in fact, the ingredients are very basic.

Overshot is a twill derivative in which the blocks often follow a twill sequence. Part of the fun of overshot is that with only four shafts you have four blocks to design with instead of the two you have with summer & winter. The treadling is the same as that for a 2/2 twill but with even more variations available. Like summer & winter, overshot requires two shuttles, one for tabby and another for pattern. Therefore, it has the same considerations for relative yarn weights, sett and beat, and color choice.

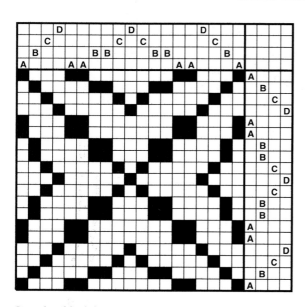

Overshot block pattern.

The pattern blocks and threading

On four shafts, overshot has four blocks available. The threading unit for block A is 1, 2, for block B it's 2, 3, for block C it's 3, 4, and for block D it's 4, 1. Notice that blocks share shafts, but not in the same way that Atwater-Bronson lace and summer & winter did. There are no separate ground shafts in overshot; all shafts work as both ground and pattern shafts. The sharing of shafts from block to block causes a slight overlapping, which permits curves in patterns. Whereas most summer & winter designs are fairly blocky, many overshot patterns utilize circles and curves.

Let's look at some block patterns first, then translate them into threading.

The block pattern at left is very simple, one in which it is easy to see that overshot is related to twill. Not all overshot patterns are this twill-like, but many are.

For overshot to work, the threading must always go from odd to even or even to odd shafts (this is necessary to be able to weave tabby, which we'll discuss more later). So, to get from block A (threaded 1,2) to block B (threaded 2,3), requires the addition or subtraction of one thread to break the 2,2 (two evens together) pairing that would exist otherwise. So, the transition threading from block A to block B would *not* be 1, 2, 2, 3 but rather, 1, 2, 1, 2, 3, or just 1, 2, 3, depending on whether you add or drop a thread. Examples are shown at the bottom of the next page, taken from the block pattern at left.

Also shown on the next page are another block diagram and its thread-by-thread draft. Because the

filled-in squares in the drawdown
represent raised warps, the pattern
weft will show in the areas that are
white. As in summer & winter, the
tabby shots in overshot are not
noted, and for the same reasons. "Use
tabby", written at the side of the
treadling, is your clue that you are to
use tabby. Other signals are the large
areas of black or white that could be
dangerously long weft floats if there
were no tabby in between. The possi-
bility of long floats may be the most
fundamental difference between
summer & winter and overshot.
When you are making up a pattern,
you can plan blocks as wide as you
want them. The problem is that wide
blocks make long weft floats. If they
are very long, they will snag easily. If
you need a wide block, but want a
good structure, put an occasional
thread on the odd or even shaft not
being used. For instance, a wide
block of 1, 2, 1, 2, 1, 2, 1, 2, 1, 2, 1, 2
would be much safer threaded 1, 2, 1,
2, 1, 4, 1, 2, 1, 2, 1, 4; the fours will
tie down the float without disturbing
the pattern much.

   To determine treadling is very
simple. I said before that the pattern
shot treadling is the same as for a 2/2
twill and that there are two wefts,
tabby and pattern. The shaft combi-

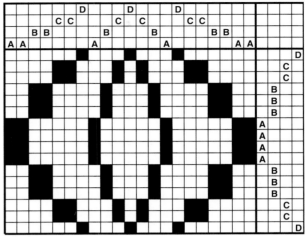

Block pattern.

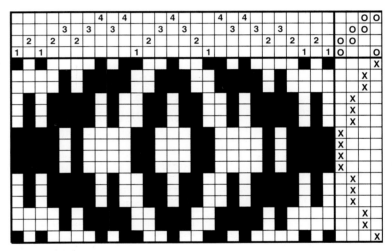

Thread-by-thread draft.

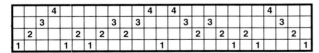

Overshot threading if you consistently drop a thread between blocks.

○ = extra thread   □ = shared thread   ◇ = both shared and extra threads. Works where they overlap.

Overshot threading if you consistently add a thread between blocks.

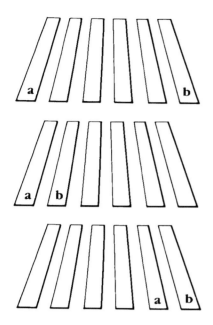

On multiple tie-up looms, there are at least three places you can tie up your tabby treadles, as shown here. Which way you choose depends solely on what feels most comfortable. Having both tabby treadles on the left or both on the right allows one foot to work only for tabby, the other foot only for pattern shots. On the other hand, many weavers tie up their outside treadles for tabby and leave them that way all the time, ignoring them when they are not needed.

nations for a 2/2 twill are 1+2, 2+3, 3+4, and 4+1; the same combinations are used for overshot. The primary difference is that when you weave a twill, you (usually) need to change which shafts are raised every time or your fabric will get mushy and not be structurally sound. With overshot, you have a tabby shot between pattern shots, so you can repeat a shaft combination as many times as you want. Having more or fewer shots in various blocks is what determines the angles, curves, squares, and other shapes that make up the patterns. You'll explore this subject further in your assignments.

Tying up the treadles for tabby

Keeping track of which shafts you raised for a tabby shot prior to your last pattern shot can be difficult. But there are some tricks to keep down the confusion.

If your loom has multiple tie-up treadles, simply remember that when the shuttle is going to the left, step on the left tabby treadle, and when the shuttle is going right, step on the right tabby treadle.

If your loom has direct tie-up treadles or levers directly in front of you, step on (or pull) the furthest left treadle (or lever) and the one that needs to go with it, when the shuttle goes to the left, and do the same with the furthest right treadle (or lever) and its companion when the shuttle goes to the right. If your loom has levers on the side, just create a link in your mind for which levers go with which shuttle direction.

Many weavers tie their outermost treadles for tabby and just leave them that way all the time, changing the middle treadles as needed (tabby isn't needed for some weaves). Years

ago, a student told me that he prefers having his two tabby treadles on one side, allowing him to use one foot for tabby and the other foot for pattern, making it easier to keep track of where he is in a treadling sequence. I tried it and agree, and now that's how I do it for most of my tabby/pattern weaving.

Tie up the pattern treadles in the same sequence as they appear in the tie-up of the draft, and then step on them in the order given.

As for what shafts to raise (or tie up) to get tabby, think back to the threading. Overshot requires the threading always to go from an odd to an even shaft and vice versa, and so your threads will always be odd-even-odd-even. To weave tabby, simply raise the odds, 1 and 3, and then the evens, 2 and 4, just as you did on your very first warp.

Yarns and related information

Your choice of yarn for overshot is important in that it will affect the dimensions of the pattern as well as how much the pattern actually shows. In overshot structure, the pattern weft is "shooting over" most of the warp. You can think of the pattern weft passing through the fabric from front to back, producing weft floats over and under the tabby background. (Occasionally you'll find areas called halftones in which, instead of floating above or below the rest of the fabric, the pattern weft is woven in just as the tabby shots are.)

The path the pattern weft takes explains in part why twice as many wefts fit into each inch as you would normally expect. For a balanced or squared pattern, the tabby weft needs to have the same picks per inch as there are ends per inch. This is also true of summer & winter, and your yarn choices for overshot can be the same as you'd choose for summer & winter.

Overshot differs from summer & winter in that the tabby background is not as integral a part of the design, and so the weft should, in a sense, hide the background. Fluffy, soft, squeezable yarns add fullness to your design, emphasizing the pattern instead of the yarn. Where the pattern weft goes from the front to the back of the fabric, it is squeezed between the tabby background threads; where the pattern weft is part of the design,

it fills out, covering the tabby shots around it. The more loft your yarn has, the more successfully it will do this.

Thickness of the pattern weft is also important. If the yarn you first try is so thin that your pattern looks sparse and unconvincing, try doubling or tripling it. If your chosen weft is so fat that your pattern is coming out much taller than you anticipated, try switching to a thinner tabby weft. Of course, you can alter the height of your pattern somewhat by how hard you pack your weft in, though this is more of a fine tuning.

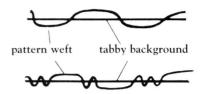

In overshot, the pattern weft is "shooting over" most of the warp as it passes through the fabric from one side to the other, producing weft floats over and under the tabby background.

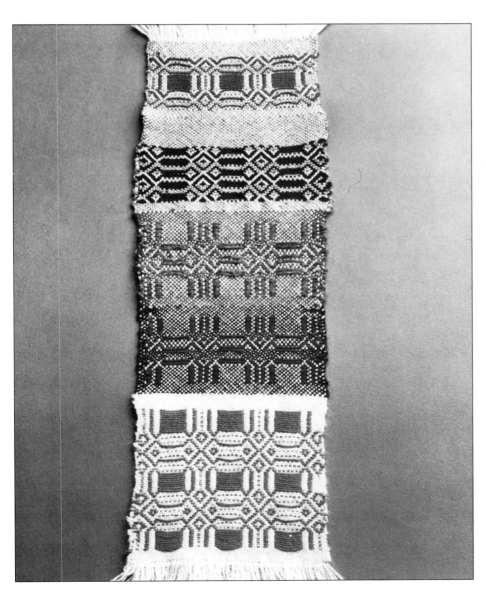

Overshot sampler. Try experimenting with different tabby colors, pattern yarns, and treadlings. Explore dark colors of pattern weft on a light colored background; see what happens when a dark tabby crosses a light colored background; try several colors of pattern wefts for different parts of your pattern; repeat over and over certain parts of your treadling, skip parts of your treadling pattern, or make up your own. *Sampler by Yvonne Stahl.*

Sett is another factor. If it's close, you won't be able to pack as much weft in, and your design will be taller. You can also change the number of pattern shots in each block, adding or subtracting as necessary to make the design taller or shorter.

How balanced, tall, or short your design is, is of importance only to you and the project. If it's pleasing to look at or matches whatever you want it to match, then it's the right height. It does not have to be balanced unless that is what you want. (I can feel the rumble of traditionalists rolling over in their graves at that statement.)

Color choice depends on how strong you want the pattern to be. A warp and tabby weft of one color used with pattern weft of another highly contrasting color will show the pattern the most. You can deviate from this as far as you like, knowing that the greater your divergence, the less the pattern will dominate. Some of the most beautiful overshot designs I've ever seen had striped warps; the pattern was very secondary to the overall effect. Try whatever comes to mind and find out if you like it. You could stumble onto something wonderful.

Miscellaneous notes

As you weave, you will need to twist the two wefts around each other at the selvedges so that the pattern weft continues all the way to the edges. When your shuttles are both on the same side, lay one down in front of the other; if the wefts don't cross over automatically as you use the shuttles, lay them down in the opposite order. The one that needs to be in front on the right may need to be in back on the left. In lieu of this, you could also use a floating selvedge, which in some cases is the only way to get a clean, even selvedge.

In both threading and treadling, your blocks can be in any order; you can go from block A to block C to block D, back to block A, for instance. Just remember *always* to thread odd-even-odd-even. Tabby is what makes this work.

There are many, many overshot patterns in books. The single most popular source is probably Marguerite Davison's *A Handweaver's Pattern Book* (Marguerite Davison, Box 263, Swarthmore, PA 19081). Remember to do drawdowns; the threading drafts are not necessarily centered, such as the pattern Periwinkle, in the drafting lesson on page 137. It is an overshot pattern, and by using tabby you can now weave it. Remember to always use tabby for overshot—several of the drafts in Davison's book leave off that notation. Also remember that Davison's book is written for sinking-shed looms, so you'll need to tie up the spaces instead of the Xs if you have a rising-shed loom. Then have fun—there are more than 300 overshot patterns in Davison's book, and many other books as well.

Your assignments

1. Choose any overshot pattern (make one up or use one of those given at the end of this lesson) and try the treadlings shown here. When there is a number greater than one in the treadling, it means to throw that many shots in that shed, with tabby in between, as always.

2. On any overshot warp, raise pairs of shafts until you find the pair that will allow the pattern weft to show on the block closest to the left edge (there will be a gap in the warp). Weave that block for as many shots as it takes to have a square block. Then find the next block and weave it to square. Then find the third block and weave it to square. Continue in this manner all the way across the warp. You'll end up with square blocks running in a diagonal line from the bottom left corner to the top right, with all kinds of interesting things

happening everywhere else. This is called *tromp as writ*, and will make your pattern look the same from all directions.

3. Choose an overshot draft and weave it once with the pattern on top, again with the pattern on the bottom. To do this, keep your treadling the same, and change from a rising- to a sinking-shed tie-up. To change to a sinking-shed tie-up, tie up the empty boxes in the tie-up instead of the ones with O's in them.

4. Weave the same pattern with at least four different pattern wefts. Try different textures, sizes and colors.

5. On one threading, weave four placemats, towels, scarves, pillows, or samples, each with a different treadling. This will give you four different patterns on one warp.

6. Choose one overshot pattern that you really like and weave something glorious for yourself!

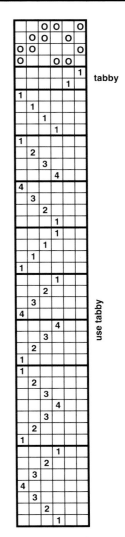

Try these overshot treadlings. The numbers in the treadling tell you how many pattern shots to throw in that shed. Use tabby in between each pattern shot. Repeat each section several times before going on to the next.

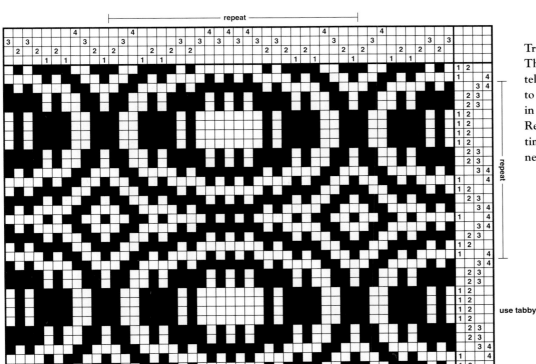

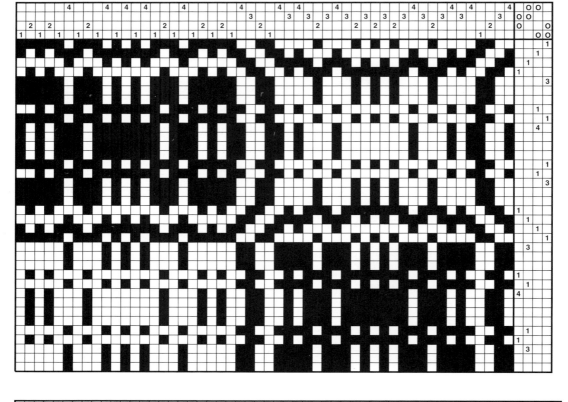

use tabby

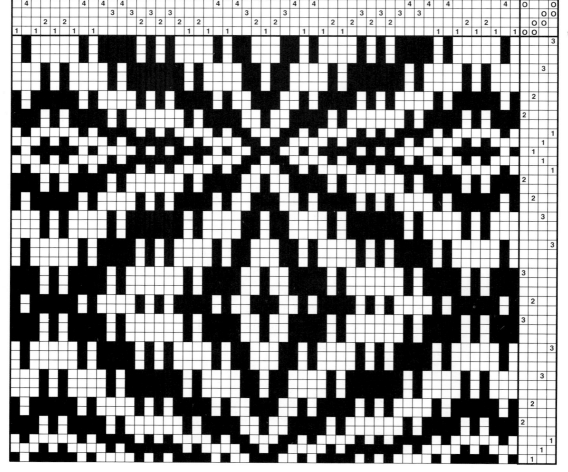

use tabby

198

Wrap Up

At the end of my classes, my students and I always have a party to celebrate. Everybody brings munchies, and we talk about what everyone has learned and where to go from here including books, looms, guilds, suppliers, magazines, and other resources. You and I can't have a party together, but if you've used this book with friends, you can have one with them. If you've used this book alone, invite over your best friends to show them what you've accomplished. They'll love it!

Most important, look at what you've done yourself, appreciate how much you've learned. How long ago was it that you didn't know anything? Now you are literate in weaving: you can plan and weave projects, read drafts, and even make up some of your own. You have a new vocabulary, which, even if you can't easily speak it yet, you probably can read reasonably well. You've come a long way—congratulate yourself!

Although this is the end of your beginning lessons, it is only the beginning of your weaving. I've attempted to give you a sound foundation, an understanding that will make it easy for you to learn more from all of the other sources of information that will come your way. Be open to them all. You will read and hear many different philosophies on weaving; my philosophy is that there are no rights or wrongs, only personal preferences. If you read or hear something you don't understand or don't like, ask for an explanation or ignore it. Sometime later it may make more sense and you can reconsider it then.

Where next? What do you want to know more about? Are you drawn toward clothing or rugs, or toward drafting and experimenting? Do you want more books or can you now take a workshop or class from someone? Maybe it's time to start over with this book and work through it again, this time learning much more because you're starting out way ahead of where you were before. You only need to plan your weaving future one warp at a time. What would you like to weave next?

Part IV is here as a reference. Look through it all; read what is interesting now. Perhaps you've been using it all along. Although it doesn't contain everything you'll need to know, it does cover many basics. Your own notes to yourself will teach you a lot more.

In closing I want to say that there are dozens of reasons why people want to weave, and for most of us the reasons change as we do. I hope that you are getting some of the satisfaction you were seeking, and that you will continue to. Thanks for including me on your weaving journey for a little while.

—*Deborah*

PART IV:
Other Useful Things to Know

People to People—Close to Home

Choosing Yarns

Sett Chart

Reed Substitution Chart

Reeds and Warp Setts

About Heddles

On Buying a Loom

Project Considerations

Finishes

High-Tech, Low-Tech—More Tools

People to People—Further Away

Suppliers & Magazines

People to people—close to home

Even the most reclusive weaver gets a welcome charge from contact with other weavers sometimes, and most weavers find the camaraderie of other weavers beneficial to their overall weaving experience. Weavers gather in several ways, each way with its own characteristics and advantages.

There are hundreds of guilds devoted to weaving and/or spinning in the United States and Canada. Membership ranges from a few to hundreds, with activities that vary according to local needs and desires. Guild projects may include weaving shows, sales of members' work, educational fairs, classes and workshops, programs, demonstrations, etc., and of course, annual picnics and parties. Many guilds publish newsletters, which may include swatches of members' experiments and discoveries. Most guilds meet once a month (some take the summer off) and many also sponsor special-interest-group meetings. Dues are nominal, considering what you get. Because most guilds do not have phone book listings, the easiest way to track them down is through area weavers or local yarn shops. Or you can contact the Handweavers Guild of America (see page 225) and ask them about local guilds.

There are dozens of summer craft schools across the country, some large, permanent institutions, others small, ad hoc organizations. Some offer only fiber courses, others a range of subjects. Classes vary in duration from a weekend to three weeks and may include living accommodations. A few offer college credit, work-study programs, or even scholarships. All include inspiration, fun, and new friendships. Many craft schools offer beginning-level classes, and for these and advanced-level classes you'll find some of the most exciting and respected teachers in the world. Craft schools are advertised in weaving and other craft magazines.

National or regional conferences can give you a shot of energy that will keep you going for a year (or more). Conferences are special in their diversity of offerings: think of lectures, workshops, and seminars as the main course, complemented by generous and equally important side dishes of shows and exhibits of textiles and supplies. Lectures, workshops, and seminars by the "big names" in the field can give you new ideas to ponder. The numerous weaving shows, each on a different theme, can inspire you and enable you to see how your work compares to that of others (it's usually better than you thought). Commercial exhibits provide an unparalleled opportunity to see, feel, and experience a vast array of yarns, equipment, books, and other weaving-related goodies—far more than you'd find in one store or even several. On top of all this, you can meet weavers from a wide geographic area with an equally wide range of experiences and aspirations. It's almost guaranteed that you won't get enough sleep, and you won't get to see and do all you want to. What *will* happen is that you'll have a wonderful time. There are 10 to 15 conferences per year, most of them in May through September, scattered around the country. You can find out about upcoming conferences from magazine ads, weaving shops, and other weavers.

You already know that I favor attending classes whenever possible.

It's not just because I think teachers are so great, but also because students have so much to offer. In a classroom, you can learn an amazing amount from your peers' interpretations of the lesson at hand, from both their mistakes and their successes. And they will learn from you; your presence is a gift to them.

Contact with other weavers, in any of the settings listed above (or any other) contributes to your weaving enrichment. Sharing ideas, celebrating successes, bemoaning (and then letting go of) disasters, appreciating discoveries, even telling bad jokes—those and much more are available to you in the weaving community, whether your participation is perpetual or occasional.

Choosing yarns

I have a vivid recollection of being confused and frustrated when, as a beginning weaver, I chose beautiful yarns but wove ugly projects without ever understanding what was happening. When I see and hear beginning students overwhelmed by the variety of yarns available to choose from, I realize once again that while these choices eventually represent opportunity for individual expression, at first the options are paralyzing. Experience will be your

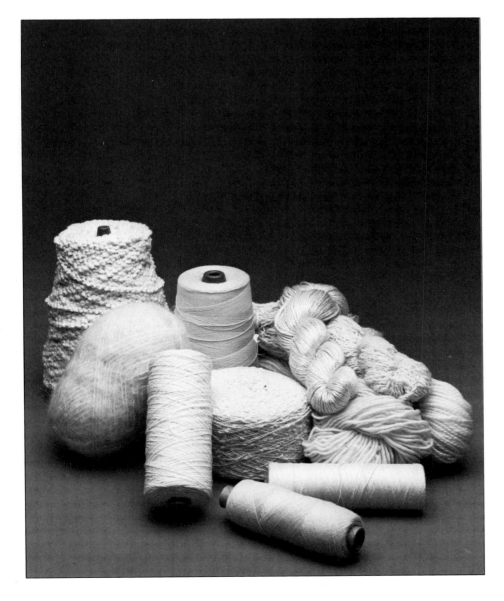

Yarn can be an inspiration. A fuzzy mohair may provide inspiration for a soft, cuddly scarf or throw; a fine linen may be just the thing for a dishwtowel or tablecloth; a bumpy cotton novelty yarn may invoke visions of a casual loom-shaped top. Ask yourself questions about your project before choosing a yarn: what will its function be, how should it look and feel, how will you plan to wash it.

best teacher. The more you weave and notice how particular yarns behave in particular projects, the more you'll see relationships, rules, cause, and effect.

Yarn is the raw material of fabric; fiber is the raw material of yarn. Every yarn is designed with a specific purpose in mind, and being able to recognize characteristics of those intended uses will greatly aid you in making successful yarn choices for your projects. You won't always use a yarn for the same purpose that the manufacturer had in mind, so the more you understand, the more easily you'll be able to make substitutions.

You can think of yarn suitability in at least three different ways. The first concerns the nature of the yarn itself: how does wool differ from cotton, a singles from a plied yarn, etc.? A second perspective comes from project considerations: what yarns are best for shawls, for rugs? And finally, from the standpoint of weaving requirements: what makes a good warp that will hold up well during weaving? What follows is a discussion of yarn that should help you answer these questions.

Fiber content

Yarn is usually divided into five categories: animal, vegetable, and mineral are all natural fiber sources; synthetics are processed from petroleum, which starts out as a liquid and is made into fiber; man-made yarns come from natural fibers that are made into a pulp and then extruded into yarn instead of being spun directly from the fibers.

Animal fibers include hair, fur, down, fleece, and silk cocoons. Wool, the fleece of a sheep, is probably the most commonly used by handweavers in North America. Weavers also enjoy the gifts of

camels, goats (mohair, cashmere, others), llamas (and their cousins, alpacas and vicuñas), dogs, musk oxen, rabbits (angora), silkworms, and numerous other critters.

Vegetable fibers come from many different plant parts and include cotton, linen, jute, ramie, hemp, sisal, raffia, coir, and others even more obscure to our culture. Mineral fibers include asbestos, which comes from a rock, and metallics such as gold, silver, and copper. Synthetics include such families as nylon, polyester, and acrylic. Man-made fibers are made from a cellulose base, for example, wood chips and cotton linters, and include rayons and acetates.

ANIMAL FIBERS

Wool

Wool is representative of the animal fibers group; the other animal fibers (except silk) are not exactly the same, but have similar characteristics.

An individual wool fiber is a hollow cylinder with scales growing on the outside, away from the sheep's body to help protect it from wet and cold. The scales are responsible for the insulative and elastic qualities that make wool such a joy to use and wear. In an acid solution, the scales close up, clinging close to the core of the fiber. In an alkaline (basic) solution, the scales open out, and in the process tangle with the scales of nearby fibers; once the fibers have entangled with each other, they can't let go. Soap makes an alkaline solution, so when wool is washed, the fibers tend to merge into each other to some degree. Sudden, extreme temperature change, vigorous agitation, and the force of a stream of water hitting the fibers also encourage this process, called fulling when it's mild, felting when it's severe. Felted fibers lock together so securely and permanently that they form a fabric, felt, on their own. (Felting is both an industry and an art form, not only an accident of the overzealous.) Fulling is desirable for many handwoven fabrics, especially yardage for clothing, for it helps stabilize the fabric and gives it a more unified appearance. It is not reversible, so use caution and don't carry the process too far.

Wool will hold up to 30 percent of its weight in moisture and still feel dry and warm, which is why it is so good for winter clothing. Because wool is a protein fiber, like your hair, washing it with shampoo instead of soap or detergent and/or rinsing it with a small dose of creme rinse or hair conditioner can add a nice softness.

Silk

Unlike the other protein fibers, silk is an extrusion, not a growing hair. The fiber is hollow but has no scales. It looks like a glass rod. The cocoon of the silkworm (the caterpillar of a moth) is made of a fine filament that is actually stronger than a steel filament of the same diameter. The finest, most lustrous silk yarns are made from reeled silk, which is obtained by unwinding cocoons. Other silks, some shiny and others with a relatively coarse-looking finish, are spun from broken or cut pieces, taken from damaged cocoons (such as ones from which the moths have emerged).

In its natural state, two basic colors of silk are white and golden. White silk, called *Bombyx mori*, after the species that produces it, is finer and softer. Tussah, the blond variety, is coarser, stronger, and less expensive. It comes from other species of worms. Within these two categories there are numerous gradations, some of which are influenced by diet.

Silk is stronger and warmer than many people expect, and more durable. It's very practical as well as spectacularly beautiful, and is growing in popularity as people discover that it is well worth the price.

VEGETABLE FIBERS

Cotton

Cotton grows on a bushy plant that produces dozens of cotton bolls, each yielding less than one-half ounce of cotton. Remember Eli Whitney and his cotton gin? I didn't appreciate this invention until I discovered that a cotton seed hangs onto its cotton the same way a cling peach pit clings to its peach, only tighter; picking these seeds out by hand had to have been a slow and difficult task.

Cotton fibers are hollow, but when picked they wilt, just as plants do, and the tubes collapse and then curl and shrivel. These convolutions provide the air pockets that contribute to cotton's warmth and softness. The mercerization process (which causes the fiber to be shiny and resist shrinkage), restores the fiber to its original form, bringing back the hollowness of the fiber and straightening it out.

Cotton conducts heat from your body and releases it into the air; that's why it is a favorite fiber for summer clothing. It is also very sturdy and can withstand tough treatment in use and washing.

Linen

Linen comes from some of the fibers in the tall stalk of the flax plant. Flax has very little elasticity, is known for its absorbency (especially after years of use), and usually produces a fabric that is somewhat stiff and always looks classy.

Linen has many of the properties of cotton, including its summer coolness. Like other cellulose fibers, linen is stronger wet than dry, making it particularly valuable for projects that are likely to be wet a lot.

Construction

Just as important as fiber content is how a yarn is made. Short fibers are twisted together to gain strength when spun into yarn. Continuous filaments (silk or nylon) are run together and twisted less, and derive their strength from their inherent qualities.

A yarn can have a lot of twist and be hard and strong, or it can have very little twist and be soft and weak. One spun yarn is called a single or singles; two singles twisted together form a two-ply yarn. While most yarns used by handweavers are 2-, 3-, or 4-ply, yarn may have as many as 24 plies. The number of plies does not necessarily tell how thick a yarn is, for this depends on the size of the original singles.

Generally speaking, a plied yarn is stronger than a singles, for it has more total twist and is also more abrasion resistant because of the twist and plying. However, a tightly twisted singles will be stronger than a loosely spun plied yarn. Look at all factors, and feel the yarn, rather than making decisions based on gross generalities.

Even before yarns are spun, the fiber goes through a variety of processes. Of greatest concern to us is the carding/combing sequence. Although each fiber is handled differently, there are some consistencies that make it all easy to understand.

The carding process fluffs fibers, be they locks of wool or bolls of cotton, so that they will be evenly distributed and can be drawn consistently out of the mass into a form called roving. Combing, which may follow carding, aligns the fibers so that they are all parallel; the longest fibers emerge from the combs in a ribbonlike strand called top, and the shorter ones fall out, often going back to the carder.

Carded wool yarn spun from roving is called woolen spun and is loftier and warmer due to its ability to trap more air. Combed wool top becomes worsted yarn; the parallel fibers trap less air, which results in a denser yarn, one that is slicker and smoother to the touch, and is usually stronger and shinier.

Cotton may also be carded or combed; like wool, combed cotton has a finer quality. Combed cottons may be mercerized—put through a caustic soda bath, causing it to swell and straighten. This process makes the cotton stronger and gives it a shiny finish that is easy to recognize. You will not find a mercerized cotton that has not been combed, but you may find a combed cotton that is not mercerized. Unmercerized cottons, called matt cottons, are usually softer and loftier. Mercerized cottons will shrink very little; unmercerized cottons may shrink quite a lot (up to 25 percent).

When flax is processed initially it is not carded, only combed. The long fibers that form top are spun while wet into line linen, a strong, smooth, lustrous, elegant yarn. The short fibers that are combed out are then carded and spun dry into tow linen, an earthy, grassy-looking yarn that is still linen, but with an altogether different appearance.

Yarn sizes

A pound of clean fiber will make a pound of yarn, but the number of yards in that pound will depend on several factors. If the fiber is spun skinny, then there will be more yards in the pound. Conversely, a fatter yarn will yield fewer yards per pound. In the most commonly used systems, yarns are assigned numbers to indicate their sizes based on yardage per pound. The higher the number, the more yards per pound and therefore, the skinnier the yarn. Thus, a size 20 is thinner than a size 10, and a size 3 is fatter than the size 10. Plying affects the relative weight and yardage, and so the number of plies is given as the second number. Common yarn sizes are 20/2, 16/2, 10/2, 8/2, 7/2, 5/2, 3/2, 12/3, 8/3, 5/3, 8/4, and 16/1. A 20/2 has twice the yardage of a 10/2; a 16/1 has twice the yardage of a 16/2, but the latter is twice as thick, being two 16/1s plied together.

Because each fiber has a different density and even worsted- and woolen-spun yarns have different densities, a 20/2 wool does not have the same yardage as a 20/2 cotton. Both are skinny though, and in the beginning that's all you really need to know. For some yardage comparisons, see the sett chart on page 210.

Novelty yarns

Novelty yarns are fun to use, add interest to some pieces, and make others really special. Novelty yarns can always be used in the weft, and as you come to understand novelties better, you can use many of them in the warp as well.

Most novelties are constructed in one of three basic ways. Some are simply a single-ply yarn spun thick in some areas and thin in others. Some consist of a core yarn with other fibers or yarns spun or wrapped around it. And some are one or two plies, possibly looped or bumped, with a thin binding thread twisted around to hold everything in place.

In considering a novelty for warp, examine whether the yarn is stable. Do the bumps or loops slide around? How strong is the strongest element? Consider how easy it will be to weave with and how successfully it will maintain its texture. A large-dent reed and large-eyed heddles will usually prevent stripping of the texture. Hairy yarns, such as brushed mohair, are strong and stable but need to be kept away from each other so that the hairs from one will not grab and lock onto the hairs of the next, preventing a clean shed or immobilizing the beater.

The first time you use novelty yarns in the warp, consider using them in conjunction with other, smoother yarns interspersed evenly across the warp. As your confidence and experience grow, add more novelty yarns. Gradually, you'll learn what will work and what won't.

Lastly, if you're weaving a fancy pattern, use a plain yarn; save the fancy yarns for plain patterns. Mixing fancy yarns and fancy patterns often results in chaos and competition, where neither shows to advantage.

Yarn packaging and conversions

Yarn comes in a variety of packages or shapes, called put-ups. Skeins, balls, pull skeins, cones, and tubes are all different shapes; the type of put-up does not indicate quantity or quality. All put-ups except skeins are made so that you can pull the yarn directly from them. Skeins need to be made into balls before using to prevent tangles, or they may be used directly if they are mounted on and pulled from an umbrella swift or its equivalent. Two reasons yarn still comes in skeins, and will continue to, is that they place no tension on the yarn (which could stress the fibers) and they look

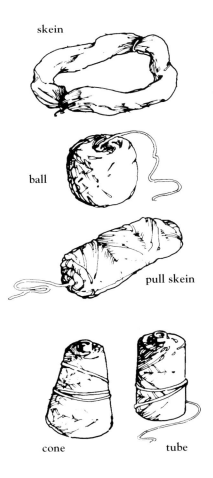

skein

ball

pull skein

cone   tube

the prettiest.

Below are some of the more common quantities that yarn comes in, along with their metric equivalents. If you're not accustomed to thinking in meters, you can figure that a skein with 400 meters has about 400 yards plus a cushion, in this case, 33 yards, ample but not excessive.

nearly 1/3 ounce	10 grams
1 ounce	28 grams
1¾ ounces	50 grams
2 ounces	57 grams
3½ ounces	100 grams
4 ounces	113 grams
8 ounces	227 grams
1 pound	454 grams
17.6 ounces	500 grams
2.2 pounds	1 kilogram

1 yard = 36 inches
1 meter = 39 inches

One of the most valuable resources you can have is Bette Hochberg's book *Fibre Facts* (Unicorn Books, 1338 Ross St., Petaluma, California 94954). It is small, easy to understand, and contains a wealth of information about fibers.

Project perspective

In choosing yarns for a project, first think about the life the project will have and the kind of abuse it will take. Use common sense in thinking about the project's requirements, then add to this your understanding of the basic yarn properties. Softness, durability, washability, abrasion resistance—which are important to the project?

Coarser fibers are usually tougher and less likely to break. Consequently, rug wools are spun from coarser wools, not softer, finer ones. In most cases, abrasion is a bigger concern than out-and-out strength. Coarser fibers are less likely to break, but longer, finer fibers are twisted into the yarn more times and will be less likely to pull out, pill, or get fuzzy.

A yarn that is too expensive or in too short supply to be used for an entire project can be mixed with another yarn to cut down on the cost and consumption. How to mix them and in what proportions depend on the pattern, the amount you have, and the effect you want.

If you have questions about the suitability of a yarn for a certain project, now is the time to ask questions of the salesperson. Keeping your own records is important too, but unless a piece is being used in your own house, you won't know how it holds up over time. Ask the people who use your weavings to let you know how well they wear, in the interests of education—yours. You can also keep a sample of a piece and abuse it as much as possible to simulate aging.

Read "Project Considerations", beginning on page 219, ask questions, keep records, and all will begin to make sense pretty soon.

Warp requirements

Possibly the most useful thing to remember about warp is that you're never pulling on only one thread—you're pulling on many at the same time. A group is stronger than an individual, so don't rule out a yarn's suitability as warp because one thread will break easily; test a bunch together. Many yarns that are soft and loosely twisted are fine for warp as long as you just keep your tension as even as possible and don't tighten it more than necessary. Be sure to use a reed with big dents that won't fray it with every beat.

You'll have the most freedom of

choice if you assume that any yarn can be warp until you find out it can't. By using reasonable care, I've come across less than half a dozen yarns I could not use for warp, some of which I didn't weave a sample with first (and regretted it).

Abrasion is probably the greatest warp killer. The friction of the reed against the yarns or of the yarns grabbing onto each other creates fuzz and eventually rubs through the yarn. Any yarn that appears to have low resistance to abrasion (scratch it with your fingernails; see how much fuzz appears) will do better if it's double-sleyed in a wider reed. If you have trouble getting the shed open, and the tendency of the yarns to stick together is hard on both the yarn and you, raise your shafts one at a time; for example, to raise 1 and 3, raise 1 alone, then 3 to join it. It's easier to lift out one-fourth of the threads than one-half. Also be sure that your beater is pulled forward so that there is as little restriction as possible on the warps as they trade places.

If you are mixing yarns in the warp, using some that are stiff with some that are stretchy, be sure to blend them as homogeneously as possible. Avoid wide stripes of a single type of yarn. Sometimes even good mixing won't be sufficient to make some yarns work together, and some will be dangerously tight while others are too loose to weave. You will have the best results if you mix only yarns of similar elasticity. To determine elasticity, stretch a yarn taut and cut off a piece one yard long. Measure the yarn in its relaxed state; the shorter the yarn, the more elastic it is. If you are using a very stretchy yarn for your warp, measure it a bit longer than calculated (see page 106) and weave it more loosely so that when the tension is released and the warp draws up, it's as long as you in-tended and the weft is packed in at the density you wanted, not tighter.

In general

Perhaps the single most important idea to remember about yarn choices and about weaving in general is that it's only yarn. The world is not going to stand still if a project is a total disaster. You can afford to make mistakes; first, because most of them can be fixed, and second, because it's one way to learn. Don't be afraid to try something new, whether you read about it somewhere or make it up yourself. If it works, you'll feel creative and satisfied and encouraged. If it doesn't, figure out why so that you don't make the same mistake again.

Experienced weavers make mistakes, have disasters, and get surprised. I'm always amazed when a beginning student assumes that teachers' weavings always work. The only way to avoid surprises is to never try anything new; but always playing safe is boring, a fate far worse than disaster in my book. Experienced weavers don't make the same mistakes as beginners, we make bigger ones!

One of the truisms about the textile arts is that you can never know it all. Some days, this concept is overwhelming. But eventually it's a relief, for if you can't know everything, you don't need to feel obligated to. If you keep this in mind, it's easier to pick and choose; to say, "This is what I want to learn next; that doesn't interest me now."

If you want to know how a particular yarn is going to behave, take a skein home and try it. Weave three different samples, wash them all, and see how the yarn acts in each one. Then write down what you've learned. Teach yourself; then you'll really know.

Things to Know

Sett Chart

Yarn Size	Yd/lb	Tabby	Twill
20/2 cotton	8,400	24–30	32–36
10/2 cotton	4,200	24–28	30
5/2 cotton	2,100	15–18	20
3/2 cotton	1,260	10–12	15
20/2 linen	3,000	20–24	30
12/1 linen	3,600	22–25	30–32
4/1 linen	1,400	12–15	15–18
20/2 worsted	5,600	20–24	28
12/3 worsted	2,160	15–18	20
6.5/1 wool	3,200	18–20	22–25
12/2 wool	3,000	18–20	22–25
7/2 wool	1,640	12–15	15–18
6.5/2 wool	1,600	10–12	12–15
1.3/1 wool	600	8–10	10–12
2.2/2 wool	550	8–10	10–12
22/2 cottolin	3,250	15–20	20
mohair loop	1,000	6–8	6–8
brushed mohair	800	4–8	4–8
linnay	1,200	10–12	15

Reed Substitution Chart

Order of Sley in Reed	5	6	8	9	10	12	14	15	16	18	20	24
0-0-1	2	2	3	3	3	4	5	5	5	6	7	8
0-1	2½	3	4	4½	5	6	7	7½	8	9	10	12
0-1-1	3	4	5	6	7	8	9	10	11	12	13	16
0-1-1-1	4	4½	6	7	7½	9	10½	11½	12	13½	15	18
1	5	6	8	9	10	12	14	15	16	18	20	24
1-1-1-2	6	7½	10	11	12½	15	17½	19	20	22½	25	30
1-1-2	7	8	11	12	13	16	19	20	21	24	27	32
1-2	7½	9	12	13½	15	18	21	22½	24	27	30	36
1-2-2	8	10	13	15	17	20	23	25	27	30	33	40
1-2-2-2	9	10½	14	16	17½	21	24½	26	28	31½	35	42
2	10	12	16	18	20	24	28	30	32	36	40	48
2-2-2-3	11	13½	18	20	22½	27	31½	34	36	40½	45	54
2-2-3	12	14	19	21	23	28	33	35	37	42	47	56
2-3	12½	15	20	22½	25	30	35	37½	40	45	50	60
2-3-3	13	16	21	24	27	32	37	40	43	48	53	64
2-3-3-3	14	16½	22	25	27½	33	38½	41	44	49½	55	66
3	15	18	24	27	30	36	42	45	48	54	60	72
3-3-3-4	16	19½	26	29	32½	39	45½	49	52	58½	65	78
3-3-4	17	20	27	30	33	40	47	50	53	60	67	80
3-4	17½	21	28	31½	35	42	49	52½	56	63	70	84
3-4-4	18	22	29	33	37	44	51	55	59	66	73	88
4	20	24	32	36	40	48	56	60	64	72	80	96
4-4-5	22	26	35	39	43	52	61	65	69	78	87	104
4-5-5	23	28	37	42	47	56	65	70	75	84	93	112
5	25	30	40	45	50	60	70	75	80	90	100	120

Warp Sett (ends per inch)

Reeds and warp setts

If you have only one reed, then you must choose yarns that will fit in that reed. If you own a variety of reeds, you can use any yarn you want and choose the appropriate reed for it. Clearly, there is more freedom with the second scenario, but reeds are expensive enough that a full set is a luxury most weavers work into only gradually.

Reeds come in a wide range of spacings, the most common being 4, 5, 6, 8, 10, 12, or 15 dents per inch. For many projects, you will sley more or fewer than one thread per dent. The change in sequence depends on the size of the yarn and how closely set you want the warp to be. By sleying two threads in each dent, a 12-dent reed yields a warp sett of 24 e.p.i.; sleying one thread in every other dent results in 6 e.p.i. To get 18 e.p.i., you'd sley one thread in the first dent, two in the next dent, then one again, then two, etc.

Although it is mathematically possible to get a sett of 10 e.p.i. in a 12-dent reed (sley five dents, skip one, sley five, skip one), it is not practical. If you have a fairly consistent sleying pattern, for example, 1/0/1/0 or 2/2/2/2 or even 1/1/2/1/1/2, the warp threads will slide into an even distribution quite successfully, if not immediately then after washing. If your doubling up or spacings, such as 1/1/1/1/0, are irregular or far apart, your threads are unlikely to shift enough to result in an even sett. Try the sleying pattern you think you need, and learn whether it will work or not. It may work with some yarns and not others. Always wash your sample as you plan to wash your finished piece to ascertain whether your warps will even out. Often, reed marks that are evident after removing your fabric from your loom will disappear with the first washing.

That fat yarns must go through widely spaced reeds is obvious. Novelty yarns, with their bumps, loops, hairs, slubs, and other protrusions, also need relatively widely spaced reeds so they won't get stripped by the reed. For a closer sett, double-sley in a wider reed. This works well, for the yarns will rest on top of one another and move about without too much abrasion.

Choosing a warp sett for any given yarn is not really as mysterious as it seems at first. A standard trick that will give you a ballpark idea of sett is to wrap your warp yarn around a ruler, compacting it tightly for an inch. Wrap the yarn as densely as you want your fabric to be, remembering that the fabric will be half warp and half weft. Your warp sett will therefore be half of the number of wraps in one inch. For example, a warp yarn that wraps around the ruler 20 times in one inch needs a sett of 10 e.p.i. to weave a balanced fabric with the same density as the wrapping. I usually prefer a warp sett slightly closer than the number I obtain from dividing by two; someone else might prefer a slightly lower number. It's a good starting point, from which you can learn your own divergence.

As you weave more samples and projects, label sheets of paper with the warp setts you use, for example, 5, 8, 10, 12, 20, 30 e.p.i. Then, as you try a new yarn, stick a piece of it onto the page for the sett you used (or decided that you should have used). As the sheets fill with yarn samples, you'll begin to see which sizes work at which setts, and eventually you'll be able to pick a good sett just by looking at the yarn.

Remember that you'll use different setts for different patterns and different projects. The yarn you set at 18 e.p.i. for a soft skirt fabric you might set at 24 e.p.i. for a tablecloth. If you were to weave lace curtains out of the same yarn, you might set it at 16 e.p.i. for a more open fabric. For a twill weave, you'll generally want to set your yarn closer than you would for a plain weave. There are no "right" setts, which is another reason that samples are so essential.

The above tips apply to balanced warp setts in particular, but what about setts for warp-faced and weft-faced fabrics? Again, type of fabric and weave structure are important factors, and using what you know about figuring setts for balanced weaves will give you a basis to work from. You know, for instance, that for a fabric to be weft-faced, the warp must be completely covered by weft, and yet the warp needs to be set close enough so that the fabric is stable. A yarn with a lot of loft will pack in easier than a tightly spun, hard yarn; consider this in determining the sett. Figuring a sett for a warp-faced fabric works similarly, though here you need to think of warp completely covering weft. Choice of yarns will be a factor here as well because a warp-faced fabric has warp ends set very closely; you don't want the yarns to stick together and prevent a clean shed.

A rule of thumb to use in determining the sett for a warp-faced fabric is to wrap the yarn around a ruler for one inch and multiply the number of warp ends in that inch by 1.5 or 2 (two or three times a normal balanced sett). For a weft-faced fabric, again wrap your ruler, this time using one warp yarn and two weft yarns, then count only the warp ends in this inch to find your sett. Keep in mind that these are only starting points. Too much depends on your materials and the intended use of your fabric for these to be hard-and-fast rules. The best way to determine the best sett for your project is to weave a sample.

About heddles

Four kinds of heddles are readily available to weavers. String heddles are the traditional heddles which were used for centuries before flat steel, wire, and inserted-eye heddles became available. String heddles are just that, string, though improved versions are now made from nylon. The latter feature specially made areas that hold the eyes open for ease of threading. String heddles are very lightweight and much quieter than metal heddles; they are flexible and will forgive a knot or a bumpy warp yarn; and they can be dyed, which is helpful for weavers with vision problems. Threading them takes more time because they don't slide along the heddle bars as easily as metal heddles will. Because most jack looms need the extra weight of wire heddles to prevent the shafts from floating, string heddles are not always desirable for this type of loom. You'll find string heddles on most countermarch and counterbalance looms; ask your loom manufacturer for more information.

Metal heddles—flat steel, wire, and inserted eye—are self adjusting in that they will space themselves out on the heddle bars after they've been threaded; string heddles need to be placed into position. Wire heddles, made from twisted wire, weigh the least of the three. Inserted-eye heddles are wire heddles with a circular ring soldered into the eye for added smoothness. Flat steel heddles are flat pieces of metal with slightly twisted eyes. Wire and inserted-eye heddles are more forgiving of knots and bumpy warps than are flat steel ones. The flexibility that protects the yarn also makes them more prone to get temporarily tangled amongst themselves on the shaft.

All metal heddles have a directional twist to the eye. You need to be aware of this when threading. When you twist metal heddles either toward you or away from you, the heddle eyes appear to be more open one way than the other (this is most apparent with flat steel heddles). When threaded correctly, the twist permits your warp to make a straight line from front to back. If you thread your warp through the wrong side of the eye, the thread will bend; this will cause wear on your warp end and possibly cause it to break. Your heddles will be a lot easier to thread if they are all mounted on the heddle bars in the same direction. When they are side by side, they should nest inside one another. If some or all of your heddles are hanging so that you have to reach around and thread them from the far side to make the thread go straight, you can reverse the heddles by turning them upside down. If all of the heddles need to be reversed, you can remove the top and bottom heddle bars (with the heddles still on them) from the shaft frame, turn the whole unit over, and put the heddle bars back into the frame. In the worst case, half of your heddles will be upside down. In this case, you'll need to slide all errant heddles (and those in the way) off of the heddle bar, flip the offenders over, and put them back—a tedious process, but worth it in the long run. See below for how to do it.

One last note on direction. If you use a threading hook, your heddles will need to face in the opposite direction from the way they should be when using your fingers. Think of this: a threading hook goes through from the side you're on to get the yarn; threading by hand means poking the thread through from the back side. If you're just beginning, you may wish to try threading both ways; when you've chosen which you prefer, you can set your heddle direction accordingly.

Moving heddles

If you need to move heddles from one shaft to the next, *do not* just slide the heddles off the heddle bars. If your heddle bars have holes in the ends, tie strong strings through the holes (if there are no holes, tape strings to the end of the bars). Then slide the heddles onto the strings and then tie the strings together to secure the heddles. You can then slide the heddles off of the strings and onto the shaft where you need them. Even if you never expect to put the heddles back on a shaft, put them onto strings anyway. Someday, someone will want to use them, and it will be much easier if they are already properly aligned. It's also a good idea to mark the bundles with the number of heddles that they contain.

To avoid moving heddles after you've started threading, take the time to make sure that you have enough heddles on each shaft before you begin threading. However, if you have an eight-shaft loom and are using only four of the shafts, and find that you've run out of heddles, you can simply start using the unused shafts. Think of shaft 5 as shaft 1, 6 as 2, etc. When tying up your treadles, just add the extra shaft where appropriate. This is one of the less renowned but valuable advantages of having more shafts.

Repair heddles

If you have made a mistake in your threading and have the right number of threads but no heddle on the shaft you want the thread to be on, you can either tie a string heddle onto the proper shaft, striving to get the heddle eye even with all the other heddle eyes, or take a pair of wire cutters (not scissors) and cut an unused heddle off the heddle bars. Bend the metal to get the heddle off, put it where you need a new heddle, and bend the metal back into place. After you've woven your piece, remove the replacement heddle and save it for when you might need it again.

Marking heddles

A trick for making it easy to distinguish shafts while threading is to paint your lower heddle bars (or heddles if you can) with paint or fingernail polish, a different color for each shaft. You can dye string heddles. Then it's easy to see which shaft to pull heddles from. The more shafts you have, the more useful marking the heddles is; with twelve or sixteen it's almost essential.

Heddle distribution

If you have more heddles than you need and you have a full-width warp, unused heddles left on the sides may abrade the selvedge warp as it passes by. To prevent this, simply space the extras amidst your warp as you thread. Thread a couple of inches, then leave a few empty heddles next to those threaded, then thread some more, then leave more empties.

On buying a loom

There are many good looms available, and all have differences, though of course, the similarities are more numerous. This section is not going to tell you which loom to buy. It will simply tell you which questions to ask.

Choosing a manufacturer

To some extent it doesn't matter which loom you buy because they all work. I suggest that you look at the manufacturer, find out how long it has been in business and/or how long it expects to be. Although looms seldom break down, you may want to replace parts broken in moving or add accessories later. That's difficult to do if the company no longer exists. However, there are well over 20 stable, reputable loom companies in the United States so you have plenty of good choices. At least seven of those sell only by mail order, so you can't see their looms at your local weaving shop. This does not make them less reliable, but it may make them more difficult to try out. If you plan to buy through the mail, look at all of the companies equally, and choose the one who responds to you the best and feels right to you.

Deciding what kind of loom you need

First consider what you want to weave. Are you going to weave only tapestries? Only rugs? Is clothing of all kinds your interest, or coverlets? North American weavers seem to have a wide range of interests, settling into a single focus for periods of time perhaps, but not forever. It's probably easier to choose a loom for one purpose only—a tapestry loom, a rug loom—but if you're versatile, you'll need a loom that is versatile, too. Make a list of the first ten things you'd like to weave. Listing the first two or three projects will be easy; those have been on your mind for a long time. The rest may take more effort, and that's good. By then you'll see if there is a pattern. Is everything on the list less than 25 inches wide? More than 40 inches wide? If it's all small stuff, don't buy a 60-inch-wide loom. If it's all rugs, don't buy a lightweight loom. If you want to weave fabric for clothing, you'll be surprised. Although commercial fabric comes in standard widths, pattern pieces are rarely more than 25 inches wide. Because handwoven fabric is custom-made, you can weave it longer and narrower than commercial patterns call for; you don't need a wide loom to weave fabric for clothing.

After loom width, the most significant question you have to ask is how complex a loom to buy. Do you need two, four, eight, or more shafts? A rigid heddle loom (two shafts) can weave a tremendous variety of projects, from shawls to blankets, wall hangings to rugs, and it costs much less than a shaft loom. If you learn to use multiple heddles, or even just one pick-up stick, you can do a lot of pattern playing as well. For speed and number of patterns combined, a loom with four or more shafts is more appropriate. One of the questions most often asked is, "Four or eight shafts?" A number of looms come with four shafts in place, with the option of adding more later. If you like puzzles and figuring things out, you'll probably want more than four shafts. If color and textured

yarns are what get you excited, then four shafts will probably be enough. If you are intimidated by the presence of unused shafts that you don't know what to do with, then by all means don't buy them—they'll spoil your enjoyment of the ones you do know what to do with.

Years ago, I was in a community where the local practice was to buy looms by weight. Whichever loom weighed the most was the one weavers bought. It was a novel approach that I think was an outgrowth of the idea that "looms need to be sturdy", which comes from rug weaving. Of course, a rug loom needs to be sturdy, as do all looms, but rug weaving puts a lot of strain on a loom that most other weaving does not. If you expect to weave one or two rugs a year but otherwise mostly much lighter fabrics, then go ahead and buy a lightweight loom and tighten the bolts after you've woven your rug. (Once a year, or more often, you should clean and tighten everything anyway.)

Consider your warping method

There are many different ways to warp a loom. Ask what features a loom has to accommodate your method. If you don't have a method yet, ask the question in general terms. Do the beams lift off? Does the back fold up or drop down out of the way? Is a sectional beam available? Can the loom be warped in a folded or partly folded position? Can the loom be folded up when it's warped, in case you need to move it? How close can you sit to the castle on whichever side you want to thread from?

Loom types

Last in the "very important" category is the type of lifting mechanism the loom has: jack, counterbalance, or countermarch. A jack loom has separate lifts for each shaft, each operating independently. You can raise whatever shaft(s) you want and the others just sit there, allowing total freedom of design. A counterbalance loom has shafts hanging over rollers opposite each other, 1 opposite 2, 3 opposite 4, and 1 and 2 together opposite 3 and 4 together. When 1 and 3 go up, 2 and 4 go down. Any two shafts can be raised or lowered, but they must work in pairs, not one against three. (While this is the theory, some counterbalance looms will give an unbalanced shed; it's not supposed to work that way but sometimes it does.) The rollers make the treadling action easy on the weaver's legs, and the raising versus lowering of the shafts is useful in separating sticky warps. A countermarch loom is one in which each shaft is counterweighted opposite the treadles. That means that you can raise or lower whichever shaft(s) you want, giving you infinite design possibilities, and because the shafts have a counteraction, the ease and antistick advantages of the counterbalanced system are maintained. Theoretically, the countermarch loom, having the best elements of both of the other two types, should be the best loom. In truth, however, each type of loom has many other features that are not necessary to the style but are traditionally associated with it, features that must be taken into account as well. With a few exceptions, jack looms have a bottom-mounted beater, countermarch looms an overhead beater. They feel entirely different, and you may develop a strong preference for one or the other.

Tie-up system

Every loom has its own tie-up system for tying the treadles to the lamms. Cords of any kind are subject to stretching, which is only of interest when they stretch different amounts. Wire connections don't stretch, but they may get bent or fall out of their holes. Other tie-up systems use chains, ropes, and other materials. Whichever you get, you will get used to and know which quirks to watch for. If you're interested in speed, then ask about the tie-up system as some are substantially faster or slower than others.

Some (and perhaps all) of the now available computer-assisted looms have electronic systems that eliminate the need to get down on the floor at all. If your body is getting creaky or is in other ways less than fully functional, this is definitely an option to consider.

Brakes

Most North American looms use one of two kinds of brakes, friction or ratchet. The purpose of the brake is to hold the beam firm so that your warp won't unroll as you weave. I'm aware of only one loom with a front friction brake; most others have a ratchet and dog (or pawl), a piece that falls into the notches of the ratchet wheel to hold it in place. A few looms have worm gears. On the back beam, there might be another ratchet or a friction brake, a drum with a cable wrapped around it. The beam won't move when the cable is holding tight, but it will move when it is released slightly. The advantage of a friction brake is that the warp tension can be adjusted infinitely;

you are not limited to the increments of the ratchet teeth. The disadvantage of the friction brake is that if the cable should get bent (perhaps in moving, but unlikely under normal circumstances), it won't work and must be replaced. Most friction brakes have a break-in period; ratchets don't. Occasionally, a friction brake won't release properly; without proper precautions a ratchet will release too quickly. Weavers generally prefer the one they have, having learned its idiosyncracies and how to work with them.

Heddles

Heddles may be made of flat steel, wire, or string. As with everything else, there are weavers with strong preferences for each. The advantage of flat steel is speed in threading and sliding around; the disadvantage is weight, not significant if you have fewer than 1000 and strong legs for lifting the shafts. The advantages of wire are flexibility—they'll flex around a snag in a yarn rather than hold firm and force the yarn to give way—and price, being the least expensive of the three. Looms come with heddles so price is no object until you want to buy more. String heddles are quiet and very lightweight. They can be purchased or tied by you. Of the several commercial varieties, those from Texsolv are rapidly taking over the field. Unlike in the olden days, string heddles now come with an open eye, eliminating their major disadvantage; avoid any that have eyes that stand closed—it takes two hands and four or five fingers to thread them. (If you tie your own, use square knots to get open eyes.) The other disadvantage of string heddles is that they don't slide easily across the shaft frame or heddle bar, important to some, irrelevant to others. A big advantage for people with vision problems is that they can be dyed, a different color for each shaft. (This is also useful when you have many shafts.) Most looms come with one type of heddle standard, but substitutes can be made in most cases. (Read "About Heddles", page 212, for more information.)

Other equipment

Other than heddles, what comes with looms varies considerably. One may come with a bench but no reed; most come with a reed but no bench. Shuttles, books, and threading hooks may be included; dealers may throw in other equipment, lessons, or shipping costs. If price is a major concern, be sure to find out what's included and what else you'll need to acquire to get started. Because many, if not most, looms are sold to active weavers, those who already own warping boards, etc., looms do not come complete with everything needed to start weaving.

Price

When comparing prices, remember that all looms are not created equal. A number of looms are designed as good starter looms, lighter weight, less expensive, some offered as kits for you to assemble. It is not appropriate to compare the price of those looms with the price of looms that are more substantial and designed for years of prolonged use. The latter will cost two to three times as much, as well they should. Decide which kind of investment you want to make, then look at the options within that range. The resale value of most looms is good. The market is ever growing, so there is a strong demand for good used looms. The very small and very large are harder to sell, the midrange easy. (Four-shaft, 36 to 48 inches wide is probably the size most sought after.)

Aesthetics

Do you like the loom's appearance? To some people, this is very important; to others, it hardly matters. If it matters to you, then shop accordingly. If you buy a loom that you think is ugly, you'll rarely look at it without its ugliness coming to mind. On the other hand, if you buy one that you think is beautiful, it will add a warm sparkle to your day every time you look at it.

Space needs

How crowded are you willing to be? Obviously, basic dimensions of loom and room are factors here, but beyond that, a loom with a low castle *appears* to take up less space because it doesn't block vision across a room. A high-castle loom that occupies exactly the same floor space will look bigger because it really is, but it is using up otherwise unused air space. If the loom is against a wall or alone in a room, this doesn't matter, but in the middle of a room, a tall loom will act as a room divider, something you may or may not want.

Other considerations

Other factors to consider when choosing a loom include size of shed, lamm system, type of wood, noise level, height of beams (if you are tall), style of bench, spacing of treadles, and portability. Read loom catalogs. Each will tout its own

strengths, and from that information you'll know what questions to ask about other looms. What one manufacturer calls a strength, another may consider of no importance; the question is, how important is it to you?

I haven't recommended a particular manufacturer or style of loom because I don't want you to buy the loom I like; I want you to buy the one you like. Thus, I've mentioned some of the things to look for, questions to ask, and factors to consider. With this information, I hope you can decide what the "right" loom is for you.

Your loom may well last you the rest of your life, so take the time you need to be happy with your purchase. At the same time, remember that the loom doesn't *have* to be a lifetime commitment; you can sell it and buy a different one if you change your mind later. In the time that I've been weaving seriously, I've sold three looms because they no longer suited my needs for various reasons. I love the loom I have now, but I have every expectation of buying another when I again live in a bigger place.

I've had students ask, half seriously, "Why don't they just make one loom, the best one, and save us all this confusion?" I suppose they could, the same as they could make just one car, one breakfast cereal, or one house design.

Whichever loom you buy, the odds are that it will be the right one for you at the time. You'll learn to use it, understand its traits and quirks, and the two of you will develop a strong bond.

"On Buying Looms" *is adapted from an article that first appeared in* Handwoven, November/December 1983.

Project considerations

During the planning stage of any project, ask yourself some basic questions. How sturdy does the fabric need to be, or how delicate? Does it need to be soft or firm? What kind of wear will it get? Will it be pulled or rubbed? Will it be washed often? Will it be exposed to direct sun for long periods of time? Does it matter how heavy or light the fabric is? Does it need to be warm?

Rugs

Before you begin a rug, ask yourself if it will be used in an area of heavy or light traffic. Will it get wet a lot such as a bath mat, kitchen rug, or mudroom foot scraper? Will it lie on a slippery surface? What will be its primary purpose: decoration, warmth, absorbency of wetness, absorbency of sound, to cover an ugly place, to unify a decor, to be a gift? How much can it cost? Is your loom so small or lightweight that you are limited in what kind of rug you can weave? (Almost any loom can weave some kind of rug.)

There are many, many different ways to weave rugs, from rag to rya. Some rugs are very heavy, some light. High-traffic rugs, such as those in hallways or near doorways, need to be durable. Rugs that go under tables, next to beds, or in other low-traffic areas can be pretty and/or warm but don't need to be as indestructible.

Some rugs are sturdy because of the yarn used, others because of the weave structure. A softly twisted yarn is not sturdy, but a sturdy weave may sufficiently compensate for such a yarn. Weft-faced weaves commonly are used for rugs, but many sturdy rugs are woven with the warp showing. Most rag rugs, for instance, which seem to last forever, are neither very heavy nor totally weft-faced.

Proper care will ensure that your handwoven rug lasts as long as possible. A pad placed under a rug will cushion it and add years to its life. If the rug will be mostly in direct sun, it may suffer sun rot—of the natural fibers, linen and cotton resist sun rot better, wool and silk worse. If the rug will be on a slippery floor, apply a rubber-cement-like backing to prevent it from sliding.

Clothing

Handwoven clothing is either loom shaped or tailored. Loom-shaped garments are constructed with very little cutting. They are mostly made of rectangles and squares and tend have an ethnic look. Tailored clothing includes fitted garments that are cut and sewn from sewing patterns. (Yes, you can cut handwoven fabric just as you cut commercial fabric.) You do need to take some care with handwoven fabric that commercial fabric may not require, but lots of weavers do it and there's plenty of information available to help you.

When planning a clothing project, weave samples at least 8 inches square so that you can feel how the fabric drapes. Wash and full your fabric before you construct your garment to avoid unexpected shrinking.

Towels, placemats, napkins, etc.

I loved it when weaving dish towels suddenly became not only respectable but almost a fad; I hope it continues. Even if it doesn't, table runners, placemats, and other table linens will always be favorite projects. They provide the opportunity to exercise a vast range of tastes in color, texture, pattern, weight, fiber, etc. Conservative or outrageous, casual or elegant, delicate or sturdy, expensive or not, household linens offer tremendous freedom of design.

What are the limits? Washability is important, whether by hand or machine. Not only do you have to choose appropriate fibers, but you also must weave them fairly firmly so that they can withstand agitation and even abuse. Towels need to be absorbent and should dry reasonably quickly. Placemat and table runner fabrics should not be so deeply textured that glasses and salt shakers tip over when set upon them. If you don't mind hand washing, wool placemats are fine, and many people prefer them. If you want to toss your placemats in with the rest of the laundry, then a nonfelting fiber such as cotton, linen, rayon, or nylon is a better choice.

Wall hangings

Over time, a wall hanging may stretch out of shape. You can minimize this deformation by mounting it so that it is well supported. If the weave is weft-faced, consider having the design work sideways and hanging the piece so that the weft is oriented vertically. That way the piece will hang from its strongest direction.

From a design standpoint, a wall hanging can be anything you want, any size, any shape. I admit I've been turned off when someone hangs a piece or sample that didn't quite work out on the wall and calls it a

wall hanging. On the other hand, a piece designed for a particular place can really enhance a room. Wall hangings conceived and born to be wall hangings that are well finished are fine art at its best.

Curtains

In planning curtains you should consider how often you will want to clean your curtains, and by what means. What do they need to match in the room? What qualities in your present curtains do you want to keep, and what do you want to improve on? How much sun will the curtains get? Will they withstand hanging for a long period of time? For small north windows these last two questions are not critical factors, but for large south windows in the Northern Hemisphere, they are. Add a lining to protect the drapes from sun rot. Wool drapes that receive intense sunlight may not last a year. How do you want the curtains to drape? If the weft is stiff, the curtains may not curve and fold well when open. A woman I know wove drapes for her sliding glass doors without doing a sample; when she hung them, the weft slid to the floor.

You can attach curtains to curtain rods in a number of ways, some simple, some fancy; the method to choose depends on your fabric and your window. Go to a drapery store or the curtain department of a home furnishing or department store for ideas.

Plan your curtains carefully so that they will be long enough; don't forget to add take-up into your warp length. (That's the voice of experience speaking—I've made at least two sets of curtains too short for their intended windows.)

Lace weaves let in light and sun, and are cheery. Double weaves, especially stuffed or with thin insulative material placed between the layers, can be terrific heat/cool savers. Waffle weaves are also good insulators, but it can be unstable—do a sample at least 12 inches square to be sure that it will work the way you want it to.

Blankets, bedspreads, afghans, baby blankets

These might be my favorite projects to weave. Because they are large, they are enormously satisfying. They are almost always much faster to weave than you expect. (My first bedspread took two months and five days—two months dreading the time it would take and five days to weave it.) Bed coverings can be heavy or light, colorful or conservative, and any of dozens of patterns. Depending on the size of your loom, afghans and baby blankets may be woven in a single piece; blankets and bedspreads will probably need to be woven in panels that are seamed together. There are many ways to make seams, some strictly functional, some decorative. Sewing by machine, sewing by hand with yarn instead of thread, crocheting, and weaving narrow bands as joining strips, are a few of them.

Is this blanket for warmth or decoration? Is it going to North Dakota or Florida? Will it be slept under or pulled back for the night? What will happen to it during the day? Is the house full of kids and animals who will play on the bed, sit on it to tie shoes, shed all over it, take naps on it as often as under it, etc., or will it be looked at but never abused? Abrasion resistance, the snaggability of long floats in some patterns, and ease of cleaning, all need to be considered in light of the life-style it will encounter.

Is a baby blanket for sleeping, grocery shopping, or dress-up? The most common concerns are washability and softness. But you should also consider flammability. Synthetics will flare and melt into skin, causing far more severe burns than natural fibers which tend to burn up and off. Because wool is self-extinguishing, it's the safest of all. Keep in mind that little babies can't push irritations away; a fuzzy or fringey blanket could be a real tickler.

There are some very soft and washable wools and wool blends. More cottons are available all the time; they are functional, fun, and elegant. Consider silk, which may seem extravagant but is actually very practical—it's durable, washable, warm, light, and beautiful.

In general

If I were to make one recommendation about project planning, it would be to ask questions and answer them. Think about what you plan to make, and question its purpose, requirements, freedoms, and limitations. Study similar goods, identify their strengths and weaknesses, and decide what you want to reproduce and what you want to do away with. Common sense is a major part of such planning, combined with your growing knowledge of yarns and weave structures and how they work together.

Finishes

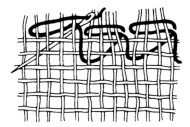

Hemstitching uses a needle and a new piece of yarn for sewing. It is easiest to do while the piece is still on the loom, under tension.

In most cases, to keep the weft from coming out at the ends of your weaving, it will need to be secured, or finished, in some way. Consider how you'll want to finish a piece while you're in the early stages of planning. Do you want your piece to have fringe? If so, how long should it be and what kind of edge or end finish do you want to give it? Will your piece have a hem? If so, how deep will it be? Whatever you decide, you will need to allow for your finishing method in your weaving plan.

Also consider your choice of yarn. Linen, for example, when used as a fringe, disintegrates quickly and will look untidy after just a few washings. Some novelty yarns, especially slick ones, have a tendency to untwist; experiment with your yarns before you begin to weave to see how they might behave as fringe. If you want to use a yarn which you feel might not hold up with wear and washing, investigate the many techniques for braiding, twisting, and knotting which will yield a stable and neat fringe. See *Finishes in the Ethnic Tradition*, by Suzanne Baiz-

erman and Karen Searle (Dos Tejedoras, PO Box 14238, St. Paul, Minnesota 55114) for many finishing techniques in easy, clear drawings.

Ask yourself if the fringe or finish will be a focal point of the overall design of your piece. Should the finish be fancy or plain? How will the finish work with the design as a whole?

Function, design, and wearability will often determine what kind of finish you choose. For example, a very long fringe that may be stylish on a shawl will be impractical and untidy for a dish towel. Blankets, shawls, and scarves all lend themselves well to fringe; placemats, runners, napkins, and tablecloths might have fringe or hems depending on your design and the yarns you choose. In weaving a garment, current styles and your own body type should play a part in determining an appropriate finish.

There are dozens of edge finishes, and you'll want to experiment and try many of them. I've included three of my favorite ones here; more are illustrated in *Finishes in the Ethnic Tradition*.

Twining is done on the loom. It forms the first and last wefts. One row is enough for security. Two rows (shown here) make a handsome edge.

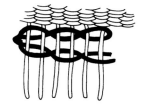 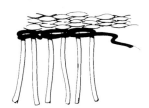

Phillipine Edge utilizes the fringe itself and is done after the piece is removed from the loom.

 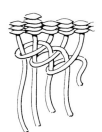 

High-Tech, Low-Tech—More Tools

Computers

Many weavers enjoy the low-tech, high-touch aspect of the craft. Ironically, the first computers were born from the technology of the Jacquard loom. Now it's all come full circle, and the addition of the personal computer as a weaving tool has expanded the craft to include folks who love the high-tech world too.

Because of the rapid changes in the availability of both hard- and software, I'll not list any specifics here. But I will tell you that there are three "computer aids" to look into if you're interested.

The first aid you might want to pursue is a drafting program. There are dozens available, all designed to speed up the design process. Though you still need to understand the principles of drafting, these programs speed up the drawdown process. You enter in the threading and treadling you want, and the program draws it. With a color monitor you can also review warp and weft color choices. To find out about the many programs available, read the ads in the weaving magazines.

Second is a computerized loom. These looms are attached to computers which have two primary functions (right now). One is to replace the tie-up system under the loom. Instead of tying up treadles, the treadling is determined by commands given to the computer keyboard. (When computerized looms first became available, one loom manufacturer told me that, to his amazement, he was selling computer looms mostly to "little old ladies with arthritis";

it extended their weaving life by years!) Computerized looms also transmit the drafting/designing features of drafting programs to the treadling. With these two functions, you weave by first sitting in front of a computer monitor playing around with a draft, and then you move over to the loom bench and throw a shuttle and beat while the computer makes the shafts raise and lower in the proper sequence to create what you just designed. (This is not totally automated: you will need to warp the loom.)

Various loom manufacturers already have or currently are designing computerized looms. Again, read the ads for what is currently available.

Finally, not connected to the loom but certainly belonging in this section, is the onslaught of publicly available electronic bulletin boards. These are essentially computerized clubs or at least conversations. As of this writing, Prodigy, CompuServ, the National Videotex Network, America Online, Arachne's Web, Delphi, Fibernet, GEnie, and the Internet all have on-line craft categories, allowing weavers and would-be-weavers all over the country—world!—to share information and ideas. While I confess to having no personal experience with these, (I'm totally low-tech, unnerved by the idea of an Information Super Highway), I find the idea exciting. For many geographically isolated weavers, and even those not isolated, it's a comprehensive way to connect with other weavers, spinners, and all other fiber types. For more information read Sandra Fish's article "Weaving Online" in the November/December 1994 issue of *Handwoven*.

Tools you don't have to plug in

I'm going to list only three of the numerous specialized gizmos and widgets designed for weavers. If you find a part of planning, drafting, warping, or weaving that seems arduous, someone has probably designed some thing to simplify the task. If no one has, perhaps you should. That's how all of these came into being.

First is Draw Partner, a manual method produced by Manuela Kaulitz for doing drawdowns faster. Describing the kit adequately would take more space than I have, so if you're interested in a low-tech, easy-on-the-eyes, quick way to fill in squares of a drawdown, write to Draw Partner, 9805 Four Seasons Lane, Louisville, Kentucky 40241.

Second is the Treadle Minder, designed by the late great Walter Schutz. Some treadling patterns are so complex that keeping track of them as you weave is a major challenge. Even if your treadling pattern is simple, unexpected interruptions can lead to confusion. The Treadle Minder, which looks something like a one-row cribbage board, can be invaluable in helping you keep track of where you are in a treadling sequence. You place a copy of your treadling pattern in a slot on the board and then keep track of where you are in the sequence by inserting a peg into spaces alongside the pattern. Throw a shot, advance one hole. You can get a Treadle Minder from Sievers Looms, Washington Island, Wisconsin 54246. (414) 847-2264.

Lastly, remember back in the warping section where I said that what stopped me from warping back to front was not being able to tie the lease sticks onto the loom successfully? Had I had a warp tensioner (loom-mounted lease sticks), my whole life might have been different—or at least my approach to warping. These are frames that attach to the back or front beam of a loom and hold up to four dowels in place, parallel to the beam and extending across the full width of the loom. The dowels act as lease sticks. They stay in place and do their job while you beam the warp.

While there have been others, the only source for this I know of at present is Harrisville Designs (PO Box 806, Harrisville, New Hampshire 03450). Though designed for Harrisville looms, this warp tensioner also fits many other looms. Ask if it will fit your loom before you buy one.

Videos

In the last ten years the world of video has exploded (like the world of virtual reality is about to; soon you may be able to weave without ever touching a loom). What was a new toy for the rich when I wrote the first edition of this book, is now almost as common as television.

Over the years I've seen at least four videos made for beginning four-shaft weavers, each with some good ideas, and many more for other aspects of weaving. The single largest source of video titles is Victorian Video Productions, which both produces and distributes videos on fiber-related topics. Of the more than 100 videos in their 1994 catalog, more than 20 of them are about weaving.

Some people learn better by watching than by reading. For this reason, I made two videos for Victorian Video Productions which cover the lessons in this book—Introduction to Weaving (which you probably don't need now) and Beginning Four Harness Weaving, which covers warping and basic weaving in ways that couldn't be done in a book (I do recommend this one to you).

To find out about what videos are available, read the classified ads in magazines and request a catalog from Victorian Video, 930 Massachusetts, Lawrence, Kansas 66044. (800) 848-0284.

People to People— Further Away

The world is getting smaller every day. You can go anywhere or communicate with anyone at speeds unimaginable in years past. Geographic distances no longer restrict who we do business with or who is considered a neighbor. It is essential therefore, that we find constructive ways to link up with people not only in our own culture but in other cultures as well. We must learn how to understand each other. Sharing common interests is one of the best ways.

While there are numerous technique-specific groups you can join, such as the American Tapestry Alliance, I especially want you to know about two more general groups.

First is the Handweavers Guild of America, founded in 1969. Formed as a network for weavers, spinners, and dyers in the United States, it has grown international in scope, with world-wide membership. HGA offers a wide range of valuable services to members, including the publication of a quarterly magazine, learning exchanges, slide kit rental, certificates of excellence, a biannual conference called Convergence (the biggest weaving conference), and much more. For information on membership, write Handweavers Guild of America, 3327 Duluth Highway, Two Executive Concourse, Suite 201, Duluth, Georgia 30096.

Second is a relatively new organization called Weave A Real Peace (WARP). Born in 1992, WARP's purpose is to build bridges and relationships between weavers (and other textile people) of the first and third worlds, or we could say to build bridges between the people who weave for recreation and those who weave to survive. WARP works on all levels: one on one, guild to coop, family to family. If you're interested, write to Weave A Real Peace, 1230 NE 70th Street, Oklahoma City, Oklahoma 73111.

Suppliers and Magazines

To locate information on suppliers, read the ads in weaving magazines. They are always up-to-date with the information and addresses you need. Below is a list of weaving or fiber-related magazines and their publishers. Each has a very different slant, so look at copies of each to decide which are best for you.

Fiberarts—Interweave Press, 201 East Fourth St., Loveland, CO 80537.

Handwoven—Interweave Press, 201 East Fourth St., Loveland, CO 80537.

Shuttle Spindle and Dyepot—Handweavers Guild of America, Two Executive Concourse, Suite 201, 3327 Duluth Highway, Duluth, GA 30096.

Spin·Off—Interweave Press, 201 East Fourth St., Loveland, CO 80537.

Threads—The Taunton Press, PO Box 5506, Newtown, CT 06470.

Weaver's—PO Box 1525, Sioux Falls, SD 57101.

Because books come and go out of print, I'm not going to give you a recommended book list. Many of my favorites have gone out of print, many new ones have come into print since this book was first published. So read magazine ads, ask your teachers and fellow guild members, go to the library of your favorite book store (if you don't have a local weaving shop) and look up what books are in print. And check again every six months. There are some great books out there, written for your pleasure and education.

Troubleshooting

Problem	Possible Causes	Solutions
Breaking selvedge threads.	Too much draw-in, beating is exerting too much pressure.	Leave more weft in shed.
	Large group of extra heddles is causing longer path, strain on sides of warp.	This time, remove heddles; next time space heddles as you thread (or decide narrower piece is okay).
Broken warp.	Uneven tension—broken threads were too tight.	Cut new one, replace broken one, and pin into weaving until woven securely. See page 96 for a detailed explanation.
	Knot that didn't fit through reed or heddle.	
	Weak place in yarn.	
Warp frays and breaks.	Sett too close.	Re-sley into larger dent reed.
	Sett okay, but in too fine a reed.	Open and close shed with beater forward.
	Yarn too softly spun for use as warp (see below for solution to this).	If wool, sprinkle with oil to keep fuzziness contained. If linen or other plant fiber, sprinkle with water.
Sagging warp makes design error and interferes with clean shed.	Uneven tension—floating threads too loose.	Hang some kind of weight on loose threads between back and warp beams to take up slack—fishing sinkers, washers, shuttles, etc.
Whole section goes loose.	Knot on apron rod loosened, or one section messed up during beaming.	Even warp tension by padding the loose section with anything from a pencil to a dish towel into the roll of warp, or cloth, depending on how much and where slack needs to be taken up.
	With a multi-yarn warp, yarn elasticity varies.	Next time blend yarns more.
	You could have too wide a stripe of one kind of yarn.	Mix warps better.
When shed is open, bottom warps are slack, tops tight, making it hard to get shuttle through without catching loose ones.	Usually a Jack loom problem. Shafts are sitting too close to neutral when at rest—heddle eyes need to be *below* a straight line drawn from beam to beam.	Adjust shafts so that those not raised have heddle eyes as far below beams as the heddle eyes of the raised shafts are above the beams.
Weft doesn't beat in straight.	Uneven tension.	Pad loose areas or hang weights off back to even up tension.
	Beater not straight to loom.	Adjust bolts on top and bottom of beater.
	Beater not quite straight due to floor not being level.	Put a shim under one corner of loom to straighten beater.
Can't beat enough weft in.	Warp sett too close; if selvedges are closer than main body, they alone can stop weft.	Resley warp looser.
		Try a different weight of weft, or a softer weft.
Weft packs in too much.	Warp sett too loose.	Resley warp tighter.
	Weft too skinny.	Use a fatter weft.
	Too much muscle in beating.	Don't beat so hard; use fatter weft.

Troubleshooting

Problem	Possible Causes	Solutions
Warp grabs around beater; beater won't move.	Hairy warp sett too close.	Resley with hairy warps far enough apart so they won't stick to each other. To get a good shed, place hairy yarns on same shaft—then they don't have to separate. Mix with other nonhairy warps.
Hairy yarns refuse to allow open shed.		Open shed one shaft at a time. Spray warp with hair spray or gel to "glue" hairs down while weaving.
Need just a few more inches of warp to finish—it's there but out of reach.	Measured warp too short.	Loosen tension a little for better shed.
	Figured too closely.	Lift reed out of beater, slide it back to castle.
	Wove too much sample at the beginning.	Extend your warp length by untying warp knots on your apron rod and running a cord through the warp knots and around apron rod, adjusting for even tension when done. In extreme cases, tie new warps to old warps so that old warp can continue forward on through heddles and reed.
Can't get a shed.	You forgot to go over the back beam—warp goes from heddles down to warp beam.	Remove back beam and slide it under warp, loosen tension on warp, lift and replace back beam.
Can't get a clean shed.	Crossed warps.	Untie, straighten, and resley from front.
	If it's a countermarch loom, the cause may have to do with adjustment of harness heights.	See loom owner's manual.
	Uneven tension.	Retie front knots.
	Tie-up cords for treadles vary in length too much.	Put cords of same length on same treadles.
Grease marks on warp.	New reeds have machine oil protecting them from moisture.	Wipe off new reeds before beginning to weave. These marks usually wash out.
Threading errors—minor.	Inattention during threading.	Tie string heddles where you need them—untie wrong warp in front, pull out of reed and heddles, rethread, resley, retie. If you need one or two additional warp threads, cut new ones, thread and sley as needed, and hang them off the back beam with enough weight to match warp tension.
	Draft has error.	
Threading errors—major.	Inattention during threading.	Hopefully you discover this right after you finished threading. Sometimes a bunch of repair heddles will solve it, sometimes you must rethread half of the warp, depending on the error. If you must rethread a lot from the front, first open a shed, put a lease stick into it behind the castle, then do the same with a second shed (tabby if you can get it). The sticks will give you back your cross so you can easily thread the proper threads. Since it's already beamed you don't want a lot of crossing over—this messes up tension. This process is no fun; usually once is enough to prevent it from ever happening again.
	Draft has error	
Pattern doesn't look right.	Proportions are off. Colors are interfering.	Change warp sett, beat, or yarns.
	Treadling error.	Check tie-ups.
		Check treadling draft.
		Check sinking or rising shed.

Problem	Possible Causes	Solutions
Something isn't right in pattern.	Threading or sleying error: open sheds and look in from the side—there may be crossed threads (between reed and heddles or within heddles) preventing some threads from going up and down when they should.	See threading errors.
Finished piece is too short.	Wrong warp calculation due to arithmetic or error in warp take-up or shrinkage.	Sometimes the piece can be salvaged or lived with. Other times it's just a good learning experience.
	Used stretchy knitting yarn which unstretched when it came off the loom.	Measure longer next time.
Desired yarn is too expensive or too weak or there isn't enough to use as desired.	Expensiveness has too many causes. Weak—designed to be soft instead of strong.	Dilute use. Combine with plainer, stronger yarn every other thread, or use it for weft only.
Finished piece is ugly.	Didn't do a sample first. Perspective, pre-conceived notion. You tried to put too many ideas into one piece so they fought each other instead of complementing each other.	Often what you think is ugly really isn't, it's just not what you expected. Put it away for a month, then take it out and look at it with a fresh eye, without expectations. It may look a lot better. If you still don't like it, you have at least two alternatives—give it to someone whose taste is different from yours, or over-dye it so it's monochromatic in a new color range that looks good. You *can* unweave it and use the yarn again.
Too many ideas.	Enthusiasm, excitement. You're an interesting person with more energy than time.	Keep notes on all ideas; otherwise, by the time you get time, you won't remember them all. Also some will later be abandoned because others were better. Some can be combined into a single piece.
Not enough ideas.	All of the above is true, but you've hit a dry spell—we all do.	Subscribe to a weaving magazine, go to an art show, ask friends what presents they would like, think about what clothing or other fabric item you plan to buy next and consider weaving it instead. Think of who in town would appreciate a handwoven donation—blankets for people in nursing homes, wall hangings for your church, banners for the football team bus, matching saddle blankets for the 4H club riding group, etc. Or just take a rest, knowing you'll weave again when the time is right.
Lack of motivation.	It's not as much fun to weave alone as to talk about it with someone interested.	Join or start a guild. Teach a friend to weave. Promise someone something you've woven.
Tired back.	Leaning over too much.	Find a lower stool for threading and a weaving seat that's a better height. Take breaks at least every 30 minutes.
Your kids are too helpful.	They're interested in you and in weaving.	Help them start their own project, on a frame, inkle, rigid heddle, or other loom appropriate for their age and interest.
Puppies or kittens destroyed your warp.	Puppies and kittens are like that.	Close the door next time.
Not enough time for weaving.	Organization and scheduling of priorities.	Read *The Creative Woman's Getting it All Together at Home Handbook* by Jean Ray Laury (Hot Fudge Press, 19425 Tollhouse Road, Clovis, CA 93611).

Index

Answers to Exercises

Completed drawdown from page 117.

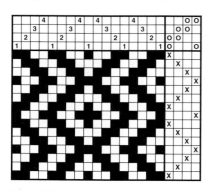

Answers to warp and weft calculations, p. 110

WARP:		WEFT:
$24 \times 6 = 144$ 18		23
$+ \quad 15$ $+ \ 1$		$\times \ 15$
$+ \quad 14.5$ $+ \ 2$		$= 345$
$+ \quad 14.5$ $= 21$		$\times \ 173$
$+ \quad 24$ $\times 15$		$= 59,685$
$= 212 \quad \times \quad 315 = 66,780$		$\div \ 36$
$\div 36$		$= 1658$
$= 1855$		

$$1855 + 1658 = 3513 \div 2 = 1756 \text{ each red and white}$$

Completed drawdowns from page 118.

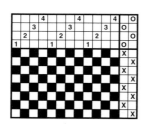

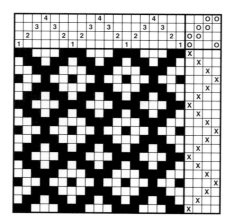

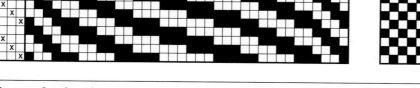

Formula for figuring your weft needs

$$
\begin{aligned}
&\text{length of one weft shot in inches} \\
\times\ &\text{shots per inch} \\
\hline
=\ &\text{inches needed to weave one inch of fabric} \\
\times\ &\text{inches to be woven (project length and shrinkage)} \\
\hline
=\ &\text{inches of weft needed to weave all of project} \\
\div\ &36 \\
\hline
=\ &\text{yards of weft needed}
\end{aligned}
$$

Formula for figuring your warp needs

project length	finished width	total length in inches
+ fringe	+ draw-in (1–2" average)	× warp ends needed
+ take-up (10% average)	+ shrinkage (10% average)	= total warp needed in inches
+ shrinkage (10% average)	= on loom width	÷ 36
+ loom waste	× warp sett (e.p.i.)	= total yards needed
= total length	= warp ends needed	

Use this formula when figuring your warp needs.